If You Only Walk Long Enough

Exploring the Pyrenees

STEVE CRACKNELL

for Veronica

First published in 2008 by Lulu.com

This edition © 2009 Steve Cracknell

Produced by Archétype Informatique
12 place Balmigère
11200 Camplong d'Aude, France
www.archetype-it.com
tel +33 (0)4 68 43 52 38

All rights reserved

ISBN 978-1-4092-6756-0

Contents

Map	vi
Notes	viii
Acknowledgements	ix
Prologue	xi
I: In the Basque country – Hendaye to Gabas	1
II: The High Pyrenees: Gabas–Luchon	55
III: Luchon–Mérens: Ariège, terre courage	141
IV: Chez les Catalans – Mérens to the Mediterranean	217
Afterword	265
Annotated bibliography	267

Legend:
- mountains
- hostels, huts, camps
- boundaries
- Pyrenean Way
- rivers

0 — 50 km

Based on the 1879, 1881 and 1888 maps prepared by J. Migeon

Notes

There is only one series of guides worth taking on the Pyrenean Way. Published by the Fédération Française de Randonnée Pédestre (FFRP), the French Ramblers' Association, the four books in the Traversée des Pyrénées series contain all the information you really need and nothing superfluous. Beware, however: the guides are not always very up to date.

Spellings: In a zone where the languages are as interwoven as the mountains and valleys there are often several different names for the same locality. I have used the versions given on the 1:25,000 IGN maps, preferring the French when there are alternatives as this is the version which has the widest distribution.

Acknowledgements

Thanks to Claude for painstakingly dissecting my photos and helping me to classify the plants. Thanks also to Paolo Mazzei for identifying the reptiles. His excellent website 'Amphibians and Reptiles of Europe' http://www.herp.it/ is worth the detour. And, to all those walkers and others I met on the mountains and in the valleys – whose names I have disguised – *un grand merci et bonne continuation*.

Alice went on. 'Would you tell me, please, which way I ought to go from here?'

'That depends a good deal on where you want to get to,' said the Cat.

'I don't much care where – ' said Alice.

'Then it doesn't matter which way you go,' said the Cat.

'– so long as I get somewhere,' Alice added as an explanation.

'Oh, you're sure to do that,' said the Cat, 'if you only walk long enough.'

Alice felt that this could not be denied, so she tried another question. 'What sort of people live about here?'

Lewis Carroll, Alice's Adventures in Wonderland

De même que les médecins ont des stéthoscopes pour mieux ausculter leurs patients, les randonneurs possèdent le sentier GR 10 quand ils veulent scruter le coeur des Pyrénées.

Just as doctors have stethoscopes better to examine their patients, walkers have the GR10, the Pyrenean Way, when they wish to examine the heart of the Pyrenees.

Pierre Minvielle

Prologue

My path leads to the east but I head west, down the beach to the Atlantic, a large yellow rucksack on my back, hairy white legs picking their way between discarded bikini tops. Taking off my walking boots and wading into the water, I fill up a tiny shampoo phial and then meander barefoot to a bar for a cooling beer, squeezing the hot sand between my toes.

How long will it take me to get to the Mediterranean? How often will I get seriously lost? I don't know: I have never walked a long-distance path before, though the idea has been maturing for several years.

From where I live, in the vine-growing Corbières near Carcassonne, I can see the Pyrenees. On a clear day, I can make out the characteristic incisor profile of Mount Canigou. In winter, dentine white with snow, it bites into the heavens. In summer it is blue-grey, shimmering. Even when it is invisible, it is still there in my mind, palpable despite the haze.

Four years ago, I started walking in the foothills, meeting people with bulging rucksacks and serious suntans whenever I ventured on to the long-distance paths. The idea of walking the whole length of the Pyrenees gradually crept into my mind. And now I am sitting on the terrace of a bar in the seaside resort of Hendaye, about to set off.

I ask myself why I want to do it. For the challenge? A middle-aged man ludicrously trying to convince himself that he is still young. No, it is not just that; the explanation is too easy. I *need* to walk. Not just

If you only walk long enough

for a couple of hours, but day after day, though I don't quite know why. I hope to stumble on some kind of an answer before I arrive at the other end of the range.

I also want to find out about my new mountain neighbours. Their history. How they live. *Why* they live.

In practical terms, the guide books tell me that I have a choice of three routes. The shortest is the *Haute Route Pyrénéenne*. It marches directly towards the watershed between France and Spain, and stays there. It only takes 40 days or so to exchange the bustling waves of the Atlantic for the torpid blue of the Mediterranean. But it makes no concessions to comfort and is technically difficult – if you decide to take in the Aneto, the highest peak, you will need crampons, an ice axe, and no fear of heights, which rules me out.

The second possibility is the Spanish *Gran Recorrido 11* which sticks to the southern slopes and is well served by hostels. It is reasonably straight, but very exposed to the sun. More importantly my command of the language is very poor. I haven't got beyond the present tense in Spanish. The GR 11 belongs to the future.

So I have decided to walk the French Pyrenean Way, the GR10, described in my guide book as a *trait d'union* – a hyphen – between the Atlantic and the Mediterranean. As hyphens go this one is rather long and not at all straight. Changing valleys once or even twice a day, it snakes up minor passes but shuns the highest peaks of the range, passing through countryside which is sometimes rugged, sometimes bucolic, but rarely banal. At the end of the day it makes a detour to sniff out a meal and a bed.

The first problem, I have been warned, is that the path doesn't exist on any map, even though some of them have a continuous red line running from west to east. Landslides, unhelpful landowners, and even the FFRP, the French Ramblers' Association, create diversions, for worse or for better. In addition, in some areas there are several different official routes, never mind the unofficial ones. Even estimates of its length vary wildly: 700km, like walking from

Prologue

London to Edinburgh? Or 866km, London to Aberdeen? I don't have the time to do it all in one year. I'll start tomorrow and see how far I get.

I

In the Basque country – Hendaye to Gabas

Hendaye to Olhette

In the morning, I check that my bottle of sea water is not leaking and set out towards the east, perfumed with summer-smelling sun cream. At first the path is bordered by palms, fig trees, and cacti but as soon as it leaves town, the vegetation changes dramatically, as if the moderating effect of the Gulf Stream only stretches as far as the urban limits. The English Cotswolds appear: sweet chestnut and beech trees, foxgloves in purple flower, pasture for sheep and cattle, and country mansions conspicuously defended by barking dogs. The houses are, however, clearly Basque, as is the temperature.

At Biriatou a few kilometres outside Hendaye I catch up with a man in the process of repacking his rucksack.

'GR10?' I ask.

'Yes,' he replies, in French.

'How many kilos?'

'Twelve.'

'Me too.'

I can't see how I could get away with less. Spare clothing, food, water. In the heat I drink three litres of water a day. I take a slug of the already tepid liquid.

My fellow walker is in his 60s. He is thin, very thin, with every detail of his leg muscles visible – like a Da Vinci anatomical drawing, it is as if his skin has been shrink-wrapped around him. These are not body-builder's all-for-show muscles, plump and fleshy; they are dense, rigid, almost additional bones. We are both going to be staying in Olhette this evening.

I continue up the ferny hillside overlooking the meandering Bidassoa river. During the Spanish civil war this was a favoured observation point for watching the fighting on the other side of the frontier. Safe in their ring-side seats, protected by a line on a map, the French spectators came here to experience death *live*. Seventy years later, France merges imperceptibly into Spain. The same rolling landscape on either side of the non-existent boundary fence. The frontier doesn't even bother to follow the watershed: Spanish raindrops flow into French rivers.

At the top of the hill the path turns east, descends again along the edge of the forest and around a small hillock, and then tumbles directly into a street of shops. This is not an out-of-town shopping mall: the buildings are crumbling disgracefully. Nor is there any of the infrastructure normally associated with shops: no domestic housing, no schools, no doctors, no town hall. No town, in fact. Just thirty or so emporiums, with a few tacky fairground stalls and restaurants. A row of decaying teeth with rotting meat stuck between them. The shop windows are stacked high with boxes and cartons with felt-tip prices scrawled on them: primarily strong alcohol and cigarettes but also just about every kind of bric-a-brac imaginable.

I have crossed the border by a few metres. Here, what little difference there is between the two countries has been distilled, concentrated, and regurgitated. French *pastis* is a top seller. Imported into Spain to benefit from lower taxes, it is quickly whisked off back to its homeland. Here, cigarettes cost half what they do in France. Long-legged dolls in frozen flamenco insist that Spain starts here, at the Col d'Ibardin, 1000 km away from their Andalusian origins. Gadgets made in Hong Kong complete the range of knick-knacks on sale. The smell of hot oil and candy floss fills the air. Yet this tawdry setting attracts thousands of shoppers every year, their buses and cars winding slowly up the hillside; careering down again packed to the gunwales with inflammables, a disaster waiting to happen.

I pass through quickly. The path wanders down the hill again, into France and then turns, climbing. It is hot, suffocatingly hot, even under the trees. In the dappled shade I almost trip over a small stone post, inscribed 'R 18'. Frontier marker, no 18. There are 602 in all. Three treaties, in 1856, 1862, and 1866, and the optimistically entitled Final Act of Delimitation of 1868 were needed to define the exact line of demarcation. The first marker is on the banks of the Bidassoa just upstream from Hendaye, and the last is hidden in a cave on the Mediterranean coast.

At this end of the Pyrenees the frontier arbitrarily separates northern Basques from southern Basques. Indeed, the Basque people is as divided as it is united – in Hendaye, the only building of any antiquity is the church, the others having been burned to the ground in repeated raids by Basques from over the border. The origin of the scission is the 1659 Pyrenean treaty, signed on the Île des Faisans in the middle of the river Bidassoa.

In the cool of yesterday evening I ambled upriver from Hendaye to see the island. On the French side grimly efficient industrial estates give way to leafy suburban gardens. On the Spanish side the bank is lined with rows of apartment blocks. In the middle is an anonymous island covered with rough scrub and self-seeded trees. The only indication of the importance of the site is a plain monument in a small clearing. Why did the French prime minister and his Spanish counterpart choose this spot for their meeting? The island, and hence the monument which might explain all this, is inaccessible.

I continue upstream to the bridge, the westernmost frontier crossing between France and Spain. This evening it is guarded only by

In the Basque country – Hendaye to Gabas

a redoubtable black cat. A series of notices explains that in the 17th century most of the island was covered by a mansion with bridges linking it to both banks of the river. It was in this building that the future of Europe was decided.

The 1659 treaty itself is a fascinating document. It starts with a half-baked history lesson and claims to resolve the border disputes which had ravaged the Pyrenees for centuries. 'The Pyrenean mountains, which in ancient times divided the Gauls and the Spanish, will from now on again become the division between the two kingdoms'. In reality the Gauls and the Spanish had never been clearly identifiable peoples. And the treaty was so loosely worded that it wasn't until 1868 that it was even possible to mark out an agreed frontier on the ground – a frontier which defies geographical logic and even preserves a Spanish enclave within France. Even so, like some arranged marriages where the husband and wife care little for each other, have affairs, frequent rows, and longer wars, it somehow worked. In much the same way, in fact, as the marriage between the 21-year-old Sun King Louis XIV and his Spanish cousin Marie-Thérèse; the contract for their marriage also formed part of the treaty.

The wedding arrangements were somewhat unusual with the couple being married by proxy on 4 June 1660, before meeting two days later on the Île des Faisans, and then marrying – in person this time – on 9 June in the cathedral in St-Jean-de-Luz on the coast.

In recognition of its historical importance, the Île des Faisans was made into a condominium: it is jointly owned by the two countries. It is administered by France from 12 August to 11 February and by Spain for the other six months of each year.

Faded red paint on one side of the frontier marker indicates that the Venta Inzola is not far away. The *venta* is a long, solid, rendered building with a string of outhouses nestling at the head of the valley. There is a bicycle shed, a small terrace, wooden picnic tables, and a concrete platform running down one side. It looks rather like a disused but well-maintained railway station, but the topography of the area rules this out. A dirt track disappears to the south into Spain; to the north the only access is by the Pyrenean Way. Postcards, drinks, snacks, and souvenirs are on sale, but not today: a chalked sign announces that the establishment is closed this week.

Ventas, once the haunt of smugglers, are part of Basque folklore. After the re-opening of the frontier following the Second World War, and above all with the increasing ownership of motor cars, the number of 'semi-professional' smugglers decreased as the opportunities for amateurs increased. The *ventas* transformed themselves into grocers, tobacconists, cafés, bars, and restaurants. But the tidal wave of the European single market has left these shopkeeper buccaneers all but shipwrecked and it is only the differential taxes which make their trade economically viable. That, and the tradition of a Sunday trip into the countryside.

Trudging up the hill, I am overtaken by an old man.

'Is this the way to Olhette?' I ask.

'Yes. Just, tag along with me,' is the reply as he strides off. I struggle to keep up, quickly overheating and exhausting the few reserves of strength I have left.

'The Venta Inzola is closed this week,' I call after him, desperately hoping to slow him down, 'but it doesn't look as though it can do much trade anyway.'

'You're wrong, usually it is full of people.'

'What food like?' I gasp.

'Very good. Pilar grills the meat on a wood fire. And a meal only costs 15€.'

The roller-coaster path crosses yet another watershed. I can now see houses in the distance.

'Where come today?'

'Olhette. I'm just doing a little circuit for the afternoon. And you?'

'Hendaye. GR10.' Finally, he slows his pace and we stroll down to the hostel.

In the Basque country – Hendaye to Gabas

A single-storey, stone-built structure, the hostel has recently been renovated. Mature plane trees provide shade for the immaculate, juicy lawn. Scattered around is an impressive collection of nostalgia – wickerwork beehives, an impossibly clean, red-painted plough with a white coulter, a seeding machine, a cider press, a wooden wheelbarrow, and a wooden sledge with a long pole designed to be drawn by horses. At the back of the house are traditional haystacks, like shaggy-topped mushrooms, somewhat the worse for wear, only for show. The only things which are in their natural place and condition are the *lauzes*, thin stone slabs which mark the edge of the garden, creating a low fence. Inside, the dining room is bestrewn with horseshoes, stirrups, and cow bells. Strings of garlic and peppers hang from the ceiling.

My feet divested of boots and socks, I ask the owner for a drink and, wiggling my toes, sip it in the garden contemplating the outrageously contrived decoration. With a beer in one hand and my feet propped up on a packing case, it is unambiguously *perfect*.

The walker I met in Biriatou arrives shortly after me.

'I always walk slowly,' he comments. 'I'm Paul. *Comment tu t'appelles?* – what's your name?'

Paul has silvery grey hair and glasses to match. His old-fashioned look and slightly protruding top lip remind me of a former British prime minister, though the resemblance stops there. He is wearing a dark blue flannel tee-shirt with a turned-down collar, two buttons at the front, and red and white striped hems – the kind of tee-shirt which you could buy in the 1970s and wear for 30 years without it fading. His beige shorts have turn-ups and ironed creases. He takes his boots off and replaces them with shockingly modern white trainers.

Later, we are called for dinner in a converted barn and sit down at the table. Paul almost disappears. Like a child, his head barely pokes up over the table top, though I hadn't noticed that he was especially small. I look to see if he has been given a particularly low chair, but no, it is the same as mine. Then I realise that he is crouched forward. When he is carrying a rucksack his hump disappears.

Hendaye to Olhette

We both eat greedily. Paul has just retired. With 30 years of long-distance walking behind him, he is much more experienced than I am, though he has not done the Pyrenean Way before. We are both hoping to reach the Pic du Midi d'Ossau before 4 July.

After dinner I saunter down the road in search of the centre of the village but there doesn't appear to be one. The houses are spread over a large area and are named, not numbered. They are immense, built of stone, with half-timbered façades, the wood often painted red. I suppose that a few centuries ago when the houses were built, the ground floor was used for the animals and labourers, the first floor was occupied by the family, and the second floor was filled with grain and hay, but I still don't manage to fill all the available space. Despite the troubled times which the Basque country has witnessed, the architecture suggests peace and prosperity over a long period. There are no run-down hovels. Either they never existed – which seems unlikely – or were so decrepit that they have completely disappeared. Only the houses of the rich survive, I conclude.

It is only later that I discover the explanation. In the Basque country, at least until the French revolution of 1789, the family house, the *etxe*, had a significance far beyond that attributed to it elsewhere in France. The rules of inheritance and customary law were specifically designed to maintain the integrity of the *etxe*, an idea which encompassed not only the building, the land, and the family, but also a way of life. Property which had been in the family for three generations or more was, with few exceptions, inalienable. That is to say, the 'owner' didn't have the right to sell it; it had to be passed on to future generations. This applied to the house, the land, the furnishings . . . everything. It all had to be passed down to the eldest child – male or female.

The importance of the *etxe* was such that, on its name plaque, the house often addresses the world in the first person: [Built] in the year 1769, I belong to the parish of Ispaster, for instance. In the 12th and 13th centuries, when surnames first came into use, families habitually took the name of their house.

And the influence of the *etxe* wasn't just limited to this mortal world. Associated with the house was a grave in the church and a designated path linking the two. The grave belonges to the *etxe* and not to the family. As recently as 1941 the courts resolved an argument between two sisters over who had the right to sit in the family pew, cooling her feet and dripping candle wax on the tomb of her ancestors. The court decided in favour of the one who was living in the family house.

In principle, the occupants of the *etxe* would be an old couple, a young couple (their children), any unmarried children of either couple, and the servants. The farm was worked by the household in common.

So when the zealous revolutionaries descended from Paris to impose their idea of a centralised egalitarian state they met with considerable resistance. The law of northern France stipulated that every child had the right to a share in the family property, not just the oldest one. But the local lawyers went out of their way to ensure that marriage contracts, specially designed wills, and lifetime donations all worked towards preserving the unity of the *etxe*.

This is why the houses are so imposing. It is as if the house is living and the family members are merely visiting, passing from the building above the ground, along the tearful path to the church, to the cold silent room below its floor. The rules of inheritance also meant that the land was kept as a single viable unit, each farm well-spaced from its neighbours, the whole system creating and maintaining a stable society.

A stable society? At the expense of those who didn't fit in. An eldest child couldn't marry another eldest child. They each had obligations to different *etxe*. Where would they live? And younger children who married younger children were semi-outcasts in this essentially rural society. As long as the population was only growing slowly the difficulties could be accommodated; the towns and the fishing industry could take up the surplus. But this has not been the case for a long while. The *etxe* no longer has the influence it once had. Urban individualism has long since triumphed over the rural past, and the landscape, still marked by these ancient footprints, must surely change dramatically in the years to come.

I return to the hostel warmed by the last embers of the disappearing sun, to hear shrieks of laughter and splashes coming from below in the woods. Half hidden in the twilight, two men are showering themselves in the river. Shortly afterwards one of them appears, dressed in a furry black pyjama suit, shaking droplets from his hair.

'*Bonsoir.* Do you think that I could have some water please?' he asks.

'I'll show you the tap. Are you camping by the river?'

'Yes. We've just arrived from Hendaye. We are knackered. My friend is out of condition so it took rather longer than expected, with all the stops.'

They have taken 12 hours, nearly twice the time given in the *FFRP Guide.* They are each carrying 20kg.

Olhette to Ainhoa

I set out just as the sun is rising over the hills, in the direction of La Rhune. Its name means 'pasture' but it is the first hill of any significance, though only 950m high at the summit. The grassy slopes are dissected by small streams, their shallow rounded valleys emphasised in the shade cast by the low sun, like a vast green sheet being shaken out, billowing in the wind. A red-and-white striped television mast caps the rocky crag at the top of the hill.

My first encounter of the day is with a foal: long white legs, a light brown back and head, and a white star between its eyes. Its mane and tail are soft and fluffy. I approach it cautiously. It looks around nervously. It almost allows me to touch it. Then thinks better of it, and skips off ahead to rejoin its mother and the others. They are a curious collection. Some piebald, some a stunning chestnut, some grey. They are small for horses, big for ponies.

Are they Pottoks? Pottok horses have been roaming these hills for millennia, to judge by the Magdalenian cave paintings at Lascaux. More recently they were used extensively in the mines. They were never really a breed, just the horses which lived semi-wild in the foothills. They had always been crossed with other breeds, but by the 1960s it was becoming increasingly difficult to define a 'genuine' Pottok. So, in 1971 a register was created of the 29 stallions and 208 mares which seemed to meet the criteria. According to the official national association, Pottoks can be chestnut, bay, brown, skewbald, or piebald and measure between 11 and 14.2 hands. There are A-list Pottoks and B-list Pottoks. To be on the A-list you have to be able to trace your ancestry back – all of 36 years – to a mare and a stallion on the original register. But you can still call yourself a Pottok even if one of your (recent) ancestors was not one. A B-list Pottok, but still a Pottok.

Unsurprisingly, not everybody is in agreement. The Maison du Pottok in Bidarray set up its own breeding programme in 1993 claiming that a true Pottok can only be black or brown and should not measure more than 13 hands, a definition used on the Spanish side of the border. On the hillside, the herd is grazing peacefully in splendid indifference.

The path levels out two-thirds of the way up the flank of La Rhune and skirts around it. Shortly afterwards I arrive at a level crossing. In a reversal of the usual roles, I am walking on the flat and it is the railway which is climbing, to the summit. The view from the top is said to stretch from the Atlantic coast to the high peaks of the Pyrenees, a panorama which has earned it three Michelin stars.

I hate Michelin stars. Any sense of awe which might be offered by a cathedral, a historic monument, a museum, or even a view is shattered by sharing it with a crowd. And three Michelin stars guarantee a crowd: the train carries over 350,000 visitors a year. On the other hand the train itself is just right. Its electric engines don't pollute and don't make much noise; the restored wooden carriages merely creak. What noise there is, from the cogs on the train chewing into the rack between the tracks, is concentrated into a few minutes as the train passes by. And the tracks do not scar the countryside to anywhere near the same extent as a road would.

On an interpretive panel for the Pyrenean Way sited near to the crossing, the names Espagne (Spain) and Pyrénées-Atlantiques have been defaced. EHE has been scrawled over them in felt tip, and the word Euskara has been cut into the surface. EHE stands for Euskal Herrian Euskaraz – a movement set up in 1979 to promote the use of Euskara, the Basque language. Its activities range from 'correcting' monolingual road signs to working with public bodies on projects to promote the language.

The path descends between scattered *etxe* to the village of Sare – Sara in Basque. Here, wherever the name is written in capitals, the As have horizontal bars across their apex, like little berets to keep the sun off.

SĀRĀ

'Why are there lines over the As? Are they pronounced differently?' I ask in the tourist office.

'No. They are pronounced exactly like any other A. It's just the way we write them round here.'

Written down, the Basque language certainly looks very strange, full of Ks and Xs, two letters which are almost absent from French. Basque disdains the letters C, Q, V, W, and Y but revels in stacking consonants together in unpronounceable combinations. One of the reasons it looks so odd is that it is completely different from any other living language. It is not even part of the Indo-European family which groups together all the other languages of western Europe. Also, it has stayed more or less in one place for a very long time, at least 2000 years, whilst the other European languages around it were on the move or, in some cases, simply dying out.

In the Basque country – Hendaye to Gabas

There are about 650,000 Basque speakers, of whom 90% live on the Spanish side of the border. In the French Basque country, where state schools have always favoured French over Basque, young people are much less likely to know the language than their elders.

Which brings us back to Sare. It is here that the first bilingual state school classes were created in 1983. Half the teaching is done in Basque and half in French. But the number of teachers being trained in Basque – and in other regional languages – is pitifully inadequate and few children speak the language fluently.

'*Saran astia*' as the saying goes: in Sare one takes one's time, and it is only half past ten. So I leave my rucksack slumped tiredly in the cool shade of the tourist office and skip out under the stone arches into the sun. The white walls have already warmed up and are beginning to redistribute excess heat into the streets.

I buy a small *gâteau basque* – it resembles a Derbyshire Bakewell pudding – at a stall from a young woman who suggests I visit the Basque cake museum, or the Basque house museum, or the prehistoric grotto (and museum). But I reject them all and wander around the streets. Just opposite the cake stall is a series of notices evoking the presence of English king Edward VII and, earlier, of the Empress Eugénie. (She was Spanish; her extravagant fandango on the top of the Rhune in 1859 scandalised the court.) Also the long-disappeared tramway, the time when 6000 spectators came to watch *pelote* – a kind of outdoor squash – being played for two whole days, and the wonderful 'authenticity' of the town.

So is Basque identity in France just a kind of quaint folklore, kept alive to entertain tourists? One Basque, a beret. Two Basques, a game of *pelote*. Three Basques, a choir? History recycled to placate a few hotheads? Nothing more than the splashes from the cauldron boiling on the other side of the Bidassoa. Or is it an important force? A memory of the past, or a hope for the future?

I eat a lazy lunch washed down with a bottle of wine, accompanied by the sound of Basque spoken at the next table, and then totter unevenly down the cobbled street to the river. The stone walls which line the road shimmer in the heat. Beyond them, the pale yellow corn stubble is all that remains after the annual shave; but in other fields the maize bristles are still a vigorous deep green. My boots sink into the squishy tarmac and I regret the time passed in the relative cool of the morning in Sare. I could have been near my destination by now.

My left foot starts to hurt. It feels as if I have a hairline fracture precisely at the middle and on the left side of the fourth metatarsal. It has felt like that for a year now, but my doctor insists that I wouldn't be able to walk at all with a fractured bone, so I don't pay it much attention. After an age, I stop and remove my boots revealing a blister on my right foot.

At the top of a small hill there is an isolated but imposing *venta* dedicated to tiles – floor tiles, roof tiles, wall tiles, bath tiles, nothing but tiles. More tarmac takes me down laboriously to the completely unremarkable Pont du Diable. Normally, Devil's bridges have at least one incredible feature. Some span an immeasurably deep chasm, which no stone mason's scaffolding could possibly have bridged. Some are so delicate that they can only be held in place by some magical exception to the normal laws of gravity. Here the devil has contented himself with an ordinary concrete slab bridge across a lazy river. I suppose the devil must have off-days like the rest of us.

I arrive at my destination, Ainhoa, under a veiled sky in mid-afternoon. Ainhoa, like Sare, is officially one of 'the most beautiful villages of France'. As in Sare, the houses in the centre of the village are imposing three-storey structures. On my left most of them have half-timbered frontages, with stone walls on the ground floor. Each storey jetties a little further into the street. The woodwork – balconies, shutters and vertical struts – is painted either ox-blood red or a dark green, as if inspired by the local wine and the bottles it comes in. The spaces between the timbers are brilliantly whitewashed. On the other side of the street the façades are mostly plainer, with less woodwork. Traditionally Basque houses keep their backs to the wind so that they have a plain west façade and a more decorative eastern side. The differences between the two sides of the street are a reflection of this tradition. Whether they faced or had their backs to the high street was of no consequence.

The houses date to the 17th century although the layout of the town is 13th century, an early example of town planning. On a minor passage across the Pyrenees, the village owes its existence to the Prémontré monks who wished to create a new route for pilgrims to Santiago de Compostela in Spain. This afternoon it is motor cars and lorries which are trundling noisily up and down a high street lined with even more cars. The Japanese mulberry trees and decorative flower pots seem surprisingly resistant to the pollution. In the square at the south end of the road I discover some banana trees with their green hands stretching towards a sun fast disappearing behind the clouds, and I head for a hotel.

'The room costs 45€,' says the receptionist.

'Don't you have anything cheaper?' I ask.

'Yes but without a bath and there is no view.'

'I'll take it.'

'It's in the attic on the top floor. No 10,' she says, handing me the key.

This is the second time I have stayed in a hotel and the second time I have been offered room no 10.

I am lying on the bed when I hear a soft 'plup' sound in the distance. It repeats at irregular intervals so I get dressed and head in the direction of the noise. The source of the sound, the village *fronton*, is an area of tarmac about the size of a tennis court, with uncomfortable stone benches on one side and a smooth high stone wall at one end. There are two teams of two young men, each equipped with what looks like an oversize table tennis bat. They are hitting the ball – called, like the game, the *pelote* – against the wall, taking care to respect the white painted lines which divide up the court, but beyond that I cannot make out under what circumstances one round finishes, or indeed who has won. There is only a handful of spectators, so I assume this is a practice and not the real thing.

Paul arrives later and we eat together again. I study him, trying to work out how he fits together. When he sits up straight, he has the build and aerodynamics of a professional cyclist. I ask him, and he confirms that he goes cycling from time to time but not seriously. He orders a glass of wine at the beginning of the meal but only takes a couple of timid sips whilst eating. Then, after polishing off his dessert, he raises the glass to his lips and downs it in greedy slurps. He doesn't drink much water either.

'I only get through a litre a day,' he says. 'People tell me it's not enough, but I don't feel dehydrated.'

My dessert is ice cream flavoured with *piment d'Espelette*, a kind of hot pepper grown locally and named after a neighbouring village. Threaded onto strings, it can be seen hanging from beams in grocers and private houses throughout the Basque country. On the Scoville scale it is classified as level four (out of ten), somewhere between Hungarian and Cayenne.

Licking the ice cream cautiously off my spoon I have the impression that I am eating a plain vanilla ice cream but then I swallow it and suddenly fire breaks out on the back of my tongue. But the fire is quenched as soon as it has started and I am left confused. I have another spoonful. Cold, hot, fire, ice. Crazy food! Capsaicin, the active ingredient in pepper, is powerful stuff but soluble in milk fat. Hence the affinity of curry and yoghurt, and *piment d'Espelette* and ice cream.

Replete, I go to bed early.

Ainhoa to Bidarray

It rained heavily during the night and is still drizzling as I unlock the front door and let myself out. The road out of Ainhoa is lined with crosses, 14 of them, leading up to an oratory, Notre Dame d'Arantze, on the hill slope above. Scattered in the porch of the oratory are a rucksack, an assortment of camping equipment, and a blue sleeping bag laid on the hard concrete. A face pokes out of the middle of the heap. Perhaps this is the young American woman that Paul met yesterday. She is walking the Pyrenean Way alone, camping. I leave her to sleep on.

Opposite the oratory is a row of three crosses stuck in the ground with life-size painted figures nailed to them. Their vividly pink torsos and legs and insecure loincloths seem indecent in the half-light, like Dylan's 'flesh-coloured Christs that glow in the dark'. Facing them, like the congregation in a church, is an altogether more sober spectacle: a score of gravestones, decorated, but without names. The graves themselves, if indeed these are graves, are completely flat and sealed by the same luscious turf which covers the surrounding hillside. Some of the stones are in the form of a cross, but the majority consist of a simple trapezoidal stone base surmounted by a circular stone panel, decorated with incised geometric patterns. The patterns include crosses but most stones have little obvious Christian meaning.

There were a few of these *stèles discoïdales* in the churchyard in Ainhoa dotted amongst the more usual burial vaults. Worn by the elements, they seem to be making no attempt to defy time. Their friable stone and mysterious patterns speak of human fragility, insecurity, and incomprehension in the face of destiny, in sharp contrast with the visually arrogant, status-conscious polished-granite family tombs which dominate modern French cemeteries.

The Pyrenean Way now follows a cart track skirting around the hill, climbing imperceptibly. The *FFRP Guide* tells me that I can see the Atlantic port of St-Jean-de-Luz but I am cloaked in low cloud and can see only a few metres ahead. My map tells me that, after two days' walking, I have progressed a grand total of 16km from the coast.

There are no fields here, no walls, just rough pasture, bracken, and scrub. But the side of the track is newly planted with saplings, still in

Ainhoa to Bidarray

their protective plastic tubes, tied to stakes much stronger than they are. The line stretches for over a kilometre. In a future summer maybe these trees will provide welcome shade, but today the rain is dribbling down my face and glasses.

Further on, through the woolly atmosphere, I can hear the hum of engines, and the grating sound of gravel against gravel as it is displaced by rubber tyres. The noise seems to get closer, passes in front of me, and then stops abruptly.

The cart track descends. I can smell diesel fumes and, coming out of the cloud, I see a collection of four-wheel drive vehicles parked at the pass. Half hidden behind them, a man shouts something unintelligible in Basque. Murmured replies, then silence. A rustling, a metallic squeak, and then the plaintive bleating of a sheep, taken up by innumerable other ovine voices. I am greeted by the lanolin smell of wet fleece, and the nauseous stench of trampled sheep dung.

There are four small wooden-fenced pens, partly hidden under the oak trees. Two are full to bursting point with a heaving mass of discontented sheep, one is completely empty, and one contains three trestle tables. Next to each of the makeshift operating tables stand two men, each holding a vicious looking instrument in one hand. In front of each man, on the table, is a sheep, its four feet tied together at the ankles, resigned, as yet uncomplaining. The apron of the man who seems to be in charge is still a pristine white.

I walk up to the enclosure and say '*bonjour*'. The foreman replies, also in French. There are 200 sheep, he tells me, and the seven men will take all day to deal with them. Behind him the men start snipping, one hand holding a sheep by the ear, the other holding the shears, biting into the fleece. The first sheep has just been finished. As soon as its legs are untied it slips off the table and is shown to the awaiting empty pen. It shrugs its shoulders, waggles its rear quarters, and skips off like a lamb.

The foreman passes me the shears to look at: a strip of iron bent into a U-shape with opposing blades at the terminals. Squeeze the

U and the blades cross and cut. Release the pressure and the blades spring apart. They are identical to shears that I have excavated on archaeological sites in Britain. They reached technical perfection in the Iron Age, over 2000 years ago, and have not evolved since.

The workers are systematic and quietly efficient but at fewer than 30 sheep a day each they will not go down in the history books. The world record holder, New Zealander Darin Forde, sheared 720 ewes in a single day – using electric shears, naturally.

'We also treat them for diseases and ticks,' says the foreman, showing me a freshly exposed backside where the ticks are feasting. He slaps a dollop of noxious, sticky, black tar on them and smears it around.

'It's now and in July that the ticks start to attack, so we have to treat them before it gets too bad.'

If the ticks are bad for sheep, they can be even worse for people. In 1989, my friend Gaby had a nasty bout of influenza. His temperature rose and he ached all over.

'One day I noticed that I didn't have any sensations in my left foot. It was like a lump of lead dangling off the end of my leg. I went to my GP and he asked me if I had been bitten, if I had noticed any sore patches.'

Gaby had been walking. He remembered a bite and the subsequent rash.

'The ambulance came to fetch me straight away. The doctor at the hospital took some blood samples and came back a couple of hours later. I asked him "Is it bad?" and he replied "We'll try to save you." "What are my chances?" I said. "Better than 50%" he replied.'

The paralysis spread. At its worst, the only thing which Gaby could move was his head, but he did make a full recovery.

Ticks, the temperate-climate equivalent of mosquitoes, carry Lyme disease. It has a variety of symptoms ranging from a rash and fever through numbness, arthritis, and encephalitis to cardiac problems, so sufferers can find themselves branded as hypochondriacs. It has been around for millennia but the symptoms are so diffuse that it was not identified until the 1970s. In France, the Pasteur Institute estimates that there are 5000 cases every year, only the drier coast of the Mediterranean escaping.

'Do you have problems with Lyme disease?' I ask the sheep shearer.

'Not here. I've never heard of anybody round here catching it,' he replies blithely.

Skirting Mont Bizkayluze, I am below the clouds and above the mist in the valleys. Sometimes they meet. Sometimes rain falls. In the distance I spot an immense white residence, the Ferme Esteben, said to be a 'basic' hostel. I had imagined a tumbledown shepherd's cottage but this is a mansion on a grand scale. The only thing which seems to be lacking is a welcome. 'Private property', 'Keep out', say the signs hung on the pristine barbed wire fence which has been strung across the path, creating a considerable detour. Has the hostel been bought by a rich businessman and turned into a private residence? Paul is due to stay here tonight. Perhaps it was a condition of planning permission in this unforgiving wilderness that the owners continue to take in bedraggled strangers. If I get to see Paul again, I will ask him.

At the pass at the Col d'Espalzam, a run-down dry-stone shed dug into the hillside overlooks the river valley. The roof is like a giant jigsaw puzzle which has been broken up and thrown into a heap, the huge, thick slate slabs half falling into the gaps between the rafters. I clamber over the mossy wooden fence which bars the doorway, look warily at the roof, and search for a space between the piles of sheep dung to eat lunch.

From the hut, the path descends abruptly into the valley, 'a difficult section' according to the guide. I am unimpressed until I slip on the wet grass and fall forwards, overbalanced by my rucksack. On my knees, I look over the drop. My left hand finds a rock and I push backwards and restore my balance, collapsing in an unstable heap, my rucksack pressed against the slope behind me. My knees are still bent, my legs crushed underneath me, but I can't get up. One leg at a time, I ease my feet forwards until I am sitting down properly and can undo my rucksack. I shut my eyes and breathe deeply. I don't know how I'm going to manage when there are real precipices.

My walking stick has tumbled down the slope. Gingerly, I chase after it and then stuff it into my rucksack. If it gets stuck in a small crack it is more of danger than a help.

At Bidarray, an hour later, the hostel is already fully booked. This turns out to be a stroke of luck, as the owner also has an empty three-bedroom apartment, with bath, real leather sofas, and a fully equipped kitchen, all for me at the same price as a bed in a dormitory at the hostel.

In the early evening I watch a game of *pelote*. This time there are no bats. The boys – teenagers – are using their hands; their palms and wrists are protected by bandages. Apart from the obvious, where the ball falls too short or too long, or hits the wall too low, I am still unable to understand who has won a point. When the game finishes I ask one of the spectators to explain it to me, but get lost in the complexity of it all. There seem to be three basic games, with a bat, with bare hands, and with a *chistera*, whatever that might be, but lots of different ways of playing. Like tennis, it is descended from the *jeu de paume* which was played all over France in the 16th century, but unlike tennis it has never quite achieved Olympic status. Although exported by emigrants, with its impenetrable rules it has remained quintessentially Basque. If there really is an authentic Basque identity north of the Pyrenees, its heart must beat to the rhythm of a *pelote* ball against a *fronton*.

In Bidarray there are two *frontons* and, as if that isn't enough, the west wall of the church, in dirty pink sandstone, is the same shape. Stone is also used in the houses here. Some of the front doors have substantial stone jambs and lintels that run all the way up to the roof, enveloping the first floor window as they pass by. At Ainhoa, Sare and towards the coast, the carpenter was the most important worker on the building site. At Bidarray, the foreman was a mason.

Bidarray to St-Etienne-de-Baïgorry

I leave at 8 o'clock, and head south-west through the pastures. For once the Pyrenean Way is making no compromises. There is a mountain nearby and even though it is in completely the wrong direction the path seeks it out.

'*Sente de crête très aérienne* – very exposed ridge path.' I've been looking at this description for some days. I'm not very good on heights and I definitely don't like exposed ridges. There is an alternative route but this seems rather wimpish. What is the point of walking in the mountains on your own if you don't confront the dangers? I decide not to make a decision.

Some of the fields have already been mown. Pale greenish yellow stubble alternates with green dampness. The sky is a morose grey with a few fanciful wisps of cloud sneaking up the valleys. The path climbs relentlessly and after an hour I reach a junction. The left-hand fork climbs steeply and then gets lost in a mess of rock. It seems to be heading for a cliff face. The right-hand fork climbs timidly and then follows the flank of the mountain through the heather to a grassy plateau.

The Pic d'Iparla is my first mountain. At 1044m above sea level it is only officially a mountain by 44m, but still it is higher than Scafell Pike in the Lake District, the highest peak in England. It would be a shame not to rise to the first challenge.

I take the easy option and the right fork, and half an hour later the deviation has brought me back to the main path which now runs along the top of the cliff. Looking back, the 'exposed ridge path' appears remarkably ordinary. I can even see a man skipping along it. Shortly afterwards he overtakes me. In tee-shirt and shorts, he is visibly well

In the Basque country – Hendaye to Gabas

past 60, and running. He reaches the summit and turns round without stopping but by the time he has reached me he has slowed down a little. He has come from Bidarray, he says. He set out at 9 o'clock.

'Excuse me,' he pants, 'but I must get back for breakfast.'

The Pic d'Iparla itself is an insignificant bump on the ridge, but walking along the cliff edge, picking my way between the rock slabs, is exhilarating. To the west the air is clearer and I persuade myself that I can see a silver reflection of the sun on the Atlantic. But to the south the clouds are black and menacing and soon the wind increases and the rain arrives. Peat squelches under my boots. Rain drips from my hat. My glasses are steamed up. I huddle in a cave. Wring out my socks. Force lunch down. Shiver. I just want to get off the mountain before the storm arrives.

The path down into the valley becomes a track, a slippery red scar. A gigantic black slug slithers by. For the last two days I have had ample opportunities to examine the local slugs. Without exception enormous, fat, and smugly unaware of their likely destiny, those on the road into Bidarray were black, just as they are here. But those on the Pic d'Iparla were a disgusting speckled yellowish brown.

In St-Etienne-de-Baïgorry in the valley there is a hostel outside the village but I want to be comfortable so I trudge from one hotel to another. They are either fully booked or ridiculously expensive and crawling with Americans. I take refuge in a bar where four old men are playing cards, speaking to each other in Basque. At the counter a group of people in their 20s and 30s are chatting, switching from Basque to French and back again every few words. The barman directs me to a hotel in Beherekokarrika. (Said out loud it sounds much nicer than it looks written down.) I had passed by the hotel earlier, thinking it was shut; it is merely run-down.

The owner looks at me suspiciously. 40€ a night, paid in advance. I ask to see the room first.

'OK. No 4 on the first floor, with shower and toilet. The key is in the lock. I'll wait here for you.'

St-Etienne-de-Baïgorry

The key isn't in the lock but I push on the door and it opens. The electric light is already on and the curtains are drawn. The bed covers have been pulled down to the bottom and the pillows have been piled up in the middle but, aside from the residual perfume filling the room, there is no other sign of the occupant, nor of her profession.

I go down the stairs.

'It's fine but the bed hasn't been made.'

'Oh? Try no 7. No. That's taken. I've got one with a toilet and bath down the corridor, on the second floor, if that would do. 30€. Go and have a look at it. It's no 10,' he says, handing me the key.

I seem to be the only guest in the hotel and I don't want to sit at a lonely table in the middle of the vast empty dining room so I go out in search of somewhere to eat and end up at the expensive hotel I had earlier rejected. The restaurant is plush and the food is superb, *foie gras* accompanied by a glass of Jurançon, *mignons de veau* with red Irouléguy wine from the Domaine Ametzia, but too rich for my stomach and I am too tired to really appreciate it.

St-Etienne-de-Baïgorry

I have decided to have a day's rest, so my fifth day on the Pyrenean Way begins with a visit to the bakery. In the shop, the baguettes are stacked up in wooden cases behind the counter with the regulation price, 70 centimes, clearly displayed. One of the baguettes has already been cut in half and I ask for the remainder.

'Seventy centimes,' says the baker, turning away to wipe some crumbs off the counter. I look at the price. I look at my half baguette. The baker looks up expecting me to pay, and I look at him. Several seconds pass in silence.

'Sorry, I should have said 35. I was thinking about something,' he mumbles.

In the Basque country – Hendaye to Gabas

Giving him the money I say, 'Yes, perhaps you were thinking that I was a foreigner.'

'Not at all. That's not the way I work.'

On the opposite side of the road, in the pharmacy, I buy plasters, sticky bandages, and a new invention, liquid skin. I left home with a first-aid kit capable of coping with minor battlefield disasters but the predicted tendonitis, diarrhoea, and blisters on my heel have not appeared. Instead the blister on my little toe has come back, deeper down.

I retreat to the hotel and hack off the dead crust with a blunt pair of scissors. The liquid skin and an impossibly large bandage complete the operation, but my feet no longer fit into my boots, so I hobble off to the supermarket to buy a pair of flip-flops.

I spend the day wandering aimlessly. In this village surrounded by mountains, the banana trees seem incongruous: but then St-Etienne-de-Baïgorry is only 160m above sea level.

In the evening when I come down from my room, Paul is already sitting at the solid wooden table in the back room of the hotel. The Ferme Esteben, he says, was fine, except that he had needed to ask for blankets. Two other walkers come in. I look discreetly at their legs. Strong muscles, skin somewhere between burnt red and tanned brown; weathered sober faces. Jean-Paul has a full beard but Richard is freshly shaved. They started at Hendaye on the same day as Paul and I. They have the easy familiarity of old friends who have been walking together since they were young, but as they talk I realise that they have only known each other for four days. They met by chance on the first section and have been keeping in step ever since.

The door opens again and another man walks in. He is conspicuously black: few black people are to be seen on the mountains, and he is wearing a black sleeveless tee-shirt and tight black shorts. He asks quietly if he can eat, though he is not staying at the hotel. I place his accent somewhere in rural northern France, but not in the Parisian suburbs or indeed in any large town: his French is too mellifluous. He has a few day's growth on his chin and a similar length on the top of his head; mostly black hair but with a few white strands. An angular face, without wrinkles though he must be about my age. He introduces himself and shakes hands. Big hands, like the rest of him.

'We are camping at the hostel but I wanted to eat a proper meal. Grégory is eating from a packet tonight,' says Aimé. 'We left Hendaye four days ago.' He is hoping to do the whole of the Pyrenean Way before the beginning of August. His friend will accompany him for the first two weeks.

We eat omelettes, duck *confit* and chips, *gâteau basque* and ice cream, far from the refined food of yesterday evening but more satisfying.

St-Etienne-de-Baïgorry to St-Jean-Pied-de-Port

In the cool of the new day, I cross the modern bridge over the *baïgorry*, the red river. It is not really red but the rocks over which it passes give it a reddish tinge and give the town a way of distinguishing itself from all the other St-Etiennes. Incidentally, the Revolutionaries of 1789 renamed Baïgorry: the 'red river' became the 'hot gates' – Thermopyles. Like their new names for the months of the year, the name didn't stick.

The valley is shrouded in mist but the path soon rises above the puffy clouds revealing harsh crumpled mountain ridges separated by shadowy valleys under a washed-out watercolour sky. On the hill slope I catch up with a walker. With his mop of untamed dark brown hair, sideburns, angular features, and long neck he looks like a character from *Astérix the Gaul*. He is wearing a shapeless turgid green hat, just like mine.

'Have you seen my friend?' he asks me.

'The tall black man?' I guess.

'That's him. He's not particularly tall though. People just think that he is.'

In the Basque country – Hendaye to Gabas

'He passed in front of the hotel when I was tying my laces. He must be about five minutes ahead of us.'

This must be Grégory. Gradually, I realise that he is the man who asked for water on the first evening. We spot a figure moving quickly along a road above us so he dashes off to catch up.

Five identical white Renault mini-vans are parked at the pass. Four of them speed off in different directions as I approach. 'We meet up here every morning for a chat after checking out the sheep,' explains the old man at the wheel. The dogs in the back confirm the story. 'We're bringing them closer to the road for shearing next week,' he continues.

At the top of the Munhoa the wind is blowing hard and I have to put on all the layers of clothing I possess, but eating lunch later in the valley just outside St-Jean-Pied-de-Port I take off my tee-shirt and sunbathe.

St-Jean-Pied-de-Port is a major crossroads for walkers. Two paths – two cultures – intersect here and then go their separate ways. Profane meets Christian. Altitude meets distance. Clay meets tarmac. As well as being one of the few towns on the Pyrenean Way, St-Jean-Pied-de-Port is also the last resting place in France for pilgrims crossing the mountains on their way to Santiago de Compostela: 'pied de port' translates as 'at the foot of the pass'.

In the hostel, lying on a bed in the middle of the day, resting his bandaged feet, is an Indian man in his 50s. Married to a Dutch woman and living in Holland for 35 years, he started walking at Le Puy 36 days ago. He calculates that he is about halfway. It is not a pilgrimage: he is not even Christian. He is simply walking to allow himself time to think, and incidentally collecting sponsorship to educate Dhalit children in the village where he was born. He hopes that a walker he met a few days ago will catch up with him so that they can cross the Pyrenees together. It is one of the longest and most arduous sections on the whole route.

I go into town and cross the river Nive – the same river which passes through Bidarray. Here it is lined with houses, their overhanging wooden balconies reflected in the still water. The bridge and the balconies are festooned with baskets of flowers. A neatly laid cobbled road leads under the stone arch, through the town wall, and up the hill between an extraordinary array of ancient stone-built or half-timbered structures, mainly shops, restaurants, and hostels. The shop fronts are for the most part unobtrusive; some coordinating authority seems to have decreed that any exposed woodwork must be painted a uniform reddish-brown.

Heaped against the door of one of the hostels are a couple of tattered rucksacks, one red, one blue. They each have a pierced scallop shell – the emblem of pilgrims on the road to Santiago de Compostela – tied to them, and a pair of worn walking boots and a stick complete the pile. Kit left temporarily on the doorstep at the end of the day by hikers too tired to drag it upstairs? There is something wrong. They are exactly the right elements in exactly the right place. It is not a random collection of equipment but a carefully coordinated new-fashioned inn sign.

In the last 20 years St-Jean-Pied-de-Port has rediscovered its vocation as a staging post on the Chemin de St-Jacques de Compostelle, as it is known in French. St Jacques – St James in English, Santo Iago in old Spanish – was one of the first Christian disciples. He reappears providentially in Galicia in northern Spain around AD 825, when bishop Theodomirus identified an ancient tomb as his last resting place: at the time Spain was divided between followers of Muhammad and Christ, after the Moorish invasions of the 8th century. Gradually the tomb became an emblematic rallying point for Christians and the first pilgrimages began. By the early 12th century, with the first crusaders having taken Jerusalem, Santiago de Compostela was being actively promoted as a holiday destination for the politically aware Christian faithful. Through them, Spain would also be brought back into Christendom. The process took several centuries, but 1492 was a momentous year for Spain. In the same year that Columbus 'discovered' America, the catholic King Fernando and Queen Isabella finally took control of Granada, pushing the Moors back across the Straits of Gibraltar. For hundreds of years the Pyrenees had metaphorically divided Europe and Africa. Now Spain was set to become a truly European power.

Half way up the main street of St-Jean-Pied-de-Port there is a stone arch leading into an attractively shady room. This is the home of the Friends of the Chemin de St-Jacques. Sitting behind one of the desks is Pierre, a Parisian. Newly retired, and with a girlfriend who lives on the coast, he likes to come down and help with the centre.

'I would say that the majority of walkers have some kind of spiritual motive, but not necessarily a Christian one.'

'Does this cause problems in Spain, in those hostels run by the church?'

'No, not as long as the walker keeps his *credencial* up to date.'

I look at the chart behind him. In 1996, just 1,264 visitors passed under the arch to get their *credencial*, pilgrim passport, stamped; in 2003 there were 18,196 of them. The Pyrenean Way is much less popular. I reckon I have met just about everybody who set out from Hendaye at the same time as me: Paul, Aimé, Grégory, Richard, Jean-Paul, and the American woman. Allowing for a couple of campers who are keeping to themselves this makes nine people walking eastwards; I have seen no more than two a day walking in the other direction.

'Why are so many people doing the Chemin de St Jacques? Obviously it isn't a sudden explosion in the number of faithful.' I say.

'Several reasons. The paths became a World Heritage site in 1998 and then 1999 and 2004 were holy years, when the saint day falls on a Sunday. Then there is the shorter working week and a snowball effect – with a lot more television time. But above all I think it is the increased number of hostels, which means that shorter walking days are possible.'

All the passes over the Pyrenees have been used by pilgrims at one time or another but of the four main routes, three, from Le Puy, Tours, and Vezelay converge just before St-Jean-Pied-de-Port. The other, from Arles, passes over the Col de Somport. Pierre has done the route four times, once running the 2200 km from Basle in 45 days. He is thin – weighs 62 kg, he says – and keeps his rucksack down to 6kg.

The past is filtered and distilled to become history, and the paths over the Pyrenees are the funnels through which it is poured into the still. Many armies have marched through here. Many lives ended here. Much history was written here. In AD 778, St-Jean-Pied-de-Port saw the army of Charlemagne return, defeated, from one of the earliest attempts to kick the Moors out of Spain. His nephew Roland was ambushed at Roncevaux just over the border and killed by the Basques. But history has distilled this and removed some of the more unpleasant facts to give us the epic *Song of Roland*, written around AD 1100, at the very start of the crusades. In this version Roland was killed by the Moors; Charlemagne then returned to Spain and inflicted a crushing defeat on them. Neither is true, yet it is the *Song of Roland* which has captured the popular imagination over the centuries. Even so, not everybody was convinced by the myth: all the main pilgrim routes avoid the Basque heartland on the coast, preferring the dangers of the mountains.

St-Jean-Pied-de-Port to the Route de Phagalcette hostel

In the morning, I walk through the town, past the Vauban fortress, and head south. Here the Pyrenean Way and the Chemin de St Jacques follow the same itinerary. They are waymarked from time to time by short painted stripes: a white stripe on top of a red one. When the FFRP was looking for a suitable sign to indicate the new long-distance paths, it borrowed the existing markings of pilgrim routes. The white stripe represents the sacred spirit which guides pilgrims as they walk with their head in the clouds. The red stripe represents the flesh: feet covered in blood. It is a nice tale but one which I have been completely unable to confirm. Perhaps this is just another reworking of history.

I catch up with Grégory and Aimé on the lower slopes of the first hill. They are looking alternately at a map and at a waymark painted on a gatepost.

'We continued straight on, following the fence, but it is a dead end' explains Grégory.

I extract my GPS to check where we are.

'It was a good trick you played on me yesterday,' says Grégory grinning, as we wait for the GPS to find the satellites and I explain how it works. 'After you said that Aimé was ahead of me, I ran up the hill trying to catch him up. It was only when I caught up with Richard on the top of the Munhoa that I realised that he must be behind me! He had gone for a cup of coffee.'

The GPS is a superb tool, but it is not infallible. When you are hopelessly lost in the middle of a forest it is no use at all because the leaf cover prevents the satellite signals penetrating to ground level. Even when it works perfectly it has its limits. I once used it to follow a path across the heath, scarring myself on brambles and crushing my toes on fallen trees. I knew exactly where I was to within ten metres: on a path which was clearly marked on my large-scale map. I knew exactly how far it was to the Eiffel Tower and, more usefully, how many metres to the ford across the river. But I had to admit the evidence of my eyes. The path didn't exist any more. I was, to all intents and purposes, lost.

'Whilst you were chatting, I have been studying,' says Aimé. 'If you look carefully at the waymark, part of it has faded. We are supposed to turn left here.'

We walk together for a while, descending into the valley of Estérençuby where I leave Aimé and Grégory in the café. I climb again following the road in the direction of the hostel, the curiously named 'Route de Phagalcette'. Tiring of walking on tarmac, I just want to be able to take my boots off and sit down. I plod on, the road meandering through the forest, until I realise that I haven't seen any waymarks since the village. My map makes no sense. I can see only trees; the cartographers saw only fields. I extract my GPS but it tells me something improbable, so I stuff it back into my rucksack. In a kilometre or so I should be able to see where I am.

On the plateau, I can indeed see where I am. But I'm not where I ought to be. The GPS was right: I really am off the map.

Somewhat later, I open the gate into the yard outside the hostel. Aimé and Grégory are sitting at a wooden picnic table, complaining of the cold. The wind has blown in since this morning, crushing the clouds together to fill up the sky. Grégory has tendonitis. I give him one of my dwindling supply of anti-inflammatory tablets: for the moment my knees are holding out. The hostel owner appears at the door and offers me a beer. She has a perfect figure: we are going to eat copiously tonight.

Route de Phagalcette hostel to Bagargrak

During the night the sky above has been torn in two, the ragged edge of the sailor's trousers flapping as the wind increases. Grey clouds are blowing in from the Atlantic to the west; the blue navy is scuttling away to the east.

Far below, down in the valley, the frothy white clouds are rucked up by the rising sun. They push up the valley, building up behind the hillocks, lapping over the tops, climbing up the mountain slope behind me, linked invisibly to the bank of clouds above. It is a stunningly beautiful scene.

I press on as quickly as possible to the top of the first hill, surfing in front of the breaking waves to be rewarded by a view of the mountain range stretching away into the distance. Over there, the low sun has coloured the sky a limpid blue. But each summit has its own wisp of cloud, a smoke signal announcing the changing weather. I fancy that I can identify the Pic du Midi d'Ossau, several days' walking away. A herd of cows is ruminating disconsolately. They have understood. One by one they sit down as the dreary dampness engulfs us.

An hour or so afterwards I stumble across a hand-painted sign saying '*ardi gasna*'. A few minutes later another sign explains: '*fromage de brebis*, sheep's cheese', adding 'sausages, water, wine' and – more enigmatically for I can see nothing through the mist – 'here!' A track leads down into a slight hollow where a low building emerges out of the whiteness. Flanked by a couple of forlorn trees, the rendered stone cottage is capped by a sparklingly new corrugated metal roof. The door is ajar. Through it I can hear two men speaking in Basque.

'*Bonjour*,' I say, pushing on the door. Inside it is dark, even with the door open. Hardly any light filters through the two small grimy windows. Opposite me is an old man sitting on a stool next to a large corrugated metal tub, like the one my grandmother used for her weekly wash. One arm is plunged into the tub, apparently stirring something.

'I'll be with you in five minutes,' he grumbles and I go round the back of the *cayolar* to wait for him to open up.

Cayolars are shepherd's huts, and were an essential part of the traditional mountain economy. In the past, ownership of a *cayolar* included not only possession of the building and the adjacent land for a sheep fold but also the right to graze the sheep over a large area and to take wood for building and heating. *Cayolars* were the mountain outpost of the *etxe* down on the plain and a place for cheese-making and hospitality in an otherwise lonely environment.

The shop is a windowless room divided by a small counter, with sausages hanging from the wall behind it. Wooden shelves support rows of cheeses, about 60 in all. On the top shelf they are creamy white, those lower down are progressively more gnarled, gritty, and grey, like the man himself. He goes straight to one of the cheeses on the lowest shelf, cuts it in half and then places his knife on the rind to indicate a suitable portion. I nod in agreement.

'Three-and-a-half months old' he explains, 'is the ideal age to eat it. Any younger and it is tasteless.'

He has 300 sheep. He will have them sheared in a couple of weeks. This reminds me of my recurring preoccupation. This morning Aimé found a tick in his navel. It had bitten him 'elsewhere' as well. Paul announced that he too had been bitten but claimed that it is alright as long as the tick doesn't make its home on you. I ask the farmer what he thinks.

'The little black ones, about 2mm long, will jump out of the ferns and bite you but they don't carry Lyme disease round here,' he reassures me. 'Then there are the little white ones on the sheep, which are not good for them… Excuse me. I must go. I'm in the middle of making the cheese.'

Outside, swimming in the cold white drizzle, I am disorientated, blindly following the direction indicated by my GPS, eyes on the ground. The dampness smothers all sound apart from the swishing of my waterproof leggings against each other. Suddenly, I hear a rustling and glimpse a streak of yellow moving jerkily through the long grass. I approach the place where it seems to have stopped and part the grass.

Staring up at me suspiciously are two tiny round black eyes under inflated yellow eyelids. The wee beastie's head is diamond-shaped, or rather would be, if its nose wasn't so flat. Wide, irregular, yellow-and-black stripes run along its body and tail. It is like a big lizard but it is too fat and the colouring and the head are all wrong. This must be a fire salamander and he must be lost. At 1050m above sea level, in daytime, in open countryside, and at least 100m from the nearest river, he shouldn't be here. These salamanders live mainly lower down, near watercourses through trees, and they only come out at night. He must have strayed from the forest which I can see on the map, but which is completely hidden from view. Salamanders are a protected species but their habitat is increasingly being eroded by human activities and I've never seen one before. It needed a misty day to improve their visibility.

Finally, I surface. My head pokes out of the wet and I can once again see where I am going. To the west, the mist covers the entire landscape, but to the east the sky and even the valleys are clear. Somehow, the mountains have managed to repel the onslaught.

I am just thinking that I haven't met any other walkers all day when a fat woman, a priest, and a group of retired people come into view. I look at the map in disbelief to discover that there is a road only half an hour away. I am entering the Forest of Iraty, a popular holiday destination and the largest beech forest in western Europe. A large forest in an even larger forest. Trees cover one-third of the Pyrenees, more than a million hectares.

The hostel at Bagargrak is excellent value though rather anonymous. Clean, modern, individual rooms, lots of heating and even halogen rings on the stove, all for the same price as basic bunks elsewhere on the walk. There are two young women staying in the hostel. They are the first people I have met walking a significant section of the Pyrenean Way in the opposite direction and, apart from the elusive American, the first women on the route. They started from Gourette a week ago but had to hitch the first section because there was too much snow.

Bagargrak to Logibar

It rains 200 days a year here and in the night, the clouds seem once again to have won the battle: I spend several minutes finding the first waymark. Aimé and Grégory have camped on the only flat square of ground and are cooking breakfast in the shelter of a dry stone pen. We agree that it must be something to do with sheep, though we can't work out why there should be so many of them. As I am leaving them, Aimé says, 'Thanks for everything'. He does this at least once a day. I ask him why, but he can't explain.

I climb up the Pic des Escalliers and cross over to the northern side. The clouds are a little thinner here and I can see them being whisked past me up the cliff face and over the top. I can half imagine the vertiginous view which the map warns me is there.

Later, when I reach a road I meet a man with a white Renault van and dogs. He is herding sheep, taking them down to Larrau today and then up to the *estives*, the high pastures, for the summer. Although he is nearing retirement age, French still doesn't come naturally to him.

Barking dogs and tinkling sheep bells accompany me for much of the rest of the morning. Occasionally I hear the shepherd cry out 'Purr tchai,' but I don't see either him or the animals again. Crickets and skylarks are also invisibly present, tantalising me with their false promise of sun just a few steps away.

I walk into a herd of cows. *Blondes d'Aquitaine*, their heavy – but silent – bells hang from their necks on wide red ribbons, which complement their beige coats perfectly. Four of them are lying down, arranged like the spokes of a wheel, looking outwards over the cliff, their rumps together, protected from the cold by the clumps of bracken. Superb but stupid, indifferent to each other, indifferent to me, they look bored as only cows can look bored.

The *blondes* have taken over. The local girl was a petite country type, mousey, well used to life in the mountains. She sported a cute set of cheerfully upturned horns, reminiscent of the shape of a lyre, or so they say round here. '*Vive la vaca*, long live the cow', reads the inscription in the porch of one church. But the local girl lost out to her more flamboyant cousins brought up in the fertile meadows on the plains. There are now only 100 true Basque cows; in the 1960s there were 20,000.

Finally the path drops off the ridge down to the hostel in Logibar and I am below the clouds for the last twenty minutes. Aimé and Grégory took another route, descending directly to Larrau in the valley and then walking along the road to Logibar. They recount their day over a beer.

'Not easy in the fog, but Grégory used his GPH and we got through,' Aimé tells me.

'GPH?' I ask.

'Global Positioning Hooter,' clarifies Grégory, pointing to his nose, grinning.

'The walk wasn't much fun but it was worth it just for the café in Larrau,' continues Aimé. 'There was a tatty old sign on the street outside a house so we opened the door. Inside was a dark room with a long wooden table and an old couple at one end eating lunch. I said, "Sorry, we thought this was the café," and we were about to go out when the man said, "It *is* the café, please come in." The building used to be a *cayolar* and they want to maintain the tradition of informal hospitality rather than have an ordinary modern establishment.'

We compare wounds. My toes are now covered with blisters, despite wearing two pairs of socks and a pharmacy's entire stock of Compeed second-skin plasters.

Aimé advises: 'I'll only give you one idea for your blisters. Two pairs of socks. I won't say any more, but think about it. You will thank me.'

Aimé and Grégory push on to find somewhere to camp. I eat with Paul again for the seventh time. Once we have reviewed the day's events we have little to say to each other. We have shared details of our families, our background, our work, and our holidays. Avoided politics and religion. But we always share a table. I do wish he didn't eat so slowly.

Logibar to Sainte-Engrâce

I leave Logibar ridiculously late and regret it all day, the sun having recovered its powers. On the slopes above the hostel, gleaming white puffball mushrooms poke through the coarse grass. I break one in two and put it to my nose: hazelnuts. A worm – or is it a snake? – slithers by my feet. The suspiciously virulent yellow V on its forehead makes me think that I should have been more wary.

The path leads into the mottled shade of the forest and joins a dirt track, recently opened up for extracting timber. My map says that I should turn right but the forest is impenetrable so I continue to follow the track, increasingly sure that I am heading in the wrong direction – until I reach a gate and there is another waymark, although I am 500m from where I expected to be. A diversion I presume. Recently cut trees are piled up at the side of the track, waiting to be dragged away. The aroma of broken bark and sawdust is complemented by the peppery smell of over-ripe *cèpes jaunes* mushrooms.

Coming out of the woods, I am overtaken by a large van, slipping along the still-wet track, thumping and bleating as it goes. It stops and the sheep tumble out, clashing corkscrew horns against the sides of the van, like tourists out of a holiday coach, eager to be outside at last, but uncertain what to do next. They look around at each other, tossing their unshorn fleece out of their eyes, a little giddy from the journey, hoping for leadership or inspiration, until the shepherd and his dog chase them away onto the long grass. Unlike its bovine cousin, the Basco-béarnaise sheep is in no danger of extinction, thanks to its *appellation contrôlée* Ossau-Iraty cheese.

By lunchtime I am looking for somewhere to sit in the shade, so I try the door of the Cayolar d'Anhaou. It is open, but before crossing the threshold I go to look at the other two nearby buildings. The first is not much bigger than a large pig pen, constructed in dry stone, with the rafters tumbling dangerously into a mass of weeds. The door has disappeared. This must be the prehistoric-*cayolar*. Across the track is the 21st century chalet-*cayolar*. All new wood and shutters. Locked and unwelcoming. My *cayolar* must span the 200 years between them. Originally built of dry stone and tiled with wooden shingles, at some stage the walls have been concreted inside and out and the roof re-covered with corrugated metal sheeting.

In the Basque country – Hendaye to Gabas

I can smell charcoal as I enter. Today the air seems full of smells: it must be the effect of the damp followed by the scorching sun. The one room contains an assortment of home-made furniture, constructed from tree trunks, empty oil cans, and irregular planks, rescued from building sites. A gas oven and separate rings look as though they are in working order, though there are neither pots nor pans, nor indeed any gas. There are two double beds, one with a mattress: dusty and grey but still plausible. Basic but clean, so I settle in and munch my lunch contentedly.

I notice the smell of aniseed and looking round discover an empty bottle of Ricard *pastis*. Next to it is a bottle of Château la Roseraie St Emilion AOC 1996 with vinegary dregs still slopping about in the bottom. Ricard is not poor man's *pastis* and Château la Roseraie costs 13€ a bottle. Either shepherds are richer than they used to be or some visitors spent a well-oiled night here not long ago.

I have run out of water. When will scientists find a way of compacting it, like dehydrated food? Will they ever invent *dehydrated* water? The stream looks tempting but I don't want to drink from it. Instead I fill my hat and upend it over my head. I trudge down the exposed slope in the mid-day fire, a walk only relieved by a short section sunk between two field walls, hidden under the trees. I cross the Pont d'Enfer, Hell's Bridge – the devil seems to be going in for quantity rather than quality – and look down at the water below. If the bridge belongs to hell, the river must flow from heaven. The still waters are translucent in the shade of the bridge; in the sunlight they are coloured with the vibrant blue and turquoise normally reserved for Polynesian lagoons. I contemplate jumping in like the sailors on Captain Bligh's *Bounty*, to re-hydrate myself by absorbing the water through my skin, but decide against it.

Instead, when I reach the top of the road leading to the Gorges de Kakouéta I attack the drinks stand. An Orangina and an ice cream, followed by a Perrier and another ice cream. In the bar at the entrance to the gorges I drink a beer, followed by another beer, and then make an unwise decision: to investigate further. I can leave my rucksack at the bar; the gorges are reputed to be cool, relatively speaking.

The gorge is indeed cool, and humid. Water cascades over improbable limestone formations between cliff faces hundreds of metres high. In places the heavens are reduced to a distant ribbon between the luxuriant vegetation clinging to the sides of the canyon. I am sandwiched between a large group of retired Spanish people, carefully picking their way over the slippery rocks, and a French family anxious to progress more quickly. Borne along at their rhythm, I am unable to go either faster or slower. Suddenly the man in front stops and turns to face me.

'*¡No pasa!*' he says, stretching his arms wide apart so that I couldn't possibly go round him without falling into the river. Beyond him I can see a woman squatting in the middle of the path. I look away.

The grotto at the end of the trail is full of stalactites but they are a bit of a disappointment. These are not glistening white daggers waiting to pierce you from shoulder to hip should they fall. They are more like petrified sumo wrestlers. You would still die if one fell on you. But crushed not perforated.

I ask one of the Spaniards to take a photograph. Looking at it later I can see that it captures my state perfectly: red tee-shirt, a redder face, and the reddest of lips; dilated pupils, eyebrows raised as if they were stretching to catch up with my receding hair, and a completely inane smile.

By the time I get back to the road, I have added two hours to my walk and I am dead tired. The tarmac is melting and I am as well. I still have an hour to go. More worryingly, for the first time I am way behind the schedule for the day, even discounting the trip up the gorge.

At the hostel in Sainte-Engrâce, Paul is waiting for me with a welcoming beer. The hostel owner asks him to show me to the dormitory but he can't find it any more. The sun must have gone to his head as much as it has gone to mine.

To be honest, these mountain houses are not simple affairs. If

In the Basque country – Hendaye to Gabas

the *etxe* of the plains is a Renault Espace people-carrier with everything under one roof, the typical house here is an ageing saloon car with a roof rack. The sheep are in the car with the farmer sitting on top. Trundling along behind it is a trailer with the food; attached to the trailer is a motor bike, with its side-car stuffed with wood. The different elements of the house may be arranged in various ways but steep roofs and the use of stone are common features.

I go to visit the Romanesque church opposite the hostel. The capitals at the tops of the columns depict a range of scenes including Solomon and his queen enjoying themselves in an unreligious way, and the devil finishing off the mortal remains of a sinner. The legs and body have already disappeared into his stomach, but the arms and the head are still between his teeth.

When I return to the hostel Aimé and Grégory are slumped on the terrace drinking beer. Akerbeltz ambrée Gorrosta is an un-pasteurised amber ale made in a micro-brewery a little way down the valley. Unlike the big commercial mouthwashes, this beer has flavour. Malty without being syrupy, the black goat label has become something to seek out at the end of the day.

'Since Paul is only going a short distance tomorrow, this is the last time we will see each other. How about eating together?' suggests Aimé. We accept.

We climb the stairs to the dining room. The hostel is full for the first holiday weekend of the summer and the tables are crammed together. The food is both tasty and plentiful.

I say, 'What I like about walking is the contrast with being at work, sitting in front of a computer all day. I like being "elsewhere". And it gives me the opportunity to think about things, to put them in perspective.'

'*Moi, je pense que la marche rend con* – I think that walking makes you pig stupid,' comments Aimé, continuing: 'At first you think about your life, your relationships. Then when you have exhausted the possibilities of that you look at the scenery. You think about where you are going, how long it will take to get there and what you will eat. But after three or four days all you think about is walking, putting one foot in front of the other. Then the mind goes completely blank and you think about nothing at all. *Ça rend con.* Mind you, yesterday evening I managed to learn a page of script in half the time it would normally take me.'

Aimé and Grégory are actors, and have been playing together in a Parisian production. Grégory is an actor by training; Aimé 'just started doing it'. A bit like their approach to the Pyrenean Way. Grégory spent a fortnight walking every day to practice. Aimé, whose idea it was, simply got up last Thursday morning and started.

They ask Paul what he does for a living. It is noisy and difficult to follow the conversation. In any case I have heard it all already. My attention starts to wander.

Behind us is a group of young potholers, off to explore a new gallery tomorrow. To my left is a French family who seem to know the hostel owner. And to my right there are four men all substantially the same age and build, talking in a mixture of Basque and French. I think about how improbable we must look to them. The Englishman, the hunchback, the black, and the Gaul.

'You're not listening, are you?' exclaims Aimé, indignantly, looking at me. 'You've already switched off. You know you're not going to see us after this evening. You don't give a damn. You're already in another world.'

'No, I was listening,' I lie, unconvincingly, and then revise myself. 'I can't hear for all the noise,' I splutter. I am just too tired.

Outside before splitting up to go to bed, Grégory suggests we swap addresses. And surnames, for we only know each other's first names. Aimé M . . . writes Aimé on the back of a cigarette packet.

'That's an Arab name, isn't it?' remarks Paul.

'And . . . What about it?' snaps Aimé, stiffening.

'Nothing. Nothing at all, ' says Paul meekly.

We are all exhausted.

In the Basque country – Hendaye to Gabas

Sainte-Engrâce to Lescun

The Pyrenean Way follows a narrow valley out of the village. The overarching trees, tumbling ivy and swishing ferns, the splashing water underfoot, the exaggerated shadows cast by my lamp in the darkness and the early morning fog throw me back into the primeval soup. At the head of the valley the path winds through the forest and just before emerging into daylight deposits me in front of a row of lichen-covered stone water troughs. Next to them, carved in the native rock, is a larger-than-life head, ostensibly human but sinisterly distorted. Its mouth is wide open, and painted red as if blood were dripping out. This is the spirit of the spring: beware he who tampers with nature's gift!

> Instead of smiling at these superstitions, let's stop for a instant considering the Pyrenees as zones to be developed, ski slopes, or even picturesque landscapes… and imagine each summit, each slope, each forest, each spring, sheltering a god, a fairy, a witch. Suddenly, the countryside comes to life, is metamorphosed. Pressing an ear to the rock, one can hear the oracles of the Pic de Encantats [fairies], that petrified giant who may get up and walk at any time… Trees pursue their objectives. Above our heads, crows go about their business, on which our fate depends… reality is just the surface. Behind the immobility of the landscape the secret mechanism of the world is set into motion, the exclusive domain of the divine…

> …today, all has changed. Because in the 18th century, there came forth men from the plains, animated by another faith, that of Science… And, immediately, the Pyrenees of weeds and nasty smells are transformed into the abstract Pyrenees of books.

It is all very well understanding the scientific mechanisms – how the mountains came into being, why certain animals live there – but in the process of rationalisation we have lost something important. The mountains are no longer so enthrallingly mysterious.

I leave the forest for the short-cropped moorland grass, and brilliant sunshine. With the bank of clouds below me, I climb, avoiding the unprotected *gouffres*, natural pits, which dot the slope. Another flock of sheep stumbles out of a trailer.

When I reach the ridge and look across into Spain, the contrast with the French side of the frontier is horrifying. There is a joyful azure sky above and fluffy clouds below in the valleys, just as in France. But over the border, the mountains are injured, badly burned, irredeemably scarred. Everything is grey, that numbing neutral grey, halfway between black and white. The rocks are fissured and irregular. Some grass has regenerated but not much. The pine trees are woefully rare. As I approach the pass I can see that the damage is not restricted to Spain. Whole swathes of the mountain have been devastated. But then, when I finally reach frontier post no. 262 and walk between the lonesome pines, I can see that they have not been burned at all: the rock is *naturally* ugly.

If there is one commune in the Pyrenees which has been moulded by its geology it is Arette-La Pierre-Saint Martin. Here at the Col de la Pierre the limestone karst is like a giant drain grid, with crazy fissures to be avoided every other step. No sooner has rain fallen than it is swallowed and then digested in the bowels of the earth. The consequent scarcity of pasture and drinking water for sheep necessarily created tensions between shepherd neighbours on either side of the frontier.

It is a story of low murder and high farce. According to one version of the events, two shepherds have an argument about the right to water their sheep at a spring near here. The Frenchman, Pierre Sansoler, from the Barétous valley to the north is killed. His relatives take up arms, traverse the mountain and descend into the Roncal valley in Spain. Finding only the pregnant wife of the murderer, they kill her and cut her open, hanging the unborn boy from the branch of a beech tree along with the entrails of his mother. A series of retributive attacks follows. So much for the low murder. The high farce is contained in another version, which relates that the whole series of attacks and counter-attacks is brought to a halt by a young woman, acting alone. Hearing of the feud she takes off her clothes and covers her body with honey and then feathers. On seeing her, the belligerents are so frightened that they return meekly home.

There must be a kernel of truth somewhere in these tales because in October 1375 a meeting was called between the inhabitants of the two valleys to establish a lasting peace. The arbitrators decided that both sides had suffered equally. The Barétounais were to give the Roncalais three heifers each year, as they had done in the past. In a masterpiece of diplomacy this is described in the pact as 'for the use of the springs or to atone for the murders' – reflecting the different views of the two sides. Conflicts over grazing rights were common in the Pyrenees and there are several examples of these *lies et passeries* agreements, one even declaring that the two communities involved would never take up arms against each other, even if their respective governments ordered them to do so.

Nowadays, in a ceremony which has more meaning for tourists than local residents, the cows are led to the boundary stone – hence the name La Pierre – and given to the Spanish mayor (he gives them back later and takes the money instead). In return the Spaniards lay on a feast.

I walk down the road to La Pierre-St Martin, one of the two nuclei of the commune, and enter the village. Anything that nature can do, man can do better: the tower blocks would disgrace a Parisian suburb, never mind a Pyrenean hillside. They are monolithic, rectangular, and faceless; grey, greyer, and greyest. There are some zones of white, but the only colour visible is a kind of muddy beige. Between the buildings there are wide roads and car parks. Which blend in extremely well with the tower blocks. The village is even uglier than its surroundings.

I need to buy some food. Looking at the map last night, the village appeared big enough to have a couple of shops. But I can see nobody to ask. I try in one of the blocks, but it seems to be entirely residential – though singularly lacking in residents. The next block looks more promising. There is even a sign pointing to a bar.

I am walking up the steps into it when I meet a little girl and her mother.

'Hello,' says the girl.
'Hello,' I reply.
'Are you on holiday?'
'Yes.'
'What are you doing?'
'Walking.'
'Me, I want to go sledging.'

Even a three-year-old can recognise the essential. La Pierre-Saint Martin is dedicated to winter sports. It is of no interest whatsoever in the summer.

I walk along bleak corridors, up and down stairs (the lifts are not working) and finally discover the bar. I sit on the terrace, holding down my papers to prevent them being blown away in the wind, and sip a mineral water. According to the barmaid there are only 30–40 inhabitants at this time of year. There will be 300–400 at the height of summer and 3,000–4,000 in winter. No, there are no shops open. Actually the bar is the only place open in the whole village. But she searches around and manages to find me a couple of granary bars, for slimmers.

Not everybody shares my view of the village and its geology. It is an internationally renowned centre for caving. A vertical 330m *gouffre* drops down to the galleries, over 50km of them. The system contains some of the deepest and biggest caves in the world, stretching as far as the lake at the bottom of the Gorges de Kakouéta, where an underground river emerges. There may be no water on the surface but there are real rivers below it, where the permeable karst meets the impermeable rocks below. At one time the French Electricity Board even considered using the water for hydroelectric power, boring tunnels into the massif and financing exploratory expeditions. Evidently La Pierre-Saint Martin has hidden depths.

The commune is also known for a different geological phenomenon. Arette, its other nucleus, was the epicentre of the last significant earthquake to shake the French Pyrenees, on 13 August 1967: 5.3 on the Richter scale. One person was killed and 80% of the houses in the village were uninhabitable as a result.

The name Arette is derived from the Basque *ar*, stone. *Pierre* is French for stone. Arette-la Pierre-Saint Martin: even its name is made of rock and fissured like the landscape.

I leave the village, walking with my eyes on the ground, picking my way between ankle-twisting cracks and neck-breaking pits. There is a small patch of residual snow in a crevasse. I tread warily, remembering the warning sign: 'On 17 February 2001 Élodie and Loriane fell into a *gouffre* 35m deep whilst sledging. Now, they beg you not to stray beyond the safety barriers.'

Ahead of me is an unforgiving vertical rock face. I can't see a way through but the map is quite clear. I will have to scale the face. At the Pas de l'Osque there are only four metres to climb but it frightens me silly. If I fall off I will inevitably tumble heels-over-head down the steep incline behind me. If I am lucky I will come to rest 50m below. But there is no alternative and in a few seconds I am at the top, quivering.

Down below in the next valley I hear a whistling. A *marmotte* – groundhog – its sunbathing disturbed, is warning its neighbours. Way in front of me, there are two larger specks gambolling down the scree. I make a big effort and catch up to them.

'You're doing well today,' says Aimé.

'You're doing better. You were still sleeping when I left. I didn't even notice you overtaking me.' I reply.

'It was foggy so we decided to follow the road to La Pierre-Saint Martin. And then a milk lorry came along so we hitched a lift,' explains Grégory.

They feed me and we walk together as far as the Cabane du Cap de la Baitch. The scree is replaced by pasture. At an hour's walk from the nearest road, it must be a hard life for the couple who live there all summer, milking sheep, making cheese, and rearing pigs. No electricity, of course, but abundant clear spring water and an idyllic location.

I had set my heart on the hostel at Labérouat where the path meets the road, but it is closed so I continue disconsolately on to Lescun. I have been walking ten and a half hours. When I stumble into the village square Aimé and Grégory are already sitting on the terrace of a bar. Inevitably, they are downing beers.

'It's a dangerous drug,' I say. 'You start with a milk lorry in the morning and by the evening you're already hooked on hitch-hiking. You'll be climbing into 40 tonne artics soon, dreaming of the poppy fields in Afghanistan.'

'No, we didn't hitch,' corrects Grégory, 'we walked.'

We compare notes. They took the old path, which still has the waymarks intact, whilst I followed the official route.

Jean-Paul and Richard are also in the village. Thanks to the long haul today, we have caught up with them.

Lescun to Etsaut

In the timid dawn light, Lescun resembles a Yorkshire mining village in the depths of winter seen through a hangover. It isn't raining but the roads are running with water and the roofs are dripping methodically. Yesterday evening's honey-coloured stone has been reduced to shades of grey. Everything is out of focus. Not a breath of wind. The clouds have come down from the *estives* for breakfast.

Later on, in the next valley, I discover the base of the clouds. It is like being in the audience at the start of a play. The lights have been dimmed and we have all settled down. We are looking in the direction of the stage, waiting. The curtain shivers and then starts

In the Basque country – Hendaye to Gabas

to rise slowly. At first all we can see is a line of bright light, then the scenery – an enchanting Pyrenean valley criss-crossed with hedges, sprinkled with farmsteads, and dotted with sheep. But the curtain gets stuck at shoulder height and the actors stay in the wings. The high pastures and the sky remain hidden. Frustrated, we are all willing the curtain to rise, but to no avail. It falls again and the theatre reverts to its grey obscurity.

The rest of the day is spent in the drizzle. Eyes on the ground, I catch sight of a slow-worm slithering across the path. Finally the clouds disappear and I can see below me the twin villages of Borce and Etsaut, separated by the river Aspe. The path leads down to a new wire grid fence and then runs along the side of it for some distance. The thickness of the wire, the height of the fence, and the strength of the supporting posts all make for an impenetrable enclosure. Something is being kept in, or out. At the other end of the fence there is a notice: Espace animalier de Borce. This is a new extension to a wildlife park, the latest manifestation of the love–hate relationship between the Pyrenees and the brown bear.

Bears have always been a feature of the high Pyrenees. To some extent they were respected. *Lo Moussur*, the gentleman, was one nickname. But they were also killed and exploited. The damage they did to crops and animals led to hunting by upland farmers struggling to survive. And cubs were taken from their mothers by bear tamers to be shown at country fairs.

By 1972, however, when there were only about 40 bears left and they were no longer considered a threat, the relationship began to change. The first step was the definitive ban on hunting in that year. And in 1984 the Ministry of the Environment launched its first management plan. But if I were to choose one date to mark the changing attitude it would be 17 May 1971. On that day, some children were walking in the Belonce valley above Borce. Passing through a thicket they heard a cry and discovered a baby bear. There was no sign of its mother so they took their find back to the village. Baptised Jojo, he became something of a mascot, and lived for 20 years – a reasonable age for a bear. He then passed through the hands of a taxidermist and has since been on public display. So his fate was little different to that of a cub stolen from its mother by a 19th-century tamer. But the interest he evoked had shown that bears were a powerful symbol.

In the meantime the population had dwindled even further. Although hunting had been provisionally outlawed in 1962, poachers continued to operate. But even their activities cannot account for the long-term decline of the Pyrenean bears. One estimate puts the number of bears killed – legally and illegally – over the last four centuries at 3000, or less than 10 per year, a small figure in comparison with the medieval bear population.

It is the mountains which have changed. Before the exodus of the 19th century, agriculture was practised much higher up the valleys and the bears took their tithe of the corn and other foodstuffs. When the mountains became poorer, the bears became scarcer. Those bears who survived gravitated towards the zones where agriculture and pastoralism remained relatively active – as here in the Aspe valley.

A second environmental change is the recent return of people to the heights, with 5000km of paths created in the high Pyrenees between 1950 and 2000. Walkers like me are a nuisance to bears and don't provide any compensatory benefits.

It is not that brown bears are in danger of extinction. It is only their presence in the Pyrenees which is in question. By 1995 there were only six brown bears left in the whole of the French Pyrenees. So in 1996–1997 three bears were kidnapped from Slovenia and released in the mountains.

The newcomers mastered the environment, but their return to the peaks is hugely controversial. Having spent centuries eradicating them, mountain communities are far from unanimous in welcoming them back. The debate is wide-ranging. If there are no bears in the high mountains can we really claim that this is a natural wilderness?

In the Basque country – Hendaye to Gabas

Do humans have the right to manage the environment for their own purposes? Do bears have the right to eat sheep, or do sheep have the right to graze in peace?

A postscript to the life and death of Jojo. Now, when bear cubs are orphaned they are helped to stay in the wild. In November 2004 when Cannelle – the last pure-bred Pyrenean female – was killed at Urdos near here, her young son was provided with dumps of food to supplement his rations before winter set in. He survived. Less encouragingly, some voices are suggesting that any new introductions who 'misbehave' should be imprisoned in the wildlife park.

By the time I arrive at Borce the sun is shining, but the stone walls are still cold. The main street is dark, hidden from the sun by the high ski-jump roofs designed more for winter than for summer: the top part of the roofs is steep so that the snow doesn't stick, while the lower part is flatter so that the avalanche is projected onto the other side of the road or, frequently, onto poorer neighbours with smaller houses. Although these houses are built on the same social foundations as the Basque *etxe* of the plains, above ground there are noticeable differences. In Borce the main entrances are wide, rounded arches defined in stone. There are few windows at ground level. And where the roofs descend the gables as well as the sides of the houses, there are dormer windows illuminating the roof space.

Aimé and Grégory are sitting on the terrace of a bar. I join them for a while and then slip over the river to Etsaut. Beyond the footbridge, a disproportionately wide road embellished with new street furniture cuts a wide swathe along the valley floor. Parallel to it, a disused railway track comes to an ignominious halt in a tuft of grass.

The railway track is the relic of one of the more significant attempts to link France and Spain through the central Pyrenees. Most of the projects have consumed more paper than concrete and the idea is still divisive. For Parisian diplomats more concerned with international relations than with environmental conservation and for Spanish ministers impatient for access to European markets the Pyrenees are simply a nuisance. As the French foreign minister said in 2001 at a bilateral summit: 'The Pyrenees are not our fault...'

The Aspe valley leads to the Col de Somport. Inevitably, it attracted pilgrims on the way to Santiago de Compostela, and armies going in both directions. The emperor Napoleon III built the first road in 1859, but it was 1928 before the first French train crossed the border. One of the problems was the steep gradient. The engineers came up with an ingenious solution: a tunnel in the form of a helix, the sole purpose of which is to gain height – 60m of climbing for a tunnel 1800m long. Even so, the line never attracted much traffic and was closed down in 1970.

Instead a new road tunnel was projected. There was some support for the idea, in the hope that the improved road would open the valley up, revive the economy, and halt the decline in population. But it was the opponents of the project who captured the media's attention. Why not revive the railway, they asked. What about the pollution from exhaust fumes trapped in the narrow valley? What about the bears? The worst of it is that, although the road tunnel was opened in 2003, the road access on the French side is still substandard. And even when the road has been improved, its capacity will be inadequate, so another crossing is being planned: a rail tunnel under the Vignemale mountain, in the centre of the National Park, perhaps.

At the hostel in Etsaut, I rediscover Richard and Jean-Paul and we eat a convivial evening meal with a large group of walkers, including some Canadians. The hostels are filling up.

Etsaut to Gabas

In the dreary mist I walk towards the Col de Somport. On the road there is a snake, a yellow-and-black monkey ladder pattern running along its spine. Yellow and black shivers run along mine, but then I see that it is dead. It is probably a Seoane's viper; recently eight live ones were seen near here in a single day.

The Pyrenean Way turns its back on the road and I find myself approaching the Chemin de la Mâture. I don't relish the prospect. The path is cut out of the vertical limestone cliff, says the *FFRP Guide*, creating a ledge just wide enough for two oxen to walk side-by-side. I will see a frightening drop to my right. But I have chosen the right day – I can see nothing. I am air-bagged by the mist.

Originally, the Chemin de la Mâture gave access to the forests higher up the valley, where the centuries-old trees were felled to provide masts for the French navy. In the 18th century, the demand for wood was phenomenal – 800 log rafts were arriving in Toulouse from the Pyrenees each year. And for a short while the trees of the Aspe valley were an important natural resource.

I can imagine the difficulty of hauling the massive trunks – up to 30m long – along this narrow shelf. How many trunks fell into the void, dragging the oxen with them, the workers trying desperately to control the situation? How many men died during the construction? The account of the works, written by an engineer concerned with his place in history, omits to mention the negative side of his exploit.

The path was finished in 1772 and in six years the forest was razed. Now, except for the Chemin de la Mâture, the passing of the French navy has been obliterated.

Further up the valley, I hear a rustling. Grégory is standing in a small clearing, stretching his arms, yawning. Aimé pokes his head out of his tent. Trying to find a patch of flat ground yesterday outside Etsaut, they had followed the Pyrenean Way and walked the Chemin de la Mâture in dangerous sunshine.

I leave them to pack up and shortly emerge from the mist. At the end of the long valley ahead of me I glimpse patches of glistening snow, but for the moment I am strolling through the luxuriant pasture which marks the beginning of the National Park. When I arrive at the Cabane de la Baigt de St-Cours, the door is shut but I push it and it swings open. Graffiti everywhere, rubbish littering the floor, furniture destroyed, the ladder which should have given access to the mezzanine missing. This hut is two and a half hours' walking from the nearest road, not in a poverty-stricken suburb, but it has suffered the same fate as many an urban bus shelter.

I meet a man striding down the valley. He has recently brought his cows here for the summer. Cows don't have a herding instinct, he tells me, so for the next week he will be coming to see them every other day and bringing the more adventurous ones back until they get the idea.

At the head of the valley, just before the zigzag assault on the pass, I sit down quietly to watch a group of eleven *isards* grazing. Called *chamois* in the Alps, with the body of a goat but the grace of an antelope, at the slightest noise they will bound up the hillside, leaping from rock to rock. Piew . . . piew . . . piew. A *marmotte* whistles, and I manage to identify its brown-ochre fur against the mottled grey rock on which it is squatting before it disappears into its burrow.

Marmottes and *isards* share the same territory above the tree line and are both now thriving in the Pyrenees although their histories are different. *Marmottes* died out with the retreating glaciers, 10,000 years ago, when the advancing forests encroached on their habitat. They were first reintroduced in 1948, as a private initiative by a certain Dr Couturier, without any study of the impact they might have. The six one-year-olds and a few others released later have between them managed to populate much of the mountain range. In contrast, *isards* have always been present in the Pyrenees but by the middle of the 20th century their numbers were declining seriously, principally as a result of hunting. They were saved by the creation of reserves and there are an estimated 40,000 today.

At the top of the pass, I can see the Pic du Midi d'Ossau again for the first time since the Route de Phagalcette. Above it, burgeoning clouds. Behind it, the peaks stretching into the distance. In front of it the high pastures dropping dramatically into the forest, slumping into

In the Basque country – Hendaye to Gabas

the valleys. The mountain itself is conical, fissured down one side, the shady crevasse still filled with snow. It looks like a volcano, and indeed that is what it is, or rather was, 280 million years ago.

A quick ice tea at the Refuge d'Ayous, a downhill yomp accompanied by dozens of other walkers, tick bites at the Lac de Bious-Artigues, and the Pyrenean Way is finished for this year.

II

The High Pyrenees: Gabas–Luchon

Gabas

A year later I repack my rucksack, adding a tent, a sleeping bag, a stove, and two days' food and water. It weighs 5kg more than last year but the only unnecessary item is the half-empty phial of seawater from Hendaye. The top was screwed on tightly but somehow the water has escaped. I wrap some sticking plaster around to seal it better. Then I check the email which has arrived overnight – nothing important – turn off my computer, shut the office door, and catch a train back to the Pyrenees. The town of Pau, where I get off, is bustling with tourists.

I take a taxi up the *gave*, the valley, back to Gabas and pay the 78€ on the meter. The taxi driver gives me my change and, with a wink, a receipt for 100€. He suggests that I can use my tip for lunch in a nearby café.

Today's special is *garbure*: a chunky nourishing soup made of cabbage, lots of vegetables, haricot beans, and a few scraps of meat. At the next table the talk centres around the problems of transhumance.

'I'm transporting my horses up in a lorry this year,' says one woman. 'It's just too much trouble to do it on foot. Most of the car drivers are careful but you only need one idiot to ruin everything.'

Afterwards, walking towards the hostel along the empty main street, I pass under a road safety campaign banner inciting vigilance.

Below it, the bitumen is stratified under a pale brown coating; the hot sun is extracting the last volatile molecules from the squashed cow pats. The transition from urban concerns to rural life has been remarkably quick.

After dumping my rucksack at the hostel, I continue up the valley for an afternoon stroll to the reservoir at Fabrèges. The vertical face of the concrete dam has been daubed with paint. At first, all I can make out is a white letter R with an E below it and the painted paw print of an animal to one side. The rest is hidden behind the trees. As I advance more letters become visible until finally I can read the word REINTRODUCTIONS stretching down the concrete. The paw prints, in red, clamber up from the valley floor. This graffiti is no small achievement. The dam is 30m high and rock-climbing skills would have been essential.

The paw prints identify the species: bears. Following the death of Cannelle, the environment minister Serge Lepeltier wants to reintroduce 15 pregnant females to create a viable population. The controversy surrounding the idea is as big as the graffiti.

I ask the woman in the grocery shop at Fabrèges if they know who was behind the graffiti.

'*Non. Sinon il aurait passé un sale quart d'heure.* No, otherwise he would have had a bad time of it.'

She directs me to the lift which takes me up the mountain to the ski resort of Sagette and the terminus of the Petit Train d'Artouste. At the top, it is cold, much colder than I would have expected given the difference in altitude. A train is just coming in, balancing precariously on narrow-gauge rails only 0.5m apart. The engine looks like a child's toy which has been scaled up, its corners rounded to avoid cutting tiny hands. The open carriages behind it could be a string of shopping trolleys being dragged, rattling, across a windswept supermarket car park. It might be fun when it is warm, but today the few passengers are wrapped up in parkas with hoods pulled tightly around their heads. Shivering, they descend quickly and run into the café.

Gabas

Claimed to be the highest railway in Europe, the Petit Train d'Artouste clings to the side of the massif, following the 1910m contour in sumptuous curves to the reservoir at the Lac d'Artouste 8km away. It was originally built in 1920 for the construction of the dam by the Compagnie des Chemins de Fer du Midi. Their project was to supply hydroelectricity to their railway network, which spread over much of the south of France. Once the dam was built, the train was destined to become a tourist attraction. Publicised by the company, it helped fill the carriages of trains coming from Paris, thus paying for itself a second time.

I walk for a few minutes to the top of the hill before joining the railway passengers for a hot chocolate in the steamy café. I rub my ears to warm them up. I am tense, anxious. Do I really want to do this? Do I want to walk in these conditions for days on end? Suddenly, it all seems too difficult. It is a silly idea, an arbitrary challenge, to walk the length of the Pyrenees. It took me years to learn how to relax on a beach all day without getting bored. What a waste not to use my hard-earned skill this summer.

The first problem is tomorrow. I need to practise. Again. So on the way back I scramble onto the wall which holds the road in place. Standing up, the river on the other side seems a long way below, though the drop is insignificant in comparison with any respectable cliff. Normally, I wouldn't look down for more than a few seconds but I force myself to stare into the emptiness below. Am I a little off balance? I move my left foot backwards. I have overdone it. I correct myself. I shift my weight onto the other foot. No better. I turn away from the drop and stability returns. Not a good omen.

My father had the same problem. When we went walking, he would often warn me: 'Don't go so near the edge.' At the age of 18, with his best friend Ken, he had climbed up a ladder to the top of a gasometer for a better view over the sooty roofs of industrial Leeds. Going up was no problem, but when it came to climbing down again he needed to put a foot over the edge of the tank, out into the void to feel blindly for the top rung of the ladder. He couldn't do it. Somehow Ken coaxed him down. He realised for the first time that he had vertigo. Ken, on the other hand, realised that he didn't have a problem with heights, and went on to frighten his family for many years, climbing and occasionally falling off cliffs in the Lake District. 'I could always tell when I was going to fall off. I knew I was doing something silly, something which was too much for me,' he claimed.

Back at Gabas, the village has been transformed. A stream of lorries fills the main street. One of them, a double-decker, shudders to a halt and disgorges its cargo, first the cows from the lower deck and then the sheep from above. Fresh cow pats sizzle on the hot tarmac. The man in charge explains to me that the lorries have come up from the plain. This afternoon he will walk the animals up to the lake at Bious-Artigues. Doing the whole journey on foot tires the sheep out so he has been using a lorry for the last five years.

At the hostel, the evening meal starts with *garbure*, continues with a beef stew, and has just finished with a pear tart when the door bursts open and a man falls through it. He is wearing green-and-beige camouflage and dripping sweat. He picks himself up, stumbles unsteadily over to the kitchen counter and mutters something unintelligible to the cook who shakes her head. She calls me over to translate: although the walker is from Munich he speaks some English. The cook says that there is still room in the dormitory and food for the table, but he must eat now and tidy himself up later. The walker smiles weakly, waiting for me to interpret, and then sits down opposite me.

'I stayed at the hostel in Gourette last night,' he tells me. 'I didn't realise that Gabas was so far away. It took me a long while to get to the pass but then I thought the downhill would be easy. It wasn't. It just kept on and on.'

'I'm glad I've got two days to do it, in the other direction.'

'Is there another hostel then? Did I miss it?' His mouth drops open.

'No, but I've got a tent,' I explain. 'Where did you start from?'

'Lourdes. I'm going to Santiago de Compostela. I didn't want to follow the crowds on one of the standard Chemins de St-Jacques so I bought all the maps and have worked out my own route.'

'How much does your rucksack weigh?'

'I don't know.'

I pick it up: 'I'd say 20 kilos, perhaps more.'

'And you?' he asks me.

'Seventeen.'

I introduce him to a clean-cut American trainee priest from Denver, Colorado, who is also walking from Lourdes to Santiago de Compostela. Thankfully, they agree to team up for tomorrow. At least the German has a map – the American seems to be relying on divine inspiration. The map he has been using consists of a single wiggly black line with half a dozen place names dotted along it. On the other half of the page is an explanation, in French, of the itinerary. I realise how little French he understands when he asks me the meaning of the word *chemin* in the description.

After dinner I go outside into the twilight. Lorries are still arriving but now the combination of young undisciplined cows and young inexperienced cowgirls is creating havoc. The cows first wander into a hotel car park and have to be rounded up. Then one of them sees a track leading up to a grassy field and sets off running. Her sisters follow her in a cacophony of jingling bells and clattering hooves, splattering the fresh cow pats as they pass. The cowgirls run after the escapees shouting and waving their arms, but only succeed in driving them further into the field. It is ten o'clock; the cowgirls are also going to Bious-Artigues. It will take them about three hours, they claim.

Gabas to the Mines d'Arre

The next day I start my transhumance. Leaving the road behind I walk up the flank of the mountain under the fir, beech, and birch trees. The clearings are prettily decorated with flowers: wild chicory, St John's Wort, martagon lily, and Pyrenean iris. Then I stumble over them. In the middle of the path having messy sex, completely unconcerned about possible passers-by, and producing a disproportionately large quantity of white gunk, are two very black slugs.

The sex life of slugs is as bizarre as it is messy. The most conventional thing about it is that slugs have male and female sexual organs. Slightly less conventionally, slugs have *both* male and female organs: they are hermaphrodites. So that if you are a particularly ugly slug and self-conscious about it, or you simply don't like going to parties, you can have babies without all the fuss of having to find a partner. If, conversely, you happen to meet a particularly attractive slug and after a bit of preliminary cuddling you jump into the nearest flower bed: beware. The problem isn't so much deciding who should do what, and to whom, but what to do afterwards. No question of lighting up a cigarette. Slug penises often get entangled. There are two solutions. You gnaw off your partner's penis. Or you gnaw off your own. If the worst comes to the worst you can still be a happy fulfilled female slug, after all. And then there are some kinky slugs who go in for acrobatic sex, entwined around each other, suspended from a long filament, swinging wildly in mid air. But these two don't look as though they have ever tried anything so demanding.

At a bifurcation, there is a wooden signpost: 'Corniche des Alhas. *Passage vertigineux*'. I have already read the *FFRP Guide*: 'The Corniche des Alhas is crossed by a path carved in a granite cliff which overhangs the Soussouéou gorge. Narrow, in places damaged by avalanches, this path can be considered vertiginous, even dangerous, although equipped with a handrail.'

This is what I was practising for yesterday. I really don't like the sound of it. Clinging onto the handrail nailed into the cliff with my right hand, looking over the drop by my left foot. One foot in front of the other on a narrow ledge. No room to pass if I meet somebody coming the other way. One slip, and even with a hand on the rail I will be left dangling over the void. With a heavy rucksack on my back, will I be able to pull myself up again? There is an alternative route, but this is my first day. I really must.

By the time I arrive at the start of the corniche, my back is locked solid, as if the pelvis and spine are a single bone. My hands are tingling. My arms and legs trembling. My stomach is churning over. This is stupid, I don't *need* to do this. Even now I can retrace my steps and bypass the problem.

I see the start of the ledge. I tell myself it will only take ten minutes. Like going to the dentist, in a few minutes it will all be over. One way or another. At first it doesn't seem too bad. The path is a bit narrow and the edge a bit crumbly. I take care not to bang my head on the overhanging rocks. Then there is a passage through the trees. Fine so far. I don't know how the trees manage to hang onto the slope, but they look comfortingly secure. And then… and then… that's it, I am at the end of the corniche. All the tension flows out of me, from my neck, down my arms, down my back, down my legs. I burst out laughing, uncontrollably. I have to sit down. Was that vertiginous? I regret not having tackled the 'very exposed ridge path' on the Pic d'Iparla.

After four hours' walking I reach the Cabanes de Cézy where crickets are chirping in the late morning warmth. There are four stone huts and even a house for the shepherd. Roofs, walls, and doors are intact, all that is needed for a night on the mountains. I could have comfortably squatted in any one of the huts overnight and carried much less kit. The *FFRP Guide* is annoyingly badly informed on this point.

I eat lunch outside one of the huts and then look around the other side to discover a *Marie Celeste* meal. A tin with a good chunk of pâté remaining, a wheel of camembert with one portion untouched, and half a slice of Emmental cheese, still in its plastic wrapper, garnish an improvised hearth. It is as if the meal has been hastily abandoned, but there is no sign of the diner. I bury the detritus under a stone.

The High Pyrenees: Gabas–Luchon

Across the valley, the Petit Train d'Artouste emerges from the tunnel and tootles happily as it trundles along in the sunshine.

The path – a former mule track – climbs slowly through the ferns leaving the limestone behind. The rock under my feet is now friable, reddish-brown, and mineral-rich. I climb up an enclosed valley which opens out into a small grassy plateau cradled by a string of high, angular peaks. On the tops, the clouds are forming, dissolving, and re-forming, decoratively. The only sound, now that the wind has dropped, is the piew-piew of *marmottes* as they scuttle away. The hillside here is pockmarked with their burrows, each one with a little mound of earth at its entrance. Higher still there are some larger holes, also with spoil tips: the mines of the Société des Mines d'Arre et d'Anglas which operated for a few decades around the end of the 19th century. With the passage of time, even these spoil tips have blended into the rocky landscape.

On the plateau there are a couple of low stone walls outlining the remains of rectangular buildings. I pitch my tent on the flat ground near to one of them and sit with my back against a rock, cushioned on the short-cropped grass, reading about the history of the site. Initially the ore – blende containing zinc, iron, magnesium, and traces of silver – could only be extracted during the summer months but, in an attempt to improve productivity, at the end of 1882 the company decided to lodge the workers here throughout the winter. Mining continued comfortably underground as the snow fell outside. The accommodation was well constructed and there was food for many months. Then, suddenly, on 18 November in the middle of the night, an avalanche roared down the mountain pulling out the rocks in its path and tumbling onto the sleeping quarters. Sixteen workers were killed and four badly wounded. The few survivors descended the valley with great difficulty but the bodies had to be left until the following spring.

Winters here must be impressive. A little distance away I can see a small pond still surrounded by snow. Icy cornices drip into it, chunks falling off to become miniature summer icebergs.

Gabas to the Mines d'Arre

I go in search of the spring marked on my map. I don't find it, but down in the valley there is a collection of huts by a stream. One is in ruins, another intact but dilapidated, and the third pristine, with a solar panel and an aerial on the roof. There is washing hanging on a line outside. Nearby, a couple of donkeys are munching their way across a rectangular enclosure. There is also a ramshackle construction built on metal poles, with cages and chairs, roofed with plastic sheeting.

As I approach the huts, two collie dogs appear, barking. The top half of a door opens with a metallic squeak and a man sticks his head out. From his greying hair and the exuberance of his moustache, I put him in his 50s. Through the door I can see that the walls are decorated with children's drawings.

'I hope I haven't disturbed your siesta,' I apologise.

'No, I was just sorting letters ready for the post,' he replies.

'Could you tell me what that is for?' I ask, pointing to the raised metal structure.

'For milking sheep. I'll be going to fetch them back shortly.'

He takes his sheep out to pasture each morning and brings them back at night for safety, as he has been doing in the summer for the last forty years. He doesn't seem particularly inclined to chat – he has only been here for a week – so I leave him in peace. As I am climbing back up the hill to my tent I notice three walkers – two adults and a child – and a donkey making their way up the valley to the hut. The postal service.

The clouds are no longer disappearing as quickly as they are forming. They hug the cliffs for a little while and then lose their grip and slip down the slope towards me. I eat and then get into my sleeping bag. Starting to doze off, in the half-world between consciousness and sleep, a dim memory comes back to me.

One moonless night, aged 13, I was camping in safe rural England when I was woken by a noise outside. Heavy breathing. Something scraping against the canvas. A large shape, bigger than the tent. The canvas was ripped apart. Then there was a crunching, crackling, slobbering noise. Inside the tent. Squeezing to the other side, I felt around for my torch and turned it on. But there was nothing to see, except for a mangled packet of digestive biscuits and a hole. Then I heard a whinny from outside and remembered that there were horses in the field. One of them had managed to detect the biscuits through their cellophane wrapping and the canvas. The worst of it was that, when I got home, my parents blamed *me* for the hole.

I get up and hide the remaining food under a stone, well away from the tent. Surely a hungry bear will be more interested in a herd of sheep than a lonely walker.

Mines d'Arre to Gourette

By dawn, the wind has returned and blown the clouds away. The valley of the Soussouéou is still in deep shadow but the sun is already warming the Pic du Midi d'Ossau to the west, starting at the top and working its way down, colouring the cliffs a Barbara Cartland pink.

Crossing a slippery snow field on the way, I climb up to the pass at the Hourquette d'Arre. As the name indicates, I have left the Basque country behind and entered Gascony. This is one of those names which looks impenetrable at first. Translated into French it becomes even more baffling. Hourquette becomes *fourchette* and Arre becomes *rocher*. The rocky fork doesn't seem to make any more sense, unless you make a leap of imagination. This is not a fork lying on a dinner table, but a fork in the rock – a narrow passage, somewhat narrower than a pass, somewhat wider than a crevasse. The *rocky fork* is the highest point on the Pyrenean Way so far. Behind me, on one side of the pass the wind is blowing furiously; on the other it is calm.

The path twists down to the Lac d'Anglas, an extravagant, vivid blue jewel in a lurid mossy emerald setting. In the distance, I see a colony of perhaps 30 *marmottes* gambolling in a hollow, bounding up and down amongst the flowering rhododendrons, running away and then returning to the fray. I approach cautiously, but one of them flies away! They are not *marmottes* but vultures. More exactly *vautours fauves*, griffon vultures, and much bigger than I thought – two or more metres across from wingtip to wingtip. Looking up, I see that more are arriving, circling high above, scrutinising the scene. On the ground, one runs up the hill flapping its wings ineffectively, more to keep the other vultures at bay, than to take off. It has a lump of something red in its beak and blood splashed down its long, fine, white neck. A white and inappropriately fluffy collar protects its mottled brown plumage from the dribbles.

The others set up a kind of hoarse jabbering which becomes more intense as I approach, and then, in a dramatic whoosh, a menacing, flapping, dark shadow rises into the sky. They have left behind them a corpse. The leg bones have been stripped clean but the ribs are still splashed with drying blood. Little remains of the innards, except for a large brown, fleshy, oozing bag. The wool has been stripped back from the neck to reveal a pink and as yet undamaged throat. The head, except for the eyes, is intact. The stink keeps me from examining the carcass more closely.

Vultures are gregarious creatures. Leaving the colony at dawn, on a bad day they may travel up to 100km in search of food, spreading out over a large area but keeping visual contact with each other. Their excellent eyesight allows them to spot a dead *marmotte* 3km away. Once they have identified their objective, their cry and sudden descent invites the other guests, and the feast can begin. In principle, vultures only eat dead animals – sheep, lambs, calves, and wildlife. But recently, livestock farmers have started saying that they also attack weak newborn lambs and calves, and even their mothers, exhausted by giving birth. There are only a handful of reports each year, which seems a trivial number when compared with a livestock population measured in hundreds of thousands. But the whole question has given rise to a heated debate, second only in acrimony to the debate surrounding the reintroduction of bears.

The High Pyrenees: Gabas–Luchon

Has the number of attacks increased following a population explosion which has left the vultures short of food? Should shepherds once again be allowed to leave the corpses of dead animals to the capable claws of nature's avian undertakers? Or are the attacks reported more often because farmers can now claim compensation? Or perhaps because they are lumped together with bears on the list of undesirable wild animals which naïve townies wish to foist on hard-working country folk?

There is also the big question of nature versus nurture. Vultures are naturally carrion eaters. They have strong beaks and featherless necks enabling them to penetrate deep into the entrails of a cadaver without spoiling their plumage, but their claws are useless for attacking living animals. And once on the ground they are ungainly lumbering monsters, incapable of mounting a serious attack. Could they really have *learned* to kill weak animals? Can we expect them to distinguish between a stone dead animal – which is theirs by right – and one which is merely 'resting'?

Humans and vultures have coexisted in the Pyrenees for a very long time. Twenty-five thousand years ago, a Palaeolithic musician carved a flute from a vulture's wing bone, leaving it for archaeologists to discover in a cave in the Pyrenean foothills north of St-Jean-Pied-de-Port. This was well before the first pastoralists took possession of the mountains. So, initially at least, vultures must have been feeding on dead bison, *isards*, deer, and so on. But over the years, the combined efforts of hunters and livestock farmers have reduced the number of wild animals, whilst at the same time increasing the number of domestic ones. In the process, the farmers also cleared the forests creating wide open spaces which can easily be inspected from the air, one of the prerequisites for vulture survival.

In the 19th century, vultures were still to be seen in many areas in the south of France but by the 1970s there were only a few score left. Years of deliberate and accidental poisoning had nearly exterminated the last colonies in France. There were also fewer undisturbed cliff habitats available for nesting. And then there was the impact of the hygiene regulations insisting that dead sheep and cattle must not be left to rot where they died. Having first eliminated vultures' wild food resources, shepherds were now obliged to remove the substitute which they had unwillingly provided over the millennia.

From being self-sufficient, vultures on the French side of the Pyrenees had become reliant on human intervention, and now they were suffering from malnutrition. The Pyrenees were at the northern limit of their distribution: it wouldn't have taken much to push them back over the frontier. Yet it didn't take much to encourage them to stay.

Hunting was outlawed and a winter feeding site was regularly supplied with the carcasses of dead animals brought down from the mountains by livestock farmers. The measures to protect *isards* and the reintroduction of *marmottes* followed by their spectacular increase in numbers may also have had an influence on the vulture population. But most important of all was the creation in 1974 of the Réserve naturelle de nidification des vautours fauves, a nature reserve specifically set up to protect the nesting sites. By 1997 vultures were becoming so common in the Ossau valley that they were competing with other birds for nesting sites, so the ONF stopped feeding them. There are now around 500 in the Pyrenees not to mention a small reintroduced colony in the Causses in the Massif Central.

Like bears, they have been harnessed to promote the mountains, particularly the Ossau valley where Vulture Cliff is a tourist attraction. Here visitors can watch the nesting sites through the intermediary of a remote controlled camera.

Initially independent, vultures have gone through a phase of dependence on humans. Are we now working our way – vultures and humans – to a kind of uneasy symbiosis?

My feet are already playing up: I have blisters on my right heel and on one toe. And my knees are giving out warning twinges, so I slow down and rest frequently on my way to the next village.

The High Pyrenees: Gabas–Luchon

The outskirts of the ski resort of Gourette are as degraded as those of Arette-La Pierre-St-Martin. The combined blades of thousands of skis have cut ugly gashes through the pine forest. A few stalks of grass are starting to knit together the rocky grey scars but the wounds will never heal before next winter's massacre. The buildings are unimaginative Stalinist blocks designed to accommodate a maximum of holidaymakers at a minimum of cost.

Unlike its cousin, however, Gourette has an impeccable pedigree. Not only was it a scion of the bourgeois spa town Eaux-Bonnes where Eugénie took the waters before she married the emperor Napoleon III, but it was also here that a group of Pyrenean alchemists set up their laboratory and first discovered how to turn snow into gold. In 1903 Henri Sallenave carried out one of the first Pyrenean experiments in downhill skiing on the slopes above Gourette. By 1909, the Concours International, held here, was a focus for the best European skiers, but it was the presence of the Spanish king Alphonse XIII which really attracted attention. (Henri Sallenave was by now also a pioneer aviator, and had organised the 3-month stay of the Wright brothers in his native Pau. Alphonse XIII went to see them too.) The king stayed at Eaux-Bonnes because there were no hotels on the mountain itself. Indeed, it wasn't until the 1930s that the first facilities began to be constructed at Gourette and the resort didn't really grow until the local council took an interest in the development of the site in 1963. Snow had acquired a new importance, becoming *or blanc* – white gold – reflecting the eternal values of the mountains and their mines.

Although the outskirts of the town were deserted, the centre is bustling with clapping crowds pushing against the crash barriers which line the road as it winds its way through. I can see literally hundreds of cyclists climbing the hill. They each have a number stuck on the back of their tee-shirt, and a Velcro bracelet wrapped around their right ankle. Nearly all the competitors seem to be in their 40s; there are very few women. Nos 2053, 596, and 4575 pass by, teeth clenched.

I talk to the wife of one of the competitors, who is there to support her husband and his cycling club. They have come down from Angoulême for the event, l'Étape du Tour. Organised by the cycling magazine *Vélo* every year, it follows the route which will be taken a week later by the professional Tour de France. At 7 o'clock this morning, she tells me, there were 7885 cyclists on the starting line at Mourenx, 108km away. She points out the new white lines on the road, and the spotless state of the tarmac.

'It wasn't like that two weeks ago, when we came to do a reconnaissance,' she tells me.

'What are the ankle bands for?' I ask.

'Timing. It takes half an hour for the racers to set off so they each have a chip which means they can be timed individually.'

It is now 12:20 and the radio in the bar announces that Laurent Marcon has just crossed the finishing line. He passed through Gourette nearly two hours ago. Those who are labouring through the village now still have 70km to do and the *voiture balai* is brushing at their heels. Though the highest point, the Col d'Aubisque, is only 5km away, there is still 400m of climbing.

They say that professional cyclists dance on their pedals as they climb up hills but those who are passing in front of us are sitting firmly on their saddles. As we watch, two competitors look at each other, nod, and put their feet on the ground. They throw their cycles against the barrier, walk to the terrace of a café, and order beers.

The town centre looks quite prosperous, at least today, with several cafés and restaurants, sports shops, and a supermarket doing a brisk trade. But it is the names of the hotels which give the game away: the Boule de neige (Snowball), the Face nord (North Face), and the Glacier are not principally aimed at the summer market.

I go to the tourist information office. Behind the counter there are three young women. I am the only tourist.

'Is there a launderette here?' I ask. I haven't many spare clothes, and I want to keep on top of the problem.

'No. There is one in Laruns.'

I also want to send my tent and sleeping bag back home. I won't need them any more.

'Can you tell me how to get to the post office? I thought I saw a sign on the way in.'

'No. It's only open in winter. There is one in Laruns.'

The card in my digital camera is rapidly filling up.

'Is there anywhere I can transfer photos to a CD?'

'No. You could try Laruns.'

'A bank? A pharmacy?'

'No. They're only open in winter. There are some in Laruns, though.'

This is beginning to sound like one of those language learning tapes where you have to ask a series of standard question and then try to understand the reply. Except that in this case the reply is always 'no'.

'Are there any buses to Laruns? Taxis?' I try, and instantly regret it.

'No. You'll have to hitch.' I am almost pleased that there are no taxis in Gourette. At least I get to learn a new word, *autostop*.

'There's nothing here, is there?' I suggest, hoping to elicit a different reaction.

'That's right,' is the reply.

However, I have no difficulty in thumbing a lift to Laruns and back again. Hitching is the one thing which does work in Gourette in summer, presumably because the inhabitants know that very little else does.

Gourette to Arrens-Marsous

In the morning, within ten minutes I have lost the path, so I decide to take a compass bearing up a small but increasingly steep valley. Initially the ferns are knee high but they soon become taller. When finally I reach the plateau, the surface is dissected by huge crevasses filled with thorns and small birch trees. After a few minutes of clumsy hopscotch, I finally locate the footpath, coming from a completely different direction. Evidently the route has been changed.

The path descends to a road. I have the possibility of walking along the liquefying asphalt following a contour or the more interesting alternative of dropping down further into the valley and then climbing out of it again. The point of departure is clearly identifiable on the map, but I can't find it, so I go to a nearby hut. Outside it, under the porch, a tall, handsome young man is sitting on a small stool, leaning against the wall, sunning himself. He is wearing a large white apron which covers him from chin to ankles. The slightly acrid smell of cheese-making wafts out of the door.

'Yes, it is difficult to see, but it *is* right by the bridge,' he tells me. Back at the bridge, I part the undergrowth, discover the path, and walk down to the river, through a colourful patch of flowers: delicately frayed pink wild carnations intertwined with the vicious blue spiky flowers of the Pyrenean thistle.

The path lunges headlong into the woods but I follow it suspiciously; soon it has vanished in a mess of cow pats. I struggle through to the other side, back into the shimmering mid-day furnace, and walk over a patch of bare soil and dead vegetation. Then I slip. Underneath the soil there is a thin layer of snow. Underneath the thin layer of snow there is a very big void spanning a nearly dry stream bed, creating a bridge high enough to ride a horse through. The earth and bracken which protect the snow from the sun must have been clawed out of the hillside last winter as the avalanche gathered momentum. I should have known. This is the Cirque du Litor. *Lit tort* in Occitan means the tormented avalanche, giving the image of snow and ice thundering down the slopes from all directions.

A shepherdess later tells me: 'Avoid snow bridges. Gilbert, a shepherd friend of mine, fell through one and broke his back. If I hadn't being going to visit him that day, he would have died.'

The High Pyrenees: Gabas–Luchon

The path starts to climb again and I start to overheat; my hat is nowhere to be found. Wiping my forehead with my handkerchief, I decide I must do something. I look at my handkerchief and spread it over my head, but it falls off so I tie it to my glasses, knotting it above my ears, and set off again.

An easy stroll takes me down the valley to a very large building balancing on a very small knoll, like a snail on a marble. The architecture – all rounded corners, gangways, and balustrades, rendered and painted cream, evoking the bridge of a cruise liner – signals an origin between the wars. Six storeys high, the building curls round the hillock, a recently mown lawn curls round the building, and a road encircles both of them. I open a door, mount the stairs and clump along a curved corridor but there is nobody around. The sliding glass doors of the reception area open automatically as I approach but nobody comes out to greet me. The snail has left home. After some searching I find a plaque which explains that this was a hospice for wounded soldiers, and has become a centre for handicapped adults. But where have they all gone?

On the top of the knoll, protected by the hospice on three sides, is the golden chapel of Our Lady. Built during the counter-reformation it is a baroque monument to decadence. Even if the Protestants were going in for simplicity in their places of worship, this was no reason for the Catholic church to follow suit. The result is a chapel bedecked with gold leaf. There are some touching details, like the quarrelling disciples at the Last Supper on the reredos. But the overall effect is grotesque, particularly when juxtaposed with the hospice, where for decades men and women have been struggling merely to exist. There, in the hospice, decadence is not an option.

My destination for today is Arrens, only ten minutes' walk away. In the village, everything is in its place. The newly painted, recently re-roofed cottage has a freshly mown lawn and a professionally trimmed privet hedge. The mill leet is constrained in a concrete channel. The paving stones on the medieval hump-back bridge have been re-laid and carefully concreted to avoid tripping. The mulberry trees are evenly spaced. There is no rubbish. It is pretty; but also artificial, unnatural. It is difficult to believe that people really *live* here. There are none of the cow pats of Gabas. Nor the ice cream wrappers of Gourette. Even the topography has been tamed. The flat valley floor is an astonishing 500m wide.

The only hat remaining in the newsagent's looks as though it might have been worn in colonial Sudan, and it is too big for me. The shop assistant says that they sell lots of them, and insists that it suits me. I tell him that I would look less ridiculous wearing a knotted handkerchief tied to my glasses. But at least it will shade my neck, so I buy it anyway.

The hostels in the village are full so I go to the inn and ring the bell on the desk in the gloomy reception area. An old woman, her white hair pulled back from her forehead and tied into a top-knot, shuffles out from one of the rooms at the back, bent over her Zimmer frame. She is wearing a long black dress with a high neck. She doesn't seem to notice me but the woman who is following her says hello in passing and then helps her charge to sit down on a stiff-backed chair in an even darker corner. Yes, they have a room. Yes, there will be *garbure* for supper. No, there is no alternative.

Arrens-Marsous to the Lac d'Ilhéou

Walking out of the town, I discover a ramshackle house, with a derelict car in the garden, teeming with cats, startling evidence of rebellious individualism. The path crosses over a small rise into the long, pleasant valley-garden of Estaing and heads back for the hills.

Just before the Lac d'Estaing there are two curious beehive-like stone structures, side by side, next to the path. Each of them has a small rectangular opening in one wall, just over a metre high and, inside, a stone seat with a circular hole. There is no door. Looking through the hole I can see running water: part of the flow of a stream has been diverted to flush out this primitive toilet – in the middle of the countryside. I try sitting on the seat but the opening is so small that I have to bend double in order to fit in. It doesn't seem very practical.

Somewhat later I discover the real explanation. These are not toilets but refrigerators. The hole is designed to take a bucket of milk still warm from the sheep. The stream and the current of air provide the cooling effect, enabling the shepherd to chill the milk quickly.

The Lac d'Estaing itself is completely unruffled. *Estaing*, I should explain, means lake in the Gascon dialect of Occitan.

Sometime in the 19th century, two cartographers are surveying the valley. They approach a fisherman at the waterside and ask him its name.

Fisherman: 'Estaing.'

Cartographer 1: 'But surely it has another name to distinguish it from all the other lakes round here.'

Fisherman: 'No. We just call it the lake. It is the only one in the valley. There isn't any other name.'

Cartographer 2: 'Just put down "Estaing"'.

Cartographer 1: 'I can't do that. When we get back to Paris they will ask us what it means. When we tell them that it means 'lake', they won't believe us. Worse still, they will send us back here again. I've had enough of these mountains and the fishermen who are too stupid to invent real names.'

Fisherman: 'You're frightening the fish with your philosophical discussions. Bugger off!'

Cartographer 2: 'Just put down the Lac d'Estaing. In Paris they won't know that it means Lake Lake. They will think that Estaing is a village or something. They won't know that it doesn't make sense.'

So they put down Lac d'Estaing. Now that the technique was well honed they had no problem further along the Pyrenean Way with Ilhéou, Gaube, and Aumar. So there were now four Lake Lakes within a short distance of each other. But Paris got wise. They were banished just over the border into Spain; but they took their revenge, secretly insinuating the Valley Valley (Val d'Aran) onto their maps.

It is very hot, so that by the time I reach the top of the pass into the next valley, I am flaking and sit down near to a herd of cows. They are behaving strangely. It is a perfect summer's day. Clearly, it is not going to rain. The grass looks juicy and the cows should be dispersed across the hillside ruminating contentedly. Instead, they are gathered together in a compact group, heads up, looking across a ravine which runs down the slope. On the other side of the ravine I can see something jumping about, flying in and out of the abyss: a flock of vultures, feasting. The cows look on, powerlessly.

Down in the valley, on the shores of another lake, the tables outside the hostel are full with walkers finishing their meals. I buy a glass of beer and slump against the wall of the terrace.

A gust of wind caresses the silky turquoise shallows, brushing them with ephemeral fingerprints. Above the lake, dominating it, the rounded peaks are grey, tired, and worn, smooth except for their geological wrinkles. The snow-flecked upper slopes are half hidden by rivers of scree – rocky torrents in perpetual movement, needing only the heat of a sunbeam to unhinge their precarious equilibrium and send them crashing down the incline. It is only lower down, by the shore, that grass and heather have installed a relative stability. The pink wild roses bloom gaily; the few sombre pine trees struggle along wearily. It is a quiet, unassuming beauty. This is not the ostentatious spectacle of the Pic du Midi d'Ossau. This is nature being modest, hinting at her powers. Look, she says, in winter, those ripples become waves, those patches of snow become avalanches. Given time, those mountains will disappear. For now, I am taking it easy.

The hostel is perched on the rocky plug which dams the lake, the Lac d'Ilhéou. Like a traditional A-frame tent, the roof nearly reaches the ground and the gables are vertical. Visually, the hostel is all roof. The architects have pushed its incline beyond the limit of the reasonable, using a slope which would be more normal on a church spire. Clearly, snow will not stick, and the sun's rays will quickly heat the dark slates. The ground floor consists of the kitchen and dining room, the first floor is the dormitory, and the manager's quarters are crammed into the attic. The food is good; the *garbure* excellent.

Ilhéou. The lake was renamed the Lac Bleu in the 19th century. The hostel, built in 1970, is officially called the Refuge Ritter. But these names have slipped into oblivion like the snow off the roof. The Refuge Ilhéou stands defiantly on the shores of the Lac d'Ilhéou. Perhaps because the name is pronounced exactly like the French *il est où?* – where is it?

Lac d'Ilhéou to Cauterets

I wake up feeling off-colour, and not for the first time. A churning stomach ache is the least dramatic of the symptoms. But it is sunny and I don't have far to go, so I quickly forget about my defective digestion. The trail curves gently down the valley, intersecting from time to time with the dirt track used to supply the hostel. Grey patches of paint signal the way. Painted on the equally grey rocks, they blend into the natural surroundings much better than the usual red and white ones. Of course, they are not *supposed* to be waymarks; they are supposed to hide them. They cover the oversized splodges which were painted before the FFRP imposed its standard size, but they function just as well as the normal ones.

I see a group of walkers some distance below me on the track.

'The path is over here,' I call out to them, pointing at my feet.

'Where...?' The rest of their reply is lost in the breeze. One of them points up the valley towards the hostel.

'It's here,' I insist indicating the path with a broad sweep of my arm.

They continue pointing along the track, so I dump my rucksack and scramble across to meet them.

'You must have missed the turning a little while back,' I explain.

'No. We wanted to take the easy route. The GR10 is too steep, too uneven,' they reply.

I stump off back to my rucksack. When I get to the turning, I tear up the fern which is half hiding the waymark. Do people really prefer walking along roads to paths? Does effortless walking really compensate for dull uniformity? Perhaps we need a Campaign for Real Paths.

In the woods just before the town of Cauterets, the sun filtering through the leaves is accompanied by strange sounds: regular dull thuds, a series of burps varying in intensity and pitch, and occasional metallic crashes. Today is 14 July. A brass band is celebrating the French national holiday.

Cauterets is full of bunting and the streets full of holidaymakers. All the shops are open, but the one which interests me most is the pharmacy. I am looking for cures, appropriately enough in a town which has been dedicated to medicine from its earliest days. The thermometer outside the pharmacy reads 32°C. Inside, I ask for plasters, sun cream, Imodium, toilet paper, and the address of the nearest doctor.

'No, it's not the *garbure*,' the doctor reassures me. 'You've suddenly started using a lot of energy and replacing it with large quantities of food. Your metabolism will take a while to get used to the idea. I'll prescribe you something to settle you down.' I tell him that it will be four days before I get to the next village so he adds some anti-inflammatory cream 'in case your knees start playing up again'.

My next stop is the Bureau des Guides to ask about walking conditions on the next section. In a few days I will reach the highest point on the Pyrenean Way in the shadow of the Vignemale mountain and I have heard that there was a lot of snow last winter. If there is too much I will take a short cut.

'Yes, there's still lots of snow on the Vignemale, but the pass is not a problem,' says the girl behind the counter. 'Just in case you are interested, the snow makes climbing the Vignemale easier. If you want to do it there's a guide going on Sunday,' she adds hopefully. 'Since you'll be staying at the Refuge de Bayssellance you'll be half way there.'

'But I've never used crampons, and in any case I haven't got any.' The Vignemale is the highest peak on the French side of the Pyrenees. Climbing it involves crossing the Glacier d'Ossoue.

'The guide will bring some with him and show you how to use them.'

I look at her suspiciously. 'What about an ice axe? You need an ice axe, no?'

'Absolutely. Jean will bring one with him as well.'

So the rendezvous is fixed for 8 o'clock, in three days' time, at the Grottes Bellevue. I was intending to be there tomorrow; I will have to slow down. Sitting in a café afterwards, I wonder how I have managed to sign myself up for this – the final assault on the summit involves hands-on rock climbing. It must be something to do with the group of walkers sticking obstinately to the track this morning.

The Bureau des Guides is a venerable institution, dating back to 1862. Like the other major Pyrenean health spa resorts of the era, Eaux Bonnes, Luz-Saint-Sauveur, and Luchon, Cauterets was starting to organise activities for a new kind of tourist: the mountain walker. The first one of note had arrived 70 years previously. As *Les Grands Guides des Pyrénées* puts it: 'In 1787 a certain Ramond stuck his nose in … His ascents, numerous scientific observations, and detailed reports started a Pyrenean revolution in its own right … A revolution born elsewhere, launched by strangers, but surviving thanks to mountain people: guides and porters'. Curiously, the new way of looking at the mountains had coincided with the French Revolution.

The conquest of the Vignemale well illustrates the place of the local guides at that time. In 1792 a group of shepherds under the direction of Louis-Philippe Reinhard Junker climbed to the top as part of a survey to map the frontier between France and Spain. Their names are unknown. It was another 45 years before the next recorded visit to the summit, by Henri Cazaux, a guide from Luz-Saint-Sauveur, and his brother-in-law Bernard Guillembet on 8 October 1837. But the names which count are Ann Lister and the Prince de la Moskowa who disputed the summit in August 1838. Miss Lister, from Halifax, engaged Cazaux and three other guides, and reached the summit on 7 August, leaving a bottle with their names written on a piece of paper as proof. Four days later the Prince de la Moskowa climbed to the top, again accompanied by Cazaux, who had told him that Miss Lister had been taken ill and had not arrived at the summit. The Prince, he said, would be the first to climb the peak (and Cazaux would be better paid in consequence). When they approached the top, one of the guides rushed ahead and destroyed the incriminating bottle so that the Prince came back thinking that he was the first 'outsider' to conquer the mountain. Although he was told soon after his return that Miss Lister had beaten him, he pretended not to believe it and published accounts of his exploit on 21 August in the *Messenger* and on 15 September in *Deux Mondes*. (Later, Ann Lister extracted a confession from Cazaux, though it was many years before the truth was universally accepted.)

So, the conquest of the Vignemale is always presented as a story of rivalry between the two tourists. As usual, the guides are relegated to the shadows; the shepherds are completely invisible. It was all very well to be the first to climb a mountain, but an illiterate shepherd could never rival the status of an English 'lady' or a prince. As one Pyrenean author wrote: *le bâton ferré ne vaut que par la plume*, roughly – the pen is mightier than the walking stick. Guiding was a part-time occupation, a useful supplementary income in hard times, but insecure and without glory, and bedevilled by quarrels with clients. This, then, was the context for the creation of the Compagnie des Guides – which later became the Bureau des Guides – which set standards, determined fees and uniforms, organised insurance on the lines of a mutual society, and regulated disputes.

I sit down on a bench in the park opposite the Bureau des Guides. From my viewpoint, Cauterets appears small: trapped, crushed by the enclosing hills. Their wooded slopes nibble at the outer layer of long terraced streets embellished by delicate wrought iron balconies. This fragile shell protects the inner core of wedding cake hotels built in the second half of the 19th century. Then there is a gaudy commercial bubble but the real centre of the town is the casino, its park, and the arcade which lines the river. For the national holiday, the park has been invaded by roundabouts and souvenir kiosks but most of the attention centres on an artificial climbing wall, the *Challenge*. Painted in primary blues, reds, greens, and yellows, the shiny plastic blocks remind me of a deformed bouncy castle, an impression accentuated by the piles of soft orange mats on the ground. Of course the blocks are more solid than the walls of a bouncy castle, though the giant gecko logos are the only things to stick to them for any length of time. One after another, hopeful youngsters fall onto the mats to the applause of onlookers. It looks like some kind of a cruel joke. The handholds are either tiny plastic oysters bolted onto improbable overhangs or voluptuous bulges too big to caress and too smooth to grip.

Later the real competition starts and it is now that I realise quite how serious it is. One young man stretches across the vertical block face, leaning over at an improbable angle to reach a slight bulge in the surface to the side of him. The handhold is only big enough for a couple of fingers but he manages to use it to support himself while flinging his other arm around the opposite side of the bulge. In the same movement he swings across the block so that one foot lands on a ledge and he can haul himself up to the top. Even these competitors find the challenge difficult. Their displays of grace and power are punctuated by ungainly falls. Here it doesn't matter, but on 20 November 2004 Régis Barraque, an experienced climber, was found dead at the foot of the natural stone blocks called *la Russe*, just outside Cauterets. For this, the second edition, the *Challenge* has been renamed in his honour.

In the evening, I go back to the gardens of the casino for the continuing festivities. According to the publicity, today marks the start of the 'Festival Latino-Roc ... three days of Brazilian madness in a Latin-American ambiance'. Concerts, encounters, exhibitions, films, and shows with, this evening, the band Via Brasil on an outdoor stage of glittering aluminium, flashing spotlights, and billowing smoke. With a bewitching *joie de vivre* which sweeps all incongruity before it, the group captures the attention of the spectators and sets them bopping. Or more accurately hopping – from foot to foot. With remarkable lack of forethought the organisers have failed to cordon off an area for dancing, but it doesn't really matter. The whole park sways rhythmically.

I am soon thirsty so I grab a beer at one of the tents and go to sit down at a long table. Opposite me, finishing their desserts, are two women with festival committee name badges.

'This is the second year. Before that, there were just the usual events – local bands, outdoor meals, stalls – just like all the other towns in the area. Nobody came from outside,' says Nathalie, the older of the two.

'Why Latino, then?'

'I don't know. Do you?' she asks her friend, Aurélie.

'No. I don't think there was any particular reason. Perhaps it was inspired by the festival at Vic-Fezensac.'

'Has it brought more people into the town?'

'Last year there were loads more. There are not many today because there are things going on everywhere. But I expect the town will be overflowing tomorrow and Saturday.'

Even today the park is full, though many must also be attracted by the fireworks which are about to start.

Nathalie continues: 'It's the young people who have organised it and I think it is a good thing. It's different from the usual local events. *It isn't Gascon*. Don't get me wrong. I was born here. I'm proud to be Gascon and I think preserving our culture is important. But we don't have to be Gascon *all* the time.'

Cauterets has evidently changed. George Sand complains in 1825 that she has been asked to sing *Ebbene, per mia memoria*. 'Did I come to Cauterets to go out to *soirées* and rediscover Paris in this country of eagles and chamois?' Eight years later the young architect Eugène Viollet-le-Duc is more violently disgusted by some of the visitors. The worst ones, he says are the rich old men who have come to take the waters.

> They go to pick up girls at Pierrefitte to take them to Barèges. They count on the evening shower to cleanse themselves of the day's debauches. They know that a summer by the waters compensates for a winter of dissolution. They are masters of debauchery; they keep themselves going with good wines, sulphur baths, and pure air. Take that away from them and their legs will refuse to work, their emaciated features will turn pale, all their limbs will lose their strength and rot. Yes, we have seen men like that this evening. Oh, beautiful mountains, air so pure, were you created to preserve the life of such wretched creatures?

Hippolyte Taine (1855) is somewhat more scathing about the efficacy of the waters:

> This town has several springs. The Source du Roi cured Abarca, king of Aragon; the Source de César, so they say, restored the great Caesar's health. One must believe in history just as one must believe in medicine.

... in the time of François 1, the waters of Eaux-Bonnes cured wounds; they were called the waters of the gunners... Now they cure chest and throat problems. In a hundred years perhaps they will cure other things. Every century medicine takes a step forward.

Cauterets to the Plateau du Clot

After breakfast, I repair my feet, line my stomach wall with chalk, and slather a layer of white cream on my knees before going outside. As I have only a short distance to walk today I have decided to visit the Maison du Parc National first.

The exhibition seems to be largely about survival. Not what to do when you trip over and discover that your toe bone is no longer attached to your leg bone. Nor what to do when you find that snow is not a first-class engineering material for making bridges. No, the exhibition is about surviving in the Pyrenees year-in year-out, from century to century, over the millennia, be you human, animal, or plant life.

There are numerous places in the world where life is impossible, but very few in Europe – none at all in Britain. Arctic wastes, deserts, the depths of the oceans, and the tops of mountains push life to its limits and often beyond. In the Pyrenees there are virtually no living things at 2900m above sea level. Remarkably, a few lichens and a pink algae manage to reproduce higher up, on the slopes of the Aneto.

In the realm of plants, the *pin à crochets*, mugho pine, is one of the most hardy species. It can grow at up to 2600m and lives sometimes 1,000 years. It has to, the rhythm of life is slow at this altitude. The tadpoles of the midwife toad, for instance, can take up to 10 years before they metamorphose into adults. Not a very suitable subject for primary school nature study.

The human presence in the high mountains is also precarious: a summer adventure which started as the last glaciers began to retreat and hunter-gatherers followed wild herds out of the forest. By the end of the 20th century the adventure was drawing to a close, confined to the few shepherds who still practise transhumance and live in the summer pastures with their flocks.

The next thing that strikes me is a series of four drawings, cross-sections of the Pyrenees, explaining the evolution of the landscape over an even longer time-scale: hundreds of millions of years. The first one is innocuous: layers of hot red mantle safely contained in a cool earth skin, colour coded green and brown. But then something starts to go wrong. In the second drawing the skin layers are starting to move. In the third, the earth's life blood is pushed upwards and starts to escape. The skin is dislocated, irregular, bulging. It bursts, the blood vessels haemorrhaging in streams of boiling lava, leaving irremediable scars. Only the effects of time, measured in millennia, and represented in the fourth drawing, restore a semblance of order and calm.

It looks exactly like the diagram my doctor drew explaining what would happen it I didn't have my hernia repaired. Now I understand the Pyrenees. The mountains are trapped entrails. The sulphurous hot springs are suppurating pus. The paths, roads, and railways straddling the hills are a clumsy surgeon's attempts to stitch up the damage… But perhaps I am getting my symptoms out of all proportion.

The way out of town passes in front of the Thermes César, Caesar's Baths (1844) and its monumental architecture. It then saunters along the valley before zigzagging between the trees down to a bridge. A monolithic stone building and a strong smell guard the crossing. A prominent sign reassures: 'Thermes des Griffons (Rheumatology). Smells caused by water containing natural sulphur.' I hold my breath and climb up the Jéret valley – an inexhaustible, bubbling, babbling, booming, crashing, thundering waterfall 3km long – to the Pont d'Espagne.

The Pont d'Espagne is a popular excursion destination for

motorists. Here, you can eat in the café-restaurant, buy souvenirs, walk five minutes to the Plateau du Clot, and laze around all afternoon on the river bank sipping beer from the chalet refuge. Like me. You can also go rock climbing on the natural granite blocks, or take the ski lift to the Lac de Gaube (even in summer), but even the latter seems too much effort. So I settle for dangling my feet in the water, walking barefoot, savouring the grass between my toes, and chatting to one of the guides thoughtfully stationed here by the National Park. His telescope, he tells me, is to look for *isards*, but there aren't any. In winter they will come right down to this meadow. Last winter, when the temperature dropped to −26°C, they came even further down into the valley.

In the fading evening light, I am eating *garbure* on the terrace of the chalet-hostel when a man and his dog appear. The man is wearing a black beret, a white tee-shirt, a pair of jeans, and an extravagant paunch, as though it were a fashion accessory. The dog has the bulk of a husky at both ends, though its black and white coat betrays its collie ancestry. Behind them, a flock of perhaps a hundred sheep ambles into view, followed by a bottle-green truck. The man disappears into the bar and the dog runs off.

As soon as the shepherd has disappeared, the sheep start behaving oddly, for no apparent reason. Those in the centre of the flock are standing still but those at the outer edges start walking in an anti-clockwise direction around the axis. The further they are away from the centre, the faster they walk. And those sheep which had somehow become detached from the flock return to it. It is like a giant woolly Catherine wheel but working in reverse: instead of projecting sparks as it turns, it is gaining stragglers. The dog reappears, silently putting the finishing touches to its work of art, and then sits down on a slight promontory to admire the result. The flock is now a compact, complaining mass, encircled by a single dog.

There is one sheep in the back of the truck, which I take to be too ill to do the journey on foot, so I go to look. When I get closer I see that it is not ill. It is a ram, being kept separate from the females. Tomorrow is his big day. I study his expression. Is it frustration, anticipation, disdain, boredom, or lust? Sheep don't give much away.

Plateau du Clot to the Bayssellance hostel

In the early morning dew, I climb through the woods to the Lac de Gaube. There is nobody to be seen, only the lake, the inclined strata diving into its cool depths, and the vertical cliffs and glaciers of the Vignemale far away, blocking the head of the valley.

The abbé de Voisenon, a friend of Voltaire, visited the lake in 1761. He felt 'crushed' by the mountains.

> One sees only pine trees, yews and verbena, and those things which characterise the home of a black magician; there are no birds, the silence is only disturbed by the avalanches which fall from the heights of the mountains with a frightening noise. Nature seems to shiver with horror at herself. I was always thinking that she was saying to me: 'Why did you come here with your happiness? You are bold to dare laugh in this place!'

His reaction was typical. But now, 250 years later, the Lac de Gaube is famous for its beauty and the number of visitors it attracts. Why?

In France it was Jean-Jacques Rousseau who first wrote about the beauty to be found in the frightening heights of the Alps. His *Julie ou La Nouvelle Héloïse*, also written in 1761 was to become the prologue for a movement which transformed both French literature and the French countryside. Just as the Lake District in Britain was transformed by Wordsworth and the Romantics from a dark, forbidding wasteland into a place of beauty, the French Romantics came to value the Lac de Gaube, the Pyrenees, and beyond.

Plateau du Clot to the Bayssellance hostel

The movement stressed the importance of individual emotion and imagination over intellect. It took nature as its inspiration. Mountains were no longer *horrible*. (This 'horror' was a Western concept. In the Far East, mountains had long been revered, Mount Fuji in Japan being a well-known example.)

At the same time peasants were transformed into noble creatures whose faults were the result of contact with corrupt city dwellers. Hortense de Beauharnais, Napoleon Bonaparte's adopted daughter, on holiday near here, was tricked by a young couple into promising a dowry so that they could marry. When she found out, she forgave them because the young man admitted to his lies. 'I complimented him,' she said, 'that having done wrong, he knew how to make amends.'

One didn't need to have read the classics to understand Romantic literature. Gone were the references to Horace and Cicero. Equally, scientific names were abhorred. In fact scientific accuracy was thrown out if it got in the way of a good sentence. Hugo, for example, describes the Lac de Gaube as 'Thirteen hundred feet [deep]. Our old Notre Dame could be heaped up on top of herself six times before the high balustrade of her towers would appear at the water's surface.' The lake is 130ft not 1300ft deep.

Inevitably, as the movement was pushed further and further, descriptions became over-written, losing touch with reality, and reaction set in. In 1840 Flaubert, who had dreamed of seeing the Lac de Gaube by moonlight, regretted leaving. By 1872, again in the mountains, he just wanted to get back to his green writing table: 'I would give all the glaciers in the world for the Vatican Museum. It's there that one dreams.'

But something remains. As *Le Romantisme et les Pyrénées* concludes: 'The Romantics have bequeathed us a feeling for the mountains which has become truly integrated into the human soul.'

A visit to the Lac de Gaube became one of the three principal outings for the wealthy taking the waters in the Pyrenean spa towns in the mid-19th century (the second was the Cirque de Gavarnie, two days further along the Pyrenean Way, and the third, the Lac d'Oô, is a week away).

Above the lake, the path rises slowly as the valley opens out into a long water meadow. The stream fractures into numerous lazy rivulets which merge, only to split again. Fluffy tufts of white cotton grass shake their Andy Warhol haircuts in the breeze.

I am overtaken by a man many years older than me, running. Without stopping, he tells me that he is practising for the Vignemale Race which will take place a week on Sunday.

The first Vignemale Race was in 1904. Starting from Cauterets, the competitors followed the path I am now taking up to the Bayssellance hostel, across the glacier to the top of the Grand Vignemale, going back to their starting point by a different route – a distance of 55km, with over 2300m of climbing. The winner, Jean-Marie Bordenave, a guide from Cauterets, took six hours and one minute, and lost 6.7kg in weight. The record now stands at four hours 24 minutes. For ordinary mortals it would take something like 18 hours.

The race has become one of the World Mountain Running Association's official marathons: 549 runners completed the course in 2005. Nowadays, it no longer goes to the summit – the Glacier d'Ossoue is considered too dangerous.

I climb warily across a small patch of frozen snow up to the pass at the Hourquette d'Ossoue and down the other side to the Bayssellance hostel. It is a curious structure, built as if four rowing boats have been pulled out of the sea for the winter, dragged up the mountain by some helpful Gulliver, arranged in the shape of a cross, and then turned over to protect any passing travellers. The design also means that there is always one corner which is protected from the wind. I sit down in it and eat my picnic lunch.

I am soon joined by a tall man wearing a cowboy hat, who turns out to be English. John has been rock climbing for 26 years. He has just returned from the Grand Vignemale.

'I just followed the footprints across the snow. Except just before the top, that is. I made the mistake of climbing up a steep snow corridor between the rocks. It was a little tricky, I had to use my ice axe but the snow wasn't really frozen enough. Then when I came back down I met a couple who told me that I should have stuck to the rocks.'

'You were on your own?'

'Yes. Mind you, at one point my leg disappeared into the snow. What if I had disappeared completely? The hostel manager said that the crevasses were only a problem at the end of the summer. On the way back I saw some kids and a dog just wandering around completely uncontrolled, without a rope. Some people are absolutely stupid.'

After lunch I climb the snowless *Petit* Vignemale and sunbathe. A white-winged snow finch comes to beg some crumbs; two yellow-billed Alpine choughs circle overhead. To the north, I can see all the way back down the valley to the Lac de Gaube and beyond, to the plains choked by white haze. To the east, half-way down another grey-green valley, there is a reservoir: the Ossoue dam taking its tribute of the melt waters of the Vignemale glacier. The cars parked at the dam sparkle in the sun. Beyond them a slug-trail road wanders indecisively down to Gavarnie. In contrast, all around me the mountain tops are uncompromisingly harsh and jagged, bare rock or loose scree. Except just below me, to the south, where the glacier – the Glacier d'Ossoue – has polished off the worst of the deformities, covering them with alternating swathes of snow and ice.

I can see a few dots crossing one of the bands of snow near the far edge of the glacier. There are perhaps 30 dots in several groups, descending. The first group reaches the edge of the snow and stops before risking the icy slope. They progress gingerly, but I see one of the dots moving faster than the others, overtaking them and then coming to an abrupt halt. The other dots catch up, coalesce, and mill around. After a few minutes they all set off down the slope again.

At my table in the evening we are four French, two English, one

Belgian, and three Spanish. One of the Frenchmen has two fingers held together by an ostentatious white bandage.

'I was bitten by a bear,' he says.

Seeing our sceptical looks he says: 'Would you believe me if I said a *marmotte*?'

'Not now.'

'Actually it was a lawnmower. You might not think so, but it is quite a handicap. Even though I don't need to use my hands most of the time, my feet don't seem to work as well. I keep on falling over.'

The conversation is excitingly multilingual. There is plenty of goodwill and lots of communication at a basic level – where have you come from? Where are you going to? But as soon as we start on more complex subjects, everything grinds to a halt in mutual incomprehension. Europe in miniature. Even so, Europe *is* being constructed here, in an isolated hut, a day's walk from the nearest road, just as much as it is created in the padded conference rooms of major cities.

Vignemale

At a quarter to eight, after a night disturbed by snoring, I am at the Grottes Bellevue. I put my rucksack down and look into the first of the three caves. It has been carved out of the native rock and might sleep four or five, uncomfortably. Although the floor is littered with shreds of silver and gold emergency blankets and an empty wine bottle, I regret not having slept there, *inside* the mountain. The second one is in the same state. The third one, which is partly protected by a wall, is occupied. The rustling and grunts suggest some kind of wild animal but when I stick my head cautiously into the entrance, I make out a blue sleeping bag. A voice says, '*Buenos dias*'. The occupant tells me that his companions have gone to climb the Vignemale but his nose didn't like the idea. It had been gushing blood all night so he didn't feel strong enough. I ask him about the hard hat sitting on top of his rucksack. 'That was for the rock climbing at the end, in case someone dislodged a stone and it fell on my head.'

'Excuse me,' he continues, 'we camped near the hostel last night and what with my nose and the canvas flapping in the wind, I didn't get much sleep,' and he tucks himself back into his sleeping bag.

The caves look more suitable for bears than for human occupation yet they, and four others just under the summit, have carved out the legend of the man who financed their construction: Henry Russell. With an Irish father and a French mother, Count Henry Russell Killough was born in 1834 in Toulouse. He spent his early adult life adventuring across the world but came back to his native Pyrenees definitively in 1861, at the age of 27, climbing the Vignemale for the first time in that year. In 1864 he became one of the founding fathers of the Ramond Society, dedicated to the scientific study of the mountains. February 1869 found him at the summit of the Vignemale for the third time, with the guides Hippolyte and Henri Passet. Afterwards he wrote:

> Never will I forget the short but memorable minutes which we spent up there in the heart of the winter with the certainty that no other man in Europe was breathing at our level [3298m]; childish pride, but pardonable… From the top of this celestial cathedral, I saw below my feet the Pyrenean range frozen from one end to the other. I was in the centre of a snowy paradise! I was madly enthusiastic.

By the end of his life he had climbed all the major peaks, written several books about them, and could claim to have conquered some 30 virgins. Evidently his achievements would have guaranteed him a bulky entry in specialist books, but paradoxically his almost heroic status – his legend – is built on rather less substantial foundations. Russell is known as the man who became obsessed by a mountain.

He spent 150 nights on the Vignemale, the first three being in the open air. The experience persuaded him that he needed a shelter so he had a cave, which he named the Grotte Russell, carved in the rock face at the edge of the glacier, in 1881.

> An Eskimo would have built in snow; in Switzerland they like wood; and me, I only like rock. Nothing is as warm and as solid.

But he had not calculated on the variations in the thickness of the ice which sometimes covered the shelter and sometimes left it stranded, inaccessible, way above its surface. So workers were employed to build, successively, the Grotte des Guides, the Grotte des Dames, and the Grotte du Paradis, the latter just a few metres below the summit, in much harder rock, necessitating dynamite. Finally he had the Grottes Bellevue built for times when the higher shelters were unreachable.

In *Souvenirs d'un Montagnard*, he gives the impression of an austere, somewhat misanthropic nature-lover. One formal photograph shows a tall thin man, wearing a tweed jacket, standing stiffly to attention. His face is rectangular, serious, and strong-boned. In contrast, he has a full moustache and a strangely playful, straggly wisp of a beard which doesn't seem to fit in with the severe aspect of the rest of the photo. He looks a bit like Lenin. Another photo shows him in his favourite sheepskin sleeping bag, lying equally stiffly on an irregular rocky slope.

As he freely admits, he contributed nothing to the corpus of knowledge which was being assembled by his contemporaries. In the Introduction to *Souvenirs*, clearly influenced by the Romantic movement which flowered in his youth, he wrote:

> Nature is not a laboratory: it is an entertainment and a school… The things which are least understood are often those which please the most. What is melody, harmony, love? What is Beauty? … Will we know in ten thousand years? Probably not, and we won't have lost anything.

Vignemale

Although he sought isolation on the mountains, he also welcomed company when it arrived – at least at first. In 1884 he spent nine consecutive days in his eponymous *grotte*, sometimes contemplating alone, sometimes partying, sometimes praying. He had the *grotte*, and the mountain, blessed by three separate masses in a single day. There were 30 guests, most of whom evidently had to shiver in the wind on the glacier outside.

But this church 'wedding' was not enough for Russell. He wanted the symbolic equivalent of the civil ceremony conducted by the mayor, which consecrates a marriage in the eyes of French law. In 1889 he wrote to the *préfet*, a government official, asking for a 99-year lease, which was duly accorded. Later he wrote in the *Gazette de Cauterets* 'Vignemale is my wife and my seven caves are our children.'

Yet he was by no means antisocial. In Pau, he lived a normal life for a bachelor of his background, attending balls – he was an excellent dancer – and concerts. He played the cello.

One summer Henri Brulle and other climbing friends carried a tent up to the hermit's retreat.

> They organised three delectable days for me, in ideal weather, in Asian luxury… carpet, armchairs, bedding, oriental perfumes, lanterns, and vaporisers… Never in my small snowy empire, were seen so many beautiful things, without counting the cigars, the fine wines and a ham so big that it could have served as a bench or a cushion.

Several times, he built a cairn at the summit so that his betrothed would pass 3300m, but each time the winter frosts brought it down again. By 1894, at the age of 60, he was talking of his 25th ascent as his 'Silver Wedding.' Ten years later, after his 33rd visit he said a final goodbye. He died in Biarritz in 1909.

Meanwhile it is half past eight and I am still waiting for the guide. I watch as yet another a group of walkers arrives, says hello, and passes by without stopping. Most of them have helmets attached to their rucksacks. Another half hour, I say to myself. By nine o'clock, exasperated but relieved, I have just decided to go back to the hostel when a man arrives and introduces himself. Jean sports wrap-around sunglasses, has the deeply tanned skin of somebody who spends his life outside, and evident self-confidence. Then again he is small, almost skeletal, not particularly muscular, and what remains of his hair is thin and snowy-white. He is carrying a tiny rucksack which seems to be half empty. He opens it and extracts a pair of crampons. Nobody has told him about the ice axe. In any case I won't need one, he says. He doesn't even have one for himself. Use your stick, he says. I don't dare ask about a hard hat. It is quite clear that there aren't any.

Jean is followed by a young couple and a family of four: father strolling along, mother red faced and breathless, and teenage children bounding up the track. Mother announces that she is not going any further. Full stop. She will spend the day at the hostel.

The path leads across rubble to the edge of the snow where we sit down to attach our crampons. Jean makes loops in his rope and passes them round our waists.

'The rope is a safety measure,' he insists. 'Crampons are a means of locomotion. In the Pyrenees, people often think that crampons are a safety measure, so they don't bother with a rope. If you go to the Alps you will never see climbers crossing a glacier without a rope. Just as you'll never see them walking alone.'

He leads, followed by the teenage daughter, the son, the father, me, Brigitte and finally Gérard, her husband. Gérard is the only one of us with previous experience of glaciers.

We walk onto the snow. The crampons sink in and grip well. I can hear the sound of water gurgling under the crust: from time to time there are holes and we can see the stream. We arrive at the edge of the ice.

The glacier is uneven, and grey, like a semi-petrified lava flow. The

Vignemale

ice has been crushed and churned, pushed and pulled, defrosted and refrozen through thousands of years. Where it is in the shade, its surface is chiselled ice cubes, like a gigantic sheet of coarse sandpaper specially designed to polish hard mountain rocks – or like a cheese grater waiting to peel away soft human flesh. Where it is in the sun, it is slippery. Water is already dribbling down the slope.

'The most important thing is to walk with your toes pointing outwards,' says Jean. 'Otherwise you will catch your crampons in your trousers and fall over. Where it is slippery you need to stamp the crampons into the ice. It's called walking on ten spikes.' I look at mine. I can only see eight.

'I don't like this. It's not my kind of thing. I don't like heights,' says Brigitte as we progress up the western side of the glacier and the gradient increases. All the other groups, I notice, are following a snow drift on the opposite side.

'You'll be alright. It's not difficult,' says Jean. 'I've brought hundreds of people up here without a hitch. Just look at where you are putting your feet and you'll be alright.'

'When did you first come here?' I ask him.

'Over sixty years ago. Not to the top, at that time. Just to the hostel. The roof was made of stone and every winter the cement in the joints cracked so that it had to be repaired. When I was nine, I was packed off from the Pont d'Espagne alone with two mules. I had to go up and back again in the same day.'

The first few fissures are narrow and hardly noticeable. But then we arrive at a crevasse where we have to jump across. The opposite side is much higher.

'Jump as high as you can and plant your feet flat in the ice, one foot above the other. And then run up the slope like a duck without stopping to think. Don't try to use your toes,' advises Jean. He passes, the family passes, I pass, and then it is Brigitte's turn. She jumps, plants her two feet in the side and then stops there, frozen for an instant, before slipping into the void. It narrows rapidly so she finds herself wedged between the two sides a few metres below. She starts sobbing, shaking her head. Gérard and I pull her out by the rope. Her sleeveless black tee-shirt and tiny black Lycra shorts don't afford much protection: the knuckles of one hand are red and there are long bleeding gashes in her right arm and leg.

'It's not serious,' says Jean. 'But Steve and Gérard: you must keep the rope taut. Otherwise if she falls she will injure herself. The same applies to the rest of you.'

'I should never have come. I get vertigo. I don't want to go on,' complains Brigitte.

'Don't be stupid. You *did* say you wanted to come,' replies Gérard.

Brigitte hisses something under her breath.

The next obstacle is rather more difficult. The fissure is too wide to be jumped, but there is a vertical curtain of ice, hardly wider than my instep, which runs along the middle, lengthwise. From our side, we can jump to the end of the curtain easily enough but then we will have to walk along it, one foot in front of the other for several paces before it joins the other side.

Brigitte jumps onto the ledge: 'I can't move. I can't balance. My ice axe is too small.'

She is stuck at the end of the curtain, with a vertical drop on both sides, unable to move, held in a fragile equilibrium by the rope. Her husband and I pull it taut. She is right, her ice axe is useless. It is too short to reach the ground. What she needs is a stick, but we can't move to help her.

'Spread your arms out. It'll help you balance,' shouts Jean from the other end of the rope, but she doesn't budge. He scampers down the slope and passes her a stick which she wedges against the side of the fissure. When she reaches the other side she is trembling.

'I really would prefer to walk on the snow,' she pleads, pointing at the string of walkers following the standard route on the other side of the glacier.

'I prefer to walk on the ice,' answers Jean, firmly. 'It's less risky.'

Vignemale

'Don't be such a wimp. Let's get on with it,' grumbles her husband.

'It's no more dangerous than being on a city pavement with cars speeding past. It is just that you are not used to it,' I suggest, hopefully. She is unconvinced.

Brigitte has taken the role I had allotted myself. I was the one who was going to panic. But now, for me at least, the climb has become enjoyable.

I point out a couple of climbers spidering down the vertical south face of the Petit Vignemale and ask Jean about it. 'It's not difficult,' he claims. When pressed, he admits to having climbed the nearby Couloir de Gaube. This is *the* classic route up the north face of the Grand Vignemale. Only very experienced rock climbers even attempt it.

Finally, we cross to the other side of the glacier and onto the snow. Sinking in at every step, the snow is much more tiring than the glacier, but we soon arrive at the foot of the rock face which separates us from the top. On our left I can see the entrance of the Grotte du Paradis and a lonely line of footprints climbing up a snow corridor.

'They're not making things easy for themselves. That's not the normal route,' comments Jean looking at the other groups descending from the summit. 'All the better for us. We won't have to worry about stones falling on our heads. Take off your crampons and your gloves.'

We follow him, hauling ourselves up with our hands, concentrating on the holds. After the glacier, it seems trivial. At one o'clock we are at the summit, sitting in a hollow in the rubble in the shape of a nest. All the other birds have flown. The sun is shining, the view extravagant, like yesterday. There is still no wind.

The return by the standard route, slithering across the ice and snow slurry, now more liquid than solid, is joyful. Taking off her crampons, Brigitte kisses her husband, beaming. She thanks Jean effusively: 'It was wonderful. I'm really glad I came. I was just a little bit worried at first but I'm really glad I did it!'

The High Pyrenees: Gabas–Luchon

Bayssellance hostel to Gavarnie

Below me, the valley is full of cloud, its top surface sliced off by the rising sun to reveal its hidden lining, reflecting the silver light. As I descend through the vapours, the sun rises, burning holes in the swirling mist, creating transient views of the Vignemale and its glacier. At the Ossoue dam, the clouds are thickening but open up to allow me a last fleeting view of the mountain reflected in the dank lake.

By the time I reach Gavarnie it is raining hard. The famous donkeys are lined up under their tarpaulin hangar. There are twenty or more, fully equipped with saddles, bridles, and stirrups expecting, it seems, a coach load of deranged but impermeable visitors to hire them and gallop off, *en masse*, to the *cirque*, Gavarnie's tourist attraction. The donkeys are none the happier for their day off. Nor is the shopkeeper opposite, looking out morosely from between his teddy bears and whistling polyester *marmottes*. I compare his shop with the one next door, trying to spot the differences. Identical teddy bears wear identical red berets. Perhaps there is a small difference in the range of sizes and prices. Similarly, there are plenty of possibilities of eating, but little choice. All the restaurants promise traditional local menus; all start with *garbure*. All are empty.

This is very unusual. Between 15 July and 15 September every year, the village sees 200,000 visitors. One thousand visitors for every inhabitant. Many don't get much further than the last café, stopping when they realise that the *cirque* is still an hour's walk away.

According to the tourist office, Gavarnie has maintained 'a balance between tradition and modernism. This valley has managed to preserve a certain authenticity, evolving in its ancient tradition of welcome (the rich invalids come to take the waters, the pioneers of mountaineering, the literary and political celebrities) and adapting it to the multitude of contemporary tourists' ... with all the finesse of a high-class call girl, her youth well behind her, adapting herself to the demands of a rugby team.

The rain slows a little so I walk up the valley out of the village towards the *cirque*. I am just behind a young couple, walking arm in arm.

'*Oh, la, la,* que *c'est beau* – it is so beautiful!' says the woman ecstatically, pointing to the river and the luxuriant vegetation. Her husband nods in agreement.

A few minutes later, they catch me up at the humpback bridge.

'*Oh, la, la, la,* que *c'est beau!*' she exclaims, wide eyed.

At the foot of the waterfall I see them again.

'*Oh, la, la, la, la,* que *c'est beau!*' she says emphatically.

Irreverently, I imagine her and her husband making love. I can't see her keeping quiet.

Nevertheless, the *cirque* itself really *is* imposing, even when the heights are hidden in the clouds. It is an immense natural theatre, carved out by glaciation, a semicircle of vertical cliffs and horizontal ledges, enclosed and dominated by some of the frontier's highest peaks. The *gave* bisecting the green valley floor, the stark rock face, the snow-covered scars, and the long, long waterfall have all contributed to the reputation of the *cirque* and its classification as a World Heritage Site. Victor Hugo called it variously nature's coliseum, a hippodrome, a Parthenon, a cathedral, a Kremlin, boas rolled one above the other, the mouth of a volcano, a storm trap and, beginning to let his imagination run away just a little, a Tower of Babel turned over and imprinted in the earth like a seal.

The Romantic authors of the first half of the 19th century came here in order to view natural beauty, and in writing about it they defined it. Gavarnie was given a special place in the pantheon. Hugo's effusive admiration, the concord of other great French Romantics, and the pecuniary interests of the tourist industry have together created a myth. Gavarnie is not simply a stop on the traveller's route. It has become a holy place for mountain lovers. Indeed, for many people, Gavarnie *is* the Pyrenees. Going to the Sanctuary of Notre Dame de Lourdes in the morning? Why not make a pilgrimage to one of the great natural wonders of the world in the afternoon? Bought a candle to remind you of the grotto in Lourdes? Buy a walking stick to remind you of the waterfall!

On the way to the hostel just outside the village I stop at the bookshop and weigh up the relative merits of guides to the Pyrenees. None are light enough. Then I go to look at the bronze statue of Russell which greets visitors on the road into the village. He is perched on a rock, a book in one hand, holding one of the inconveniently long sticks favoured at that time. The locals are justifiably proud of this work of art but I think that the sculptor is making a subtle but cruel joke at their expense. Russell may well be welcoming visitors, but he is quite clearly looking away from the village.

Gavarnie to Luz

The first glimpse of violet is just visible on the horizon but the stars are still twinkling; turning my back on Gavarnie, I switch on my head-torch. As the sun rises, the undulating pastures are thrown into sharp relief by its horizontal rays. A red tractor heads for the half-mown meadow where yesterday morning's hay was abandoned to the rain in corduroy stripes. The path runs horizontally, half-way up the hillside, overlooking a valley speckled with stone-built farmhouses and barns. Traditional stepped gables are complemented by corrugated metal roofs and satellite dishes.

The sides of the path are strewn with carline thistles, their huge flower heads nestling at ground level in acanthus crowns. Held down today by purple fingers, in a few days the flowers will break out in a explosion of dazzling gold. In the past they were eaten, like artichokes, by shepherds. Now they frequently decorate doorways. Crossing a stream, there is a powerful smell of mint. A few steps later it is the musky smell of wild marjoram.

The path descends a tributary to rejoin the Pau *gave*. Here, the meadows are flat and parched, in contrast with their high-mountain neighbours. In the middle of one of them, a man is picking up huge thin sheets of metal, raising them above his head, and then throwing them into the earth at his feet, cleaving it like a mad butcher. One, two, three. Pursuing his vengeance on the barren earth, he fetches another set and attacks a different part of the field. One, two, three sheets, making a thin rusty wall. Now, I can see that he has half a dozen of these walls distributed about the field. And that water is seeping out round some of them, flooding out over the grass from invisible canals.

On the opposite side of the *gave*, water is being harnessed for another purpose, and on an altogether different scale. The hydroelectric power station of Pragnères – an angular concrete excrescence – is one of the largest in the Pyrenees. The water which powers the turbines comes from the heights of the mountains in large-diameter, high-pressure pipes, surging down a drop three times the height of the Gavarnie waterfall. The electricity produced zaps away on overhead pylons. Private cableways give access to the pumping stations on top of the hills. A huge steel web with a concrete spider at its heart. But this web is at the centre of a much larger and much prettier network: reservoirs stretching from the Ossoue dam below the Vignemale, to the Lac d'Aumar, two days' walking from here, linked by underground galleries and pumping stations.

Later, I come to a junction, where the different variants of the Pyrenean Way meet up again. Cauterets is only seven hours away by the direct route. It has taken me five days. Following the track in the other direction, away from Cauterets, I descend rustic stone steps to Saint-Sauveur, an outpost of Luz-Saint-Sauveur, one of the most noteworthy of the Pyrenean spas of the 19th century. The oppressive heat drives me on, to the Pont Napoléon on the edge of the village.

The Napoleon in question was the Emperor Charles Louis-Napoleon Bonaparte, Napoleon III, nephew of Napoleon I. He only visited the central Pyrenees once, inaugurating the new railway line from Paris to Tarbes on 18 August 1859. But he and his wife Eugénie were to play a notable part in its development. He was born in Paris in 1808 and, as a member of the Bonaparte family, was forced into exile in 1816 after the defeat at Waterloo. He was politically in advance of his time, writing in 1844 'Poverty will no longer be seditious when opulence is no longer oppressive.' It was these ideas – for the urban voters – and the Bonaparte name – for the rural constituencies – which ensured his election as President in 1848. But the presidency was limited to one term of four years and Louis-Napoleon wasn't going to be constrained to a brief period of glory. On 2 December 1851 he seized absolute power, 47 years to the day after his uncle had been crowned emperor. The code name for the coup d'état was 'Rubicon'.

Victor Hugo, the writer, was one of the MPs who stood up against the coup. He was forced into exile. Hugo portrayed Napoleon III as '*Napoléon le petit*' and questioned his legitimacy, not only as head of state, but also as a member of the Bonaparte clan. 'The child of chance, whose name is a theft and whose birth is a fake,' he wrote. Which brings us back to the Pyrenees, the summer of 1807 and the visit to Gavarnie of Hortense de Beauharnais, Queen of Holland and Louis-Napoleon's future mother. The notoriously unfaithful Hortense, who made no secret of her marital problems, described her stay at the Hôtel des Voyageurs in Gavarnie as one of the happiest of her life.

Whatever his genetic heritage might be, Napoleon III was convinced of the importance of economic development so that when he came to power he took great interest in developing France's infrastructure. Paris was a major concern and it was at his instigation that the city was remodelled by Hausmann, to create the *grands boulevards*. Biarritz, at the Atlantic end of the Pyrenees, and a favourite holiday destination of his wife Eugénie, also saw redevelopment in his time. He encouraged the nascent railway industry (which was to bring tourists and patients to the Pyrenean spas). And when he and Eugénie came to the spa at

Saint-Sauveur in 1859 he was persuaded of the necessity for a new bridge. This was, and is, more a monument to Imperial glory than of any practical use. Saint-Sauveur was already umbilically linked to the nearby town of Luz by a low-level bridge over the *gave* at the northern end of the spa. The new bridge, a dramatic, high stone arch over a narrow ravine at the other end of the spa duplicates the existing one, saving only a few minutes for those heading for the mountains. It was costly to build and the wooden scaffolding risked being swept away by the merest flood during its construction. Now it serves mainly as a launching pad for bungee jumping.

More importantly, Achille Fould, minister and confidant of Napoleon, but also a local man, saw the necessity of good roads to improve communications between the spa towns. The *routes thermales*, which he persuaded Napoleon to finance, were a real boon in their time, though they are now mainly known for the high passes familiar to Tour de France cyclists: the Aubisque, the Tourmalet, and others.

Even so, Napoleon's most important contribution to the economic development of the Pyrenees was probably simply his presence: he was the most prestigious person to visit the area in some time and attracted others in his wake.

At the end of the bridge there is the usual collection of souvenir shops and cafés. I slump heavily onto a white plastic seat under a sunshade in front of one of the cafés, and have just ordered my beer and ice cream, when the inevitable miniature rubber-tyred tourist train rolls up. The waitress is slow and the train driver has already rung his bell, bellowed something unintelligible, and disappeared before I have finished my beer. So I am condemned to more walking: down the main road, then along a track, which climbs again, although Luz is well below me. The advantage of this route is the view of the town below. It is also significant for another reason. On a bluff overlooking the town of Luz stands the Solferino Chapel.

An unpretentious structure, with a simple nave and square tower, the chapel was built by order of Napoleon III to commemorate his

The High Pyrenees: Gabas–Luchon

recent victory at Solferino in northern Italy. The victory had been a bitter one. Henri Durant, an eyewitness, wrote:

> Here is a hand-to-hand struggle in all its horror and frightfulness; Austrians and Allies trampling each other under foot, killing one another on piles of bleeding corpses, felling their enemies with their rifle butts, crushing skulls, ripping bellies open with sabre and bayonet. No quarter is given; it is a sheer butchery; a struggle between savage beasts, maddened with blood and fury.

Two months later, the Emperor had concluded a peace treaty and was on holiday in the Pyrenees. In contrast, Dunant went back home and wrote about his experiences. His book led directly to the 1864 Geneva Convention and the foundation of the International Red Cross and Red Crescent Movement.

I limp down to Luz, capital of the *Toy* district in the blistering mid-afternoon heat. *Toy* has nothing to do with its English homonym. *Toy*, originally *thôys* in Gascon, is a child or youngster. Perhaps it was a reference to the stunted growth of the malnourished mountain dwellers.

In the evening I go to a concert in the fortified church of St André. The building is surrounded by crenellated walls, with a tall gate tower through which all visitors must pass. Inside, the men – it is a male-voice choir – are dressed in coordinated shades of brown – jackets and trousers, bow ties and berets – set off by stiff white shirts. They start with *Se canto, que cante?* – It sings, what does it sing? a popular Occitan song known throughout the length of the Pyrenees. It is followed by *l'Adour* (a local river), *Le Pic du Midi* (the nearest mountain), *Le Pays Toy* (their own composition), and a traditional Basque medley. They sing in perfect polyphonic harmony, in French and in the local dialect.

The conductor turns round to explain something of the choir's history. The *Orphéon*, he says, was founded in 1888. In recent years they have sung in Germany and Greece. But, he complains, there is only one singer who is under 55, and he is the son of another chorister. I look at the audience: it seems to be largely composed of tourists.

Barèges

I get up late and trundle down to the tourist office to meet Raymonde. She drives me up the Barèges valley along the road to the col de Tourmalet, overtaking panting cyclists wishing to measure themselves against the greats. She parks the van at a hairpin bend and strides off in the direction of the Pic du Midi de Bigorre, pointing out the buildings of the Observatory on top of the hill. I have arranged to meet a shepherd in his *estive*. An hour later, we find Laurent and his wife Christine surrounded by a flock of sheep. Laurent has one wedged between his legs and is applying a cream to its gums which are caked with blood and soil. He lets it go, scans the flock, and threads his way through the wool. Suddenly he leaps forward, like a rugby player, grabbing a sheep by the horn.

'Real shepherds don't need crooks,' he claims. 'You've just got to be quick.'

Laurent, who must be in his 50s, has pepper-and-salt hair and a full beard. He is wearing a bright purple tee-shirt and has a pair of binoculars strung round his neck. He has 141 ewes, 6 rams, and 10 wethers (castrated rams), and comes from his farm twice a week to check them out. Here, sheep are bred for their meat so they don't need the daily attention required by their Ossau-Iraty sisters. This morning he and his wife set out at five o'clock and, with their two dogs, Filou and Anise, have just finished rounding up the flock.

'They roam over an area of about 2sq km but I put salt cakes down here so most of them stay pretty close. When I brought them up from the valley in May they were grazing near where you parked the van but they climb higher as the snows melt.'

'You haven't shorn them yet. When I was in the Basque country they were being shorn in June,' I comment.

'No. We shear them in the autumn, when they come back down. Not too short, of course.' He uses the traditional scissors. 'If we did it in spring they wouldn't have enough protection from the weather up here.'

The sheep each have a label attached to one ear, with a number to indicate the *département*, the village, the farmer, the year of its birth, and its birth rank. This one, I can see, was the 14th lamb to be born in 2002.

'It means that you can trace the lamb you find on the butcher's slab back to the farm where it grew up. I have to keep a record of every sheep and if the inspector comes, I have to be able to produce each and every one of them.' He gets a subsidy of 20€ per year per sheep.

'What about the bears?' I ask.

'Did you see the Tour de France on the television the other night?'

'No.'

'I was there blocking the road. Papillon [a bear who died recently] cost the state 3,000€ per day, when you add up the cost of the staff, the helicopter and so on. And the compensation is pitiful. I would get about 250€ for the sale of a sheep. But if it is killed by a bear I would only get 150€, and losses from miscarriages don't get counted. Also, you've got to prove that the sheep was killed by a bear. How do you do that when the vultures clean everything up within a few hours? The only thing that the vultures won't eat is a sheep which has been killed by lightning, or by a viper.' He stops to grab another sheep and inspects its belly. 'When it's a viper, they turn blue,' he adds.

Asked about the financial side of sheep rearing, he tells me that he gets 4€/kilo because his sheep are *appellation contrôlée*, but this has extra costs: he can't use fertiliser for his winter hay and he can't use silage either. But if he didn't submit to the quality control he would only get 2€/kilo.

Some of the sheep have a semicircular mini-skirt of sacking stitched into the wool around their rear quarters.

'It's a contraceptive. Those sheep are due for slaughter this autumn so I don't want them to get pregnant. Normally, sheep farmers give them a chemical contraceptive but it's not allowed in organic farming.'

He comes from a long line of sheep farmers, but says that he will be the last of them.

'My son used to be interested in sheep until he found a girlfriend,' he muses.

We are preparing to go back down the hill when he asks me what I am doing here.

'The Pyrenean Way.'

'I hate walking. You'll never find me on the Vignemale or at the Brèche de Roland. I do it because I have to for my work.'

On the way back in the van I ask Raymonde about the economic significance of sheep farming.

'It's just folklore,' she answers.

She drops me off at a café for lunch and I then spend a happy afternoon in the botanical gardens looking at plants I have seen in the mountains and putting names to them. Overhead, red and blue hang gliders pirouette. Afterwards, I trudge down the road to Barèges.

The spa of Barèges is a long thin village clinging to the hill slope alongside the river Bastan. Not high enough above the river to avoid floods – in 1897, in particular, much of the village was swept away. Nor high enough to avoid the avalanches. It was hit in 1803 (11 dead), then in 1811, 1842, 1855 (12 dead), and 1856. However it was the avalanche of 1860 which finally made the authorities react. Just a year after the visit of the imperial couple Napoleon III and Eugénie to the village, the military hospital caring for some of the wounded from Solferino was destroyed.

The engineer Lomet had visited Barèges as long ago as 1794 and concluded that deforestation was the cause of the disasters:

In the past, all the mountains which overlooked Barèges were covered in oak... Men still living saw the few remaining trees and finished them off. The inhabitants of the plateau have destroyed everything themselves because these slopes, being the first to be freed of snow by the sun and by avalanches, provide the first spring pasture for their sheep. The day they take them there, they forget that at home in the winter they have shivered with the fear of being carried away by the avalanches which they have stubbornly provoked.

So replanting became a priority. In parallel, the military authorities conducted a series of experiments. The slopes were remodelled, an artificial forest of pickets was planted, and stone platforms and dry stone walls were constructed. The pickets were quickly swept away but the stone walls were more successful. In dividing the snow fields into independent zones they stopped the avalanche of a small area from dragging a larger area in its wake. Barèges had become a laboratory for avalanche protection. Meanwhile the village continued to suffer further disasters, in 1879, 1882, 1886, 1889, 1895, 1897, 1902, 1907, and 1939, becoming almost synonymous with the word avalanche. In Barèges there is a saying '*Un Toy ne craint que Dieu, les orages, et l'avalanche* – The inhabitants of the valleys fear only God, thunderstorms, and avalanches.'

Avalanches are a man-made problem. Nature is not malicious, merely indifferent. It isn't the snow sliding down the mountains that causes the problem. Snow has always slid down mountains. But when the Pyrenees were only inhabited by a few shepherds during the summer months, avalanches were unimportant. The zones where the snow persisted all summer, and where avalanches seemed likely, were simply avoided. It was only when the Pyrenees started to be occupied all year round that avalanches started to kill significant numbers. Although the newly popular spas attracted most of their visitors in the summer season, where they were situated in an avalanche zone – as at Barèges – there would now inevitably be a risk for the increased number of permanent inhabitants. Then there was the exploitation of mineral wealth, with disastrous consequences for the miners of the Société des Mines d'Arre et d'Anglas. And the construction of the hydroelectric dams from the beginning of the 20th century had its share of disasters. But the main problem was, and remains, the phenomenon of winter sports, growing prodigiously from 1960, and bringing with it both white gold and black marble.

Following two disasters in the Alps in 1970 the government established a safety commission. Out of the commission came an association bringing together scientists to study the composition of ice, specialists in explosives (to set off preventative avalanches), radio technicians (for finding victims equipped with transmitters), weather forecasters, rescue co-ordinators, engineers, planners, map makers (to identify the zones at risk), dog handlers, and resort promoters. Some of the resort promoters were not pleased that the association was called the National Association for the Study of Snow and Avalanches, fearing that the name would be bad publicity.

In January 2005, a 28-year-old skier and his father were taking a short cut off-piste, not far from where I have been walking today. Only the father survived. One eyewitness wrote on the Web:

> I work at the ski resort of Barèges… I saw the two people in question go into the narrow passage but I didn't see the avalanche. The father and son were skiing in parallel. Once the rescue was organised, the dogs took nearly 30 minutes to find the son, then it took another 15 minutes to reach him… Unfortunately it was too late… Many people were shocked by the accident and we hope to avoid a repetition this season. I ask you once again to be prudent. That day many people, including me, were carried away by avalanches.

The zone is known as one of the most dangerous in the area. The risk factor announced on the weather forecast was 4 out of 5. This, then, was a tragedy in the original sense of the word – a fate foretold. Yet at the same time, this professional was skiing in an even more hazardous zone. And he is asking others to be careful.

There is a ski club in Barèges called l'Avalanche – an act of defiance or a lack of tact?

At the hostel in the evening, I meet one of the men who was hang-gliding over my head at the botanical gardens.

'Three descents today from the col de Tourmalet down to the botanical gardens. I'm tired. It's not the hang gliding. It's carrying the kit to the launch point,' he tells me. 'I've been hang gliding for the past 15 years. Since I retired.'

Barèges to the Lac d'Orédon

The path leaves the road and climbs the valley quietly, visiting a series of small lakes, traversing fertile pastures, passing under twisted *pins à crochets*. After an hour's walking I am overtaken by a man in blue overalls. He is off to build a sheep fold on the plateau, he says. When I arrive, he has just woken up his colleagues, who have camped the night: they are standing outside their tents, stretching and yawning.

At the Lac de Madamète I sit down by the shore, take off my tee-shirt, and let the sun warm my back. In the stillness, I can hear the blood circulating through my ears. From time to time tiddlers jump out of the shallows: plut, plop. The lake and the sky, the same vivid indigo, are separated by a grassy hillside which descends into the water, in an unnaturally perfect reflection. On the opposite side of the lake three chestnut horses with white socks are munching steadily inside a temporary electric fence, their hooves leaving deep prints in the soft peat. Nearby there are a couple of tents but no other signs of life.

I struggle up to the Col de Madamète which separates the rivers which flow into the Gave de Pau from those which flow into the Neste d'Aure. This is not only a physical watershed but also a linguistic one. The passes are no longer *hourquettes* but *cols* and the rivers, the *gaves*, have turned into *nestes*.

I lumber down to the Lac d'Aumar and its twin the Lac d'Aubert. Our cartographers had a field day here. Both *au* and *mar* can mean lake so Lac d'Aumar could mean Lake of the Lake Lake, which makes the Lac d'Aubert, Lake of the Green Lake seem quite sensible.

I meet an increasing numbers of day trippers as I approach the car park. This is the Néouvielle Nature Reserve, created in 1935. What was once an isolated granite massif, freckled even in mid-summer by patches of snow – hence the name, meaning old snow – has become a major tourist attraction. But unlike the Lac de Gaube and the Cirque de Gavarnie, which are on the edge of the central part of the national park, these two lakes are in the very centre of the nature reserve. Their isolation was eroded by the creation of the road access for building the nearby reservoir at Cap de Long and then eradicated by the construction of a road specifically for tourists in 1970. Nowadays, each summer, the nature reserve has to cope with 150,000 visitors and their cars.

I follow the path down to the Lac d'Orédon where I book into the hostel for the night.

Lac d'Orédon to Saint-Lary

In the forest, early next day, I hear a strange feral barking but it stops after a while so I continue. I reach the first pass before the sun and look down on the Lac d'Oule, another reservoir. Water is a precious commodity in the Pyrenees. It is not that there isn't enough of it, it is just that it is in the wrong place at the wrong time. In winter there is no problem. But in summer, although there is water relatively nearby in the high Pyrenees, it needs to be channelled to the fields in the valleys and as far as the plain by the use of dams and canals. The Lac d'Oule and the Lac d'Orédon are used to water the area around Lannemezan 50km away via a canal built in the mid-19th century. The same water is also used – several times over – to produce hydroelectricity, with several major schemes being implemented just after the Second World War. The mountain streams were nicknamed *huile blanche* – white oil – oil being *the* symbol of unexpectedly discovered wealth in a world where the motor car was just beginning to make an impact.

On the hill opposite and overlooking the valley, the scenery is rather less natural. The ski resort of Le Pla d'Adet resembles a fortress or perhaps a prison, white, rectilinear, forbidding. The view *from* Le Pla d'Adet is said to be stupendous.

I walk through the comfortably old Vielle Aure to the less comfortably new Saint-Lary-Soulan. The decidedly modern church sets the tone. Its predecessor, dedicated to Saint Hilaire – hence, by deformation, the name of the village – was demolished in 1949. The replacement, with its vertical lines and steeply sloping roofs over the aisles, looks like a space ship ready to transport the faithful directly to heaven when the last trumpet sounds. Inside, it is a different story. Covering the whole wall behind the altar, a painting shows Christ rising between snow-capped mountain peaks. The only way to him and resurrection is through a harshly rectilinear concrete maze.

At the time that the church was being rebuilt, the population of Saint-Lary was only a couple of hundred. The pastoral way of life and the ancient stone buildings were crumbling. Although the road from the plain continued a few kilometres beyond the village before petering out at the end of the valley, it only served a few insignificant hamlets. In the late 1940s, the construction of the dams had brought a short-lived boom to the village but the end of that was also in sight. The prospects of tourist development were remote: the village didn't have the necessary slopes for a ski resort nor the springs for a spa.

Now, just over 50 years later, the village has been resurrected. It has a permanent population of 1024 and numerous shops. Now, the road continues into Spain through a tunnel, bringing skiers in winter

Lac d'Orédon to Saint-Lary

and clients for the spa in summer. Saint-Lary-Soulan has become the biggest ski resort in the Pyrenees with 545,000 skier-days per year. There are 24 different beds available for every permanent resident.

The village's new found dynamism is celebrated in the name of its high street: rue Vincent Mir. Mir was personally responsible for changing the destiny of Saint-Lary. A well-known rugby player, in an area where rugby is *the* sport, and a resistance worker, he was elected mayor shortly after the Second World War. His first major project was the creation of a ski resort and his great achievement was to negotiate the cooperation of neighbouring communes to the extent that Saint-Lary was able to devour the commune of Soulan in 1963. (The name Soulan derives from *soulane*, the sunny side of the mountain, a name which explains to some extent the popularity of the resort.)

His second achievement was the construction of the Aragnouet–Bielsa tunnel. The first contacts were made in 1956 but it was 1976 before the first cars emerged from the tunnel, the only cross-border passage for a distance of more than 80km.

In the meantime his daughter Isabelle had become a world-class skier, training with the 1968 Olympic team on the slopes above her home town and going on to win a silver medal. The slope where the team practised commemorates the exploit with an ingenious reworking of her name: it is called the *piste* Mirabelle.

But the village lacked a summer season to compare with its winter bustle. What it lacked was a spa. The Thermes de Saint-Lary were duly opened in 1988; the water comes from the Sources de la Garet, way up the valley. As if this wasn't enough, the Maison de l'Ours was opened in 1991. As well as a multi-media experience, the exhibition includes Bingo and Apollon, two brown bears, rescued from a circus where they were being badly treated. At least, in this concrete-walled prison, they are well looked after.

Even the victors in a rugby match leave the field with bruises and Saint-Lary-Soulan is no exception. Whilst there are some ancient buildings, many of the shop fronts on the high street look as though they would be happier with neon lights – but their owners didn't quite dare. Then there are the holiday houses, 4000 of them, empty for most of the year. And by the time of Mir's retirement the town was heavily in debt; in 1991 his business – specialising in public buildings and works – was placed in liquidation.

In one of the newsagents, above the comics, above the cookery and health magazines, above the girlie magazines, there is a blown-up model. All the folds, all the curves, all the secret corners. The Pyrenees from head to foot in three-dimensional splendour. Pornographic cartography. The lurid colours, the insistence on detail, and the plastic moulding are all revoltingly crude, like a plastic carp which sings as you walk by. But I want one nevertheless. Unfortunately, it won't fit discreetly into my back pocket. It won't even fit into my rucksack. I will have to send for it by mail order.

Saint-Lary to Germ

The road is bordered by concrete wall posts capped by giant dice balanced on one corner in a perpetual unstable equilibrium. Some of the dice will fall on a six, but not all of them. Did the owner of the house pay for it with a win on the National Lottery? Are they there to bring luck in the future? In the garden, a grey-haired woman is deadheading her carnations.

'I don't know why they are there,' she tells me. 'It was the builder's idea.' She pauses to think: 'No, I don't know why. We had the house built 40 years ago. But I've never thought about it before you asked.'

The path climbs slowly up to the top of the hill and then dives down the other side. My right knee says: 'Beware'! I stop, wait, then continue carefully down into the valley of the Luron. Here, the designer-Pyrenees are safe, lush, and carpeted. Around Balnéa, even the grass is manicured.

Balnéa is a spa which eschews any pretensions to medical utility to concentrate on soft-focus self-indulgence. The Héliantis pool, for example, is described as 'a playground in a unique wooden décor inspired by the Hoogan huts of North American Indians'. But it is closed for renovation so I have to continue. I have just left the village when my knee speaks again, this time shouting: 'No!' Tendonitis. Every time I jar my leg – almost every other step – I get a incapacitating pain. I carry on, gingerly, wondering whether I should go back to the village and get a taxi back to Saint-Lary-Soulan. The pain returns intermittently, unpredictably, and I make halting progress towards the hostel in Germ. Then one of my front teeth falls out. Unlike my leg, it doesn't give me any warning, but I eventually find it under the ferns, wipe it clean and stick it in my pocket. I had a croquet accident 30 years ago, and the resulting gap was repaired with a crown. Why now? I'm falling apart. I dismiss the pain in my left arm, – I don't want to know – and look miserably up towards the hostel.

The Centre de Montagne de Germ, as it is called, is somewhat more than a hostel. It has English-style gardens with pink peonies, hollyhocks, a silver birch tree, a freshly cut hay-smelling lawn, deck chairs, picnic tables, and a swimming pool. Today it is occupied by a party of kids with hyperactivity problems and the meal is gluten-free. For those who can eat it, there is also bread on offer, so we walkers stuff ourselves on it.

At my table there are two men who are walking from Barèges to Luchon. They are tax inspectors and seem anxious to know what I might think of the French taxation system. They ask me to compare the English and French models. In detail. Like off-duty policemen, they really want me to say: 'It's a dirty job, but we like you really.'

Germ to the Granges d'Astau

On the way through the village I pass in front of a roadside oratory 'built and restored in memory of an ancestor killed by wolves'. I walk slowly, resting five minutes every half hour in an effort to save my knees. I am beginning to wonder if they really are clinically deformed: after all, despite fierce competition, I did win the first prize in my scout troop's knobbly knee contest, at the age of 15.

The path ascends quietly through heathers and ferns. There are prickly juniper bushes and long spikes of white asphodel and, further up, patches of alpine birdsfoot trefoil, in flower, sprinkled with voluptuous miniature red-and-yellow lips. The few rhododendrons are past their best.

I slip into the next valley and meet a young man wearing hipster jeans, accompanied by a collie dog. His face is white with sun cream, and he is out of breath from the climbing. He is a shepherd he tells me, waving his crook to confirm it. He is going on to the upper pasture where he will take a siesta. His flock, lower down the valley will make its own way up when it has finished dozing. A quarter of an hour later I find the sheep and a few goats, not dozing but grazing next to the Cabane du Val d'Esquierry. On top of a prominent rock a magnificent brown Billy goat looks at me suspiciously. I approach the flock and the nearest sheep move away, bells ringing in alarm. Suddenly, from behind me, I hear loud barking. I turn round and see a large white dog, showing all its teeth, eyeing my bare legs. *Patous* are not dangerous, I have been told, *unless* you come between them and their flock.

The *patou* is a breed of Pyrenean mountain dog. Brought up with the flock as a puppy, he will protect it from attack. Until the 19th century they were a common sight in the mountains but with the disappearance of predators their numbers dwindled. In 2006 there were only an estimated 66 in the Pyrenees. Although the name derives from the Occitan *pastre*, shepherd, they are not sheep dogs, strictly speaking. They don't round up sheep; collies are better at that. But they live with the flock and are more attached to it than to human company. When the flock moves to a new pasture the *patou* will precede it, looking for any danger. In a fight with a bear they would have no chance, but bears are rare. The real purpose of *patous* is to frighten off stray dogs.

But some sheep farmers are hostile. They see the return of *patous* as part of the scheme to reintroduce bears, and reject them both at the same time.

Patous are handsome beasts. They are big and bulky – 55kg – but elegant at the same time. Their long white coat is wavy, almost silky in appearance. Shepherds receive grants for their purchase, vaccination, training, and even upkeep. But so far experiences with *patous* have been mixed, some being too aggressive towards humans, others not staying with their flocks.

My *patou* is definitely staying with his flock. I hardly dare move. I apologise profusely to him and shuffle away stiffly. The barking stops.

The Pyrenean Way tumbles through a luminous forest, the sun painting the leaves a garish green, highlighting the tree roots as they slither across the path and attempt to trip me up.

The Granges d'Astau, down in the valley, is a large car park swarming with cars and camper vans, a souvenir shop, a restaurant, a bar, and a hostel. Amidst all this clamour is a quiet little oratory: 'restored in 1959' reads the inscription over the door. The front wall, under a projecting roof, has a painting labelled St Jacobus, St James, suggesting that the oratory is dedicated to him. But although many people pass through the Granges d'Astau on a quasi-religious expedition to the nearby Lac d'Oô, this is certainly not one of the Chemins de St Jacques. The passes over to Spain are all very high and blocked by glaciers and the visitors return to the car park at the end of the day.

The oratory is one of those chapels which you can't enter but which you can inspect through a metal grill in the door. Inside, the walls are painted with figures from the Bible. All the usual iconography but with a medieval simplicity of line and colour – warm ochre, pale worn-out blue-grey, and dark mysterious green – which, for me at least, is more spiritual than any amount of baroque gold work in more recent edifices. On the wall at the back of the altar is St Catherine with a broken wheel and a young Christ, the good shepherd, sitting on a rock amid lambs and sheep (after all, we are in the Pyrenees). To my left is Mary sitting on a throne balanced precariously on the top of a mountain, with the infant Jesus on her lap. Underneath is the Latin text *Mater dei custode nos in montibus* – mother of God, protect us in the mountains. This beautiful medieval chapel is completed with a couple of saints I have never heard of: St Germana Cousin and St Aventinus. St Germana is holding her apron in front of her and letting the flower heads in it fall to the ground. St Aventinus is having an altogether different kind of experience. The scene shows a bear standing up, claws dripping blood, looking meekly at the saint – though there is no indication of the origin of the blood. There is a choir boy running away, but he is clearly uninjured. Behind the saint are a couple of worried looking, but equally uninjured, peasants.

I wonder who these saints are and why they are depicted here, but nobody can tell me, so when I get home I investigate further. St Aventinus is here because he was a local lad. He had his hermitage an hour's walk away, near what is now the village of Saint-Aventin. He was killed by the Saracens in 732. The connection with bears and choir boys remains obscure, though the village is still bear territory: a thoroughly modern bear, not necessarily with blood on his claws, but certainly with a transmitter round his neck, passed through the commune in July 2006.

St Germana, I discover, was a shepherdess, born in the village of Pibrac. The house where she lived is still standing but unlike St Aventinus she wouldn't recognise the area where she lived. Pibrac is now a commuter village on the outskirts of Toulouse. She is here in the guise of patron saint of shepherds. The flowers falling from her apron? Crumbs of bread. Mistreated by her mother-in-law, she was suspected of hiding stolen bread in her apron but when forced to open it – miraculously – rose flowers fell out. Her claim to fame was that her body didn't rot after her death, in 1601. She was canonised in 1867. 1867? So the paintings I had taken to be medieval cannot be more than 130 years old? They were painted for the benefit of tourists, not pilgrims. It doesn't detract from their beauty but I feel cheated.

Granges d'Astau to the Lac d'Espingo

I bypass the barrier which stops cars from going any further and follow the track as it climbs through the forest. There are regular path-side updates on progress, giving the distance from Luchon, the nearest spa: La Roche Soufrée, altitude 1220m, 14km 350m, Lacets de la Régulatrice, altitude 1442m, 15km 200m. *Lacets de la régulatrice* means the controller's shoelaces. The identity of the controller is not divulged, nor her role, but her shoelaces are visible ahead of me: the zigzag track which leads to the Lac d'Oô.

When Ramond first came to the area at the end of the 18th century, only the village, way down in the valley below, was known as Oô. The lake was known as Lac Séculéjo and the waterfall which feeds it as the Pich de Séculéjo. They soon became the object of excursions from the increasingly genteel spa town of Luchon. The name Pich de Séculéjo was unintelligible to the first visitors who understood nothing of the local Occitan dialect. Until some playful soul let out the dreadful truth. Pich in Occitan means 'piss'. If this wasn't bad enough, Séculéjo means cul-de-sac. This might seem an innocent name for a lake at the butt end of a valley and, in English, the expression has nuances of decorum: Wisteria Avenue (cul-de-sac). In French it means exactly the same thing, but with a subtle difference. Most of the other expressions containing the word *cul* are considered extremely vulgar: Wisteria Avenue (arse end) gives some idea of the overtones. Exaggerating only slightly, Pich de Séculéjo thus becomes the 'stream of piss at the arse end of the valley'. This was evidently too much for Parisian ladies. The lake was renamed Oô. But what the name lost in vulgarity it gained in tautology. Oô can mean 'lake'. Yet another Lake Lake was born.

Although there is nobody else around at present, later in the day the track will be full of tourists, as it has been for the last 150 years or so.

Walking up the Lacets de la Régulatrice, I can hear a regular dull hammering. As I approach the lake the noise becomes shriller and more defined: steel against stone. When I leave the forest, I can see the source of the racket: a pneumatic drill. The bridge over the river (altitude 1490m, 16km200m) is being repaired. One of the workmen is struggling to start a concrete mixer in the dry river bed. The hostel on the other side is still slumbering, with deckchairs and sunloungers piled up against one wall.

A few steps further on and I see a tiny pond girdled by a wide grey band of gravel and loose rock. Above the stony girdle, the mountains are as they should be, and the pond itself replicates them faithfully, but the effect is ruined by the dreary grey scar. Even the waterfall is looking rather wan. This is said to be one of the most dazzling vistas of the Pyrenees, reproduced in innumerable postcards. I don't remember the photographs looking like this.

I walk on a little and sit down to eat a snack by the lake. Looking back, I can see the small concrete barrier which dams the valley and holds back the waters. Only, it isn't holding back any water at all. The bottom of the dam is exposed to the air and the lake is a couple of metres lower still, so that it must be about as big as it was before the construction of the dam; indeed, as big as it was when the first tourists arrived.

The reservoir has been emptied for the benefit of the plains around Toulouse and the sun has done the rest. The tide is out. This is not a diurnal pattern but an annual one, with a high tide – 12m higher to judge by the measuring stick attached to the back of the dam – in the spring, and a low tide at the end of the summer. Undoubtedly it also makes life easier for the workers repairing the bridge.

The workman has finally managed to start his concrete mixer, joining the pneumatic drill in a discordant duet. All in all, the original names for the waterfall and lake seem reasonably appropriate.

Granges d'Astau to the Lac d'Espingo

I am ambling along a path paved with large flat stones, making walking easy, when I am rapidly overtaken by a couple of young men. As they pass, I notice that one of them has a small red portable fire extinguisher attached to the outside of his rucksack. Could they be heavy smokers, afraid of setting fire to the dry vegetation? Could they be apprentice arsonists, lighting fires, letting them burn until they are nearly out of control and then drowning them under a cloud of carbon dioxide? Perhaps they are apprentice fire-fighters. Same scenario, marginally different motivations. I try to catch them up to ask but they are going too fast. Eventually I decide that they must be afflicted by the increasing paranoia surrounding the bears. They have come up with an unusual defence in case of attack.

Higher up, on the terrace of the hostel at Espingo, it is a different world. I eat a second breakfast, *crêpes* and *café au lait*, while gazing at the irregular lake, the sluggish streams which feed it, and the uncompromising cliffs beyond, slightly softened by the enduring snow. I am going to sleep here tonight. For the last two days, I have been resting frequently to spare my knee and to stop any further dental attrition. But it is only 9 o'clock and I can leave most of my kit here. The Lac du Portillon is only two hours away and, according to the manager, there is not too much snow on the path so, despite the lack of a proper map, I continue.

On top of a rock at the side of the path there is an abandoned hat. I am just about to pick it up when Tax Inspector No. 1 appears and reclaims it. His sudden emergence out of nowhere surprises me. It is almost as if the hat were a bait and I have just been caught in a sting, revealing the source of my lavish lifestyle. However, he merely tells me that Tax Inspector No. 2 has gone on to Luchon today but that he himself has decided to go up the valley. He also tells me that he *only* likes walking in valleys, not climbing peaks, which makes me deeply suspicious. I walk slowly to let him get ahead of me, keeping an eye on his progress so that I don't catch up, but then he disappears and I am left wondering if he is going

The High Pyrenees: Gabas–Luchon

to leap out from behind a rock, this time brandishing a copy of my last year's tax return.

The path merges into scree but I can see the snow-filled valley which leads up to the lake above. I can't see any tracks, but the route is pretty obvious. From time to time, I can hear water under the snow so I use my stick to see if it will support my weight. I make slow progress, sometimes clambering on rocks to avoid the biggest drifts. The valley gets progressively narrower and, although I can see the rudiments of a path chiselled into the steep side, the snow banked against it prevents me from going any further. I am obliged to climb up a small but dangerously friable cliff to the plateau where the Portillon hostel stands next to the lake.

In the hostel I am served a Desperate Dan portion of left-over *tartiflette*, half a loaf of bread, and a jug of wine. Despite the succulent potatoes, the gooey cheese, and my considerable hunger, I fail to finish off the *tartiflette* and make no impact whatsoever on the bread.

Afterwards, lying uncomfortably on the rocks outside, I chat to Tax Inspector No. 1. He really does like looking at mountains he tells me, but doesn't feel any urge to master them. On a trekking holiday in Nepal he climbed passes at over 4000m – higher than any summits in the Pyrenees – and greatly enjoyed himself. He also tells me where to find the correct path, without suggesting that I am completely incompetent and a danger to myself and to anybody else who might have to come to rescue me. He's quite likeable really. He is called Christian.

The lake itself, which used to be known as the Lac glacé du Portillon d'Oô, is still partly frozen. From here up to the frontier ridge much of the slope is covered with snow and ice though the glaciers look less extensive than on my map.

My knee hasn't complained again. Back at the Espingo hostel in good time, I take a siesta. For the rest of the day I chat to other walkers and wander around, aimlessly contented.

Lac d'Espingo to Luchon

Below in the night-shrouded valley, the Lac d'Oô is jet black, but today its rocky, off-white girdle suggests to me an altogether brighter interpretation: a tropical lagoon enclosed by a coral reef. The path climbs steadily to the Hourquette des Hounts-Secs, the pass of the dry springs (a Gascon name, here a little bit out of place). Having looked at the map last night, I have brought large quantities of water with me. I don't want to run out: I have been told that my knee problem might be due to dehydration, so I drink copiously. As a result, I stop frequently, marking the Pyrenean Way like a dog.

At the Coume de Bourg I finally emerge into the sunny sheep pastures to find a near-naked man lying on the ground at the side of the path, sunbathing. He tells me that he has been taking *'une petite promenade digestive* – a little walk to aid his digestion'. His car is 5km away at the ski resort of Superbagnères. Yes, it was a good breakfast, he agrees.

Continuing on towards Luchon, I can see the peaks on the frontier backlit by the sun, ranged in formidable rows, surging towards me, their black crests crashing down over the grey slopes, like waves breaking in the once-again molten rocks at the end of time. The Aneto, the highest rock of them all, must be floundering around somewhere in there but I can't make out which one it is.

An unexpected noise startles me and the sunbather leaps past. 'Sorry,' he says. 'I didn't mean to frighten you,' and races ahead. He is wearing what looks likes a woman's one-piece swimsuit, but what is probably the latest thing in running gear. My chances of arriving at Superbagnères in time to hitch a lift from him seem remote.

A little while later, at the wire fence which marks the edge of the resort I see a new sign placed prominently in view of those who might wish to leave the resort's well-trodden meadows. It warns: 'Walkers, you are entering an area of high mountains, without safety barriers.

The High Pyrenees: Gabas–Luchon

You must have the knowledge and the equipment to assure your own safety.' The top half of the panel has small drawings of a friendly *isard* and a grouse. The bottom half shows a menacing bear and, separately, an unfortunate walker sliding uncontrollably down a steep mountain slope. A cynical attempt to protect the owners of the ski resort from possible legal action?

The plateau is dotted with what used to be called *canons à neige artificielle*, but on reading a notice I see, in passing, that they have been renamed *enneigeurs* and their output is now called *neige de culture*. A semantic twist: instead of firing artificial snow from cannons, the resort is now cultivating it, in snow makers. I am re-entering 'civilisation': a place where words are *written* and where connotations are considered. Evidently, the Lac d'Oô, the new name of the Lac Séculéjo, was the preface.

I sit on a wooden railing at the side of the road at Superbagnères, waiting for cars to come by. Opposite me is an immense cruise-liner hotel with a string of small shops and kiosks floating in its wake, but they are all firmly closed. There are twenty or so forlorn cars in the car park but nobody around. The town of Luchon is much lower down, through a forest with nothing to recommend it. It is hot, I am tired, and there is nothing worse for tendonitis than a long knee-thumping descent with a heavy rucksack. After half an hour no cars have passed and I am about to resign myself to walking when an elderly couple approaches. They ask me about short walks in the vicinity. We are studying the map, deep in conversation, when I see a car driving by.

But the forest is not entirely devoid of interest. About half way down there is a railway viaduct across a valley. Not a common-or-garden horizontal affair but running down a steep slope. A well-worn interpretive panel explains that this was part of the rack railway which linked Luchon to the Superbagnères ski resort, built by the Compagnie des Chemins de Fer du Midi, the same company which built the cruise-liner hotel on the plateau above, and the same company which ran the Petit Train d'Artouste: it's no use building railways if there is nothing at the end of them to attract passengers. The panel lists their numbers: in 1950 (45,000), 1960 (24,000), and 1962 (21,000), but singularly fails to explain the fall in numbers. Later, in Luchon I read the following account:

The accident

Sunday 28 February 1954 at 18:10: the 17:40 train bringing more than 130 skiers back to the valley was never to arrive. It happened half way down, at the points at Mi-Sahage which permitted the trains to pass, at an altitude of 1189m. An incident derailed the train which continued down the hill in a mad 300m race. The engine detached itself and ended up 500m lower down in the Soulan ravine. The accident killed 9 people, including an 8-year-old girl who had a bad fall at Superbagnères and who couldn't be quickly brought to Luchon, as a result of the accident.

The accident was engraved in the collective memory of Luchon. The line was modified and the route reopened... but the opening of the road in 1961 sounded the death knell of the rack railway which ceased to run at the end of the winter of 1966.

 I walk through the suburbs on flagstone pavements which echo my footsteps and occasionally make a 'gloup' noise as they move under my weight. Through the gaps I can see racing water. The suburbs – old houses, cheerfully irregular – suddenly give way to the planned town and its high street, l'Allée d'Étigny, lined with linden trees and elegant white façades leading up to the spa buildings.
 I find a doctor easily and she gives me more anti-inflammatory tablets and cream. Dentists are more of a problem. I ring all six but not one of them will take me within the next four days. I will just have to grin and bare it.

The High Pyrenees: Gabas–Luchon

In the evening I eat at a restaurant in the middle of an identity crisis. It is called the Crémaillère – rack railway – and, logically, the walls inside are covered with sepia prints of the rack railway and Superbagnères. But the glass-topped tables harbour models of tropical islands complete with palm trees, sun umbrellas, giant turtles, and, in the sea, multi-coloured fish, all naïvely executed in papier-mâché. Yet the menu relates to neither the Pyrenees nor the tropics, making great play of buckwheat *crêpes* and Brittany cider. Nearby, an establishment called the Maeva – meaning welcome in Tahitian – sells ski equipment in the winter and serves Spanish tapas in the summer. Further down the high street there is a stand selling Ben and Jerry's ice cream, a shop selling '*produits régionaux* – local produce', and the inevitable gondola display of whistling *marmotte* toys. Venerable – but recently modernised and extended – spa buildings and former grand hotels rub cornices with the steel hawsers of ski lifts. Luchon is like that: charmingly idiosyncratic.

Luchon

I am out of step with the rest of the world, so that I have finished my breakfast and walked into town well before the shops are open. The only other person around is a beggar with a black Labrador dog, arranging his life in the shade on the pavement, so I sit down with him. His rucksack is enviably small, it can't weigh more than 6kg: I would like to be able to survive with so little. When he talks, I can see that most of his teeth are damaged or missing. He is Flemish, but speaks English, French, and a little German, as well as his native tongue. He shows me a septic wound on the sole of his foot, an oversized blister running from his toes to his heel. 'I'll have to go and see a doctor,' he complains. He sleeps in a nearby garden, in exchange for painting the owner's house. He drinks too much, he insists, repeating it several times. '*Mais*,' he says, '*je ne suis pas clochard. Je suis routard, comme toi.* But I'm not a beggar, I'm a tramp, like you.'

The museum opens finally. Unlike some of the nearby businesses it is quite sure of its identity. It has not changed for 50 years and shows no sign of wishing to do so. Perhaps I am missing something, but the most recent addition to the collections seems to be the panel recounting the life and death of the rack railway.

In the 1950s the museum must have been state of the art; by the 1970s it was starting to look drab; and by the 1990s it was a disgrace to modern museology. Now it has come full circle and, like bell-bottomed trousers, has acquired a new legitimacy. The deadline for refurbishment has passed, and now it can be seen that it wasn't even necessary. The museum has transcended all that, to become, in the best Pyrenean tradition of tautology, a Museum museum.

It could still do with a little dusting and better lighting but it is a fascinating artefact in its own right, redolent of the past, part guessing game, part treasure hunt. The guessing game starts in the entrance hall with a short marble column complete with plinth and capital and, on top of it, a die balanced on one corner. I deduce that this must be a reference to Luchon's casinos and to marble quarrying in the vicinity. I ask the curator but he is unable to enlighten me: it's just decoration, he thinks.

In the first room, the most obvious exhibit looks rather grubby and worn. It is a three-dimensional model of the mountains around Luchon at a scale of ten centimetres for each kilometre on the flat. The vertical scale is twice as large. The model is covered by a web of red cotton paths with the lakes represented by fragments of glass. The peaks are punctured by cocktail sticks supporting little labels giving their names and heights, and the frontier is marked by a line of pale green ball-head pins. The result is that the model is impossible to clean. It has been collecting dust since it was first put on display in 1854.

Much less obvious is the display case devoted to the Monts Maudits – the cursed mountains – which are just to the south of Luchon. There is an account of a climbing accident and the remains

The High Pyrenees: Gabas–Luchon

of the victim: his four-pointed crampon, the sole of his shoe, a gaiter, and the bones of his right arm. A hand-written coroner's report from the time of the accident explains the circumstances and a newspaper cutting completes the story.

On 11 August 1824 Pierre Barrau, a guide from Luchon, agreed to accompany two young and adventurous engineers, Blavier and de Billy to the summit of the Pic de la Maladetta, one of the Monts Maudits. De Billy suggested, even insisted, that they use a rope. Barrau, who was 68 and much respected for his experience, replied that he had taken a German to the summit seven years previously on the historic first ascent and that a rope wasn't necessary. They were almost at the top of the glacier, within a few metres of their goal, but there was one last crevasse to be crossed. One of the engineers tested a bridge of snow with his stick and quickly stepped back: the snow was soft and ready to fall into the void. Barrau tested another bridge further along and, finding it solid, stepped onto it, only to disappear.

'I've had it. I'm sinking deeper,' he shouted for two minutes. And then: silence, a cold silence which was to engulf Barrau for over a hundred years. The Luchon guides were so horrified by his fate that they refused to tackle the glaciers in the area, including the one protecting the nearby Aneto, the ultimate challenge, for another 18 years.

More than a century later, in August 1931, two guides accompanying a group of English tourists found a body half eaten by foxes, eagles, and vultures at the base of the glacier, 1400m from the crevasse. It was identified as the indefatigable guide, who had continued his peregrinations even after his death.

More remains appeared in 1934 and Barrau was finally interred. Or, to be more precise, most of him was interred. The bone in front of me has a luggage label attached: right humerus of Pierre Barrau, who fell in the glacier of the Maladetta on 13 [sic] August 1824, found 25 August 1934 by the dogs of messieurs Baylac and Aurélien.

When I was an archaeologist – a grave robber with a clear conscience, in the words of Pierre Minvielle – I routinely handled skeletons. But there is something disturbingly macabre about this right humerus. I know its name, its reputation, even its last words.

On the opposite wall is an ornately framed list recording the conquests of the Baron de Lassus, entitled '*Avec l'aigle et l'isard* – with the eagle and the *isard*', giving the date, the name of the mountain, and its height. The photograph which surmounts the list shows the baron, debonair but serious, leaning on his walking stick. Next to him are four guides in regulation gear – a uniform invented in the middle of the 19th century because 'the sober clothes of the mountain folk were not in keeping with the image which Luchon wished to project as a luxury holiday centre.' The Pyrenees were being transformed by intellectuals steeped in the Romantic vision of the mountains, who were 'rewriting local folklore, putting the finishing touches to the shepherd's customary garb, embroidering legends, and denaturing the message of the past.' The guides are holding ice axes which reach up to their shoulders, typical of that time. They seem to be wondering what they are doing there, each looking in a different direction.

The walls of the stairs up to the next floor are decorated with posters, including one for the 1926 International ski competition which unwittingly shows how new the sport was. The woman in the poster is apparently skiing, but with her arms outstretched horizontally to either side and her legs pressed tightly together, vertical and rigidly straight. The artist has clearly never seen anybody on a real slope.

At the top of the stairs one of the rooms is devoted to local fauna: stuffed *isards*, ibex (extinct), *marmottes*, foxes, eagles… and bears. There are two bear cubs, the size of teddy bears and just as cuddly. One is sitting in a very unnatural position, on its haunches eating a pear which is held between its two front paws. The other is walking across a stone. This one has a scrap of paper next to it. The typing relates a sweet little story:

The High Pyrenees: Gabas–Luchon

La Dépêche [a local newspaper] 27 May 1952

Capture of two bear cubs near to Luchon

Some tourists walking not far from the Hospice de France early this afternoon saw two bear cubs. Fearing that the mother bear could be in the area they quickly made their way to the Hospice de France and told the manager and reputed guide Odon Haurillon.

M Haurillon, some friends, and some policemen who were patrolling nearby immediately organised a hunt.

The cubs were found without difficulty, one allowing itself to be captured easily. The other climbed a tree but was soon captured as well. The two cubs, which seem to be aged one and a half months, were brought back to the Hospice where they were given a welcome present of a bottle of milk.

And afterwards they killed them.

The last, unofficial, hand-written addition has been crossed out, but the corpses are here before me.

They killed them. Is it true? Graffiti is wild information: fascinatingly untamed and unauthorised but also personal and biased: potentially revealing hidden truths ignored by the official channels; potentially distorting facts in support of hidden agendas.

Only afterwards do I reconcile the sugary official version with the harsh graffito. Jeannot Ladrix used to hunt in the area at that time. Now over 90 years old, he explains: 'they were kept in a sheep fold, then in a hut adjoining the Hospice for nearly a year. It was an attraction for the whole valley, until one of the cubs died from poisoning. The other died a year later of diabetes.'

So one might say they were welcomed; or claim that they were killed by captivity.

In the afternoon I go to Sourcéa, part of the spa facilities, for what are called 'treatments', not that I expect them to do anything for my various ailments. I have chosen the *Rendez-vous énergie* in the hope that it will liven me up. The other clients are also healthy-looking – the afternoons are reserved for hypochondriacs and hedonists. If you are ill you come in the morning. The reception area, as might be expected, is a cross between a hotel and a hospital, with the background music and fluffy dressing gowns offset by staff who are clearly nurses, in dazzlingly white uniforms, and ubiquitous clocks.

The first 'treatment' is a Jacuzzi bath. I lie in the bath with jets of water squirting at me but any attempt to relax is destroyed by the large electronic panel on the wall opposite. The LCD panel displays incomprehensible numbers which change randomly. The only one which I manage to understand is the clock counting down the seconds to the end of this particular jet.

Within a second of the end of the last jet, the nurse comes back in. 'That's it for now,' she says. 'You can go into the waiting room. Somebody will call for you at 15:30 for the cervical mud.'

At 15:30 I am led into another small windowless room. The nurse shrouds my neck in linen bandages and then slaps hot mud onto them. I get to lie down, the heat and the mud soaking into my shoulders, in semi-darkness for precisely 12 minutes.

'You can go to the hammam and pool now, but make sure to have a shower first,' another nurse tells me. 'You must come back to reception for 16:40. There's a clock over the pool.'

At the appointed time I am led into a long, completely sealed room, hygienically tiled in white, with stark lighting. No soothing music here; I feel rather flaky after all the *soins* and would prefer to lie down.

'Go to the other end and stand under the arch, with your back to me, facing the wall,' says the nurse, a middle-aged woman with a rather abrupt tone of voice.

She stands behind a console in the shape of a church lectern, adjusts some controls, and points a high-pressure jet of water at me, aiming it up and down my back. All of it, from my neck to my ankles.

'Turn 90 degrees to the right and raise your right arm above your head. Hold onto the rail with your other hand,' she barks.

When I am sufficiently battered she turns the water off and orders me to turn round and show her my other side. I feel as though I am being examined with a critical eye. At least at this distance my gap tooth isn't visible.

I wonder what kind of bizarre experiment the doctors might be conducting here. I have just read that, in the 1930s, two radioactive springs were authorised for use in the spas – this being before the dangers of exposure to radioactivity were fully appreciated – and that doctors vaunted the health-giving qualities 'of radioactivity 15,000 times that of normal air'. Is the warder going to switch to ice-cold water and measure how many minutes I survive standing up? Is she going to turn up the pressure and flatten me against the back wall?

'Turn to face me,' she demands, 'and shut your eyes.'

When I am released, at 16:55 give or take a few seconds, a different nurse takes me up to the relaxation room in the lift.

'Are you alright?' she asks, installing me on a lounger.

I look up at the ceiling blankly.

Afterwards, I pass another comfortable night at the Lutin, a small hotel run by an English man and his French wife and decide to go home to get my teeth fixed. When I arrive there is a postcard waiting for me, from Paul, whom I last saw in Sainte-Engrâce. To judge by the postmark, he must have been walking just a couple of days ahead of me.

Aneto

The summit is empty, elemental, the air thin. To the west I can make out the sea. No, it's not possible: the Atlantic is 200km away. It must all be sky – both the cold grey layer near the horizon and the warm baby blue layer above it. To the south, in Spain, the clouds are romping over the peaks *below* us, but to the north, France is melting under the blinding sun. There is not the slightest wind today; the sun is in complete control. Beneath my feet there are jagged blocks of untamed primeval granite but no earth, no life. There is no water either, though we have just crossed ten thousand years of accumulated rain and snow to get here.

When I have got my breath back and my heart has returned to its normal rhythm, I listen. Nothing. The last natural sound – a twittering bird begging crumbs – was left behind several hours ago. I look around at the serrated landscape of mountains waiting to lacerate any rain clouds that happen by. Here, on the highest peak of the Pyrenees, nature makes no compromises and humans no impact. Almost.

'The main problem is the number of people. At the height of the summer season you get 200 people a day. They really ought to install traffic lights at either end of the Pas de Mahomet,' jokes our guide.

'You'll have a thunderstorm on your way up to the hostel and another on your way back,' my friend Alice has warned me, 'and you'll be lucky not to be blown off the Pas de Mahomet by the wind.'

It's not supposed to be like this, then.

A month after leaving Luchon, encouraged by climbing the Vignemale, I am back in the area with Claude, a walking friend. We approach our grail cautiously, circling it on all sides in the car, without actually being able to it. On the way, we notice some 'Aneto' tee-shirts for sale. 'Let's get them afterwards,' I suggest, not wanting to tempt fate.

Climbing up from the valley, we can soon see the hostel, the Refuge de la Rencluse where we are going to spend the night, but not the peak itself. The valley was green and lush but here the hillside is almost barren. Standing talking on a hillock which still has a little grass, we are nosed away by a bad-tempered mare who wants to make more room for herself and her filly. Nearby, a stream disappears abruptly into the rock: the strata here are vertical. This is the middle of the Pyrenean hernia.

By dinner time our guide still hasn't arrived so I ask the hostel manager when he might turn up.

'*A las diez, las once, o mañana por la mañana* – Ten o'clock, eleven o'clock, or tomorrow morning. You have to get up at quarter past five, eat breakfast at half past and be ready to go at six.'

During the night I wake up several times. In the haze between sleep and wakefulness, I tell myself that I need to breathe more deeply to capture the oxygen. Next morning Claude eats steadily, quietly. I'm nervous.

At quarter to six a thin young man with a tiny rucksack opens the door. He is dressed in variants of khaki, with a black sleeveless woollen waistcoat. Short curly black hair. Angular features and the slightest suggestion of a moustache. He looks competent, sharp, and determined. He introduces himself. His name, appropriately, is Pierre.

Outside, it is completely black, but somewhere ahead of us there is a formation of four moving stars, flickering. Like the three kings, we follow them; we too have lights attached to our foreheads. There is no path through the giant pink-grey-white-and-black speckled granite cubes, and at the same time there are dozens of paths. There are cairns everywhere, but no sense to them. Every step has to be calculated. The blocks are unstable, an irregular un-worn clutter. *Chaos* is the French word for it.

The sun must be rising but we are wrapped in mist. Occasionally the atmosphere coalesces into drops of rain but I can see that the clouds are thin and will disappear as soon as the sun rises above the horizon.

'Will we be roped up for the glacier?' I ask.

'We'll see,' replies Pierre.

'What about the Pas de Mahomet?'

'We'll see.'

'Are we on time?'

'Yes.'

'How long will it take to get to the top?'

'Five and a half to six hours.'

Finally, we are above the mist. To the west, the horizon is tinged pink. To the south, the Pic de la Maladeta has a sparkling-white glacier bib. It looks pretty, but this is where Pierre Barrau disappeared into a crevasse.

When we reach the Portillon Supérieur, the 'doorway' through the ridge, we discover simultaneously the sun opposite us and an immense glacier sloping steeply downwards to our left. Between us and the sun there are layers upon layers of mountain cut-outs, printed in colours graduating from the darkest black to the palest grey. On the right, three peaks delineate the horizon.

'Aneto?' I ask, breathlessly.

'The furthest one,' Pierre replies.

We cross more scree and *chaos* to the edge of a small snowfield. It's not worth putting on our crampons but the snow is frozen and slippery so I extract my ice axe from my sack and hold it ready to hook it into the ground should I slip.

'You've never been to snow school, have you?' says Pierre.

'No,' I admit.

'It is a complete waste of time holding your axe like that. And you've got it in the wrong hand. In any case if you slip an ice axe won't stop you. You'll just create a furrow in the snow.'

'What's it for then?' I ask.

'Not much really. If you slip on snow you have to roll onto your stomach, stick your arms out and your hands into the snow, and use your hands to push upwards. If you are really lucky your feet will dig in and you will come to a stop.'

I promise to go to snow school next winter.

The glacier, when we get to it, is grey and slippery, quite different to the Vignemale. We put on our crampons.

'We'll do some exercises before we start,' says Pierre.

We totter along for a few uncertain paces.

'Now we'll try running down the glacier,' Pierre continues. 'Put the whole weight of your body on the leg which is in front, bending your legs at the same time. Steve, you go first.'

This seems a little excessive, I think. We haven't yet mastered walking, and now he wants us to run. I lunge forwards.

'No. Not like that. Don't waddle. Run! You need to put your chest forwards as well, so that your weight is above your feet.'

I run like a drunken monkey, arms swaying.

'That's better,' he says. 'If you do get your crampons caught in your trousers the only way to avoid falling down is to leap into the air and land running until you regain your balance.'

He gives an acrobatic demonstration of the manoeuvre but doesn't ask us to emulate him.

'Hold the ice axe in the hand which is highest. Use it like a walking stick.'

'What do we do if we fall over?' I ask.

'Don't fall over,' replies Pierre, putting on his wrap-around sunglasses, rubbing sun cream into his cheeks, and looking up at the sky. 'Let's go.'

'I'd prefer to be roped up,' I suggest, hopefully.

'It's not really necessary.'

'I'd prefer to be roped up,' I repeat, more strongly.

'OK. But you must keep the rope taut.'

Pierre loops the rope round our waists and we set off. After a few steps he looks back.

'If you let the rope droop like that, Steve, when you fall you will pull us all down the slope with you.'

The glacier is fast disappearing, like all the glaciers in the Pyrenees. In 1870, altogether they covered an estimated 40 km^2, now there are less than 5km^2. The Glacier d'Ossoue on the slopes of the Vignemale is still 50m thick, but it is shrinking by 1.8m every year.

There is no longer enough snow to replace what melts in the summer, and here on the Aneto last winter there was even less than usual. I have seen photos where the glacier and the rocks are covered in snow all the way from the Portillon to the Pas de Mahomet near the summit. At the beginning of July, there is a comforting channel across the snow traced by hundreds of pairs of feet. It is now the end of August and all the snow has melted. There are no footprints.

'At least that means you won't fall into a hidden crevasse,' muses Pierre.

We walk across the glacier, hardly climbing at all, feet twisted uncomfortably to conform to the slope. Waddling like a duck, concentrating on every step, taking care to plant each crampon firmly in the ice, is a tiring process. We stop for a breather and I am startled to look around and discover a young couple sitting on a rock only a few paces away. Nobody else is on the glacier. This morning's stars must be heading for a different Bethlehem.

Claude slips but is stopped by crashing into my feet, which are firmly dug into the ice. She has twisted her ankle but it isn't going to stop her. A few minutes later I notice that my arms are behaving oddly. I look at Claude. Hers are doing the same thing. We are both walking with our palms facing outwards. I twist my arms back into a more natural position only to rediscover them, palms outwards, a few steps further on. There is nothing to be done. As soon as I stop consciously controlling them, my arms twist round. We are walking like ducks, with our feet splayed, and our arms following suit.

Claude's crampons have worked loose, but the slope is now too steep to stop and it is only when we reach a flatter zone that we can fix them. Here, the ice is covered with a pink dust, a kind of algae which, it appears, can live at sub-zero temperatures. At least there are now some footprints to follow.

At the top of the glacier we take off our crampons and rucksacks and wrench our feet back into a more normal walking position. We are only a few metres from our goal but between us and the summit there is a small hitch: the Pas de Mahomet. The name dates to July 1842, when Albert de Franqueville, Platon de Tchihatcheff and their guides became the first climbers to conquer the summit. It consists of a series of irregular granite blocks, like a line of giant dice which have been thrown by the gods onto the blade edge of a narrow ridge. A few have come to rest with a flat surface on top but the majority have an edge or a corner sticking upwards. There is no path and either side of the ridge the drop is vertical.

'It isn't difficult,' claims Pierre.

I insist on the rope. Claude says it would get in her way.

The first obstacle is a large almost cone-shaped rock which we have to cross by stepping delicately on the footholds in its side, clinging to its top. Then there is a crevasse to descend into and climb out of. I have half my body over the edge but I can't find the foothold.

'Look where you are going to put your foot first,' Pierre scolds me, wrapping the rope round a rock and keeping it taut.

'Not there. Your right hand is useless there. It is too low. Put it higher,' he tells Claude.

Then there is a flat block, narrower than I am, higher than any of the surrounding stones. I feel like a tight-rope walker. I look at where I am going to put my feet, concentrating hard on not seeing anything else, but I see it anyway. It is a long way down.

Claude skips along ahead of us. And then suddenly we are there, at the summit of the highest peak in the Pyrenees, 3404m above sea level. There is nobody else. Claude and I kiss, grin at each other, and amble around, empty-headed.

The view is stupendous, intimidating, unreal. Innumerable mountains clutter this dreamscape but the overarching heavens are bigger still. We are isolated, and at the same time at the centre of the world. Even for an unbeliever like me, there is something otherworldly here. Something eternal. I'm not sure what it is, nor what it might mean. All I know is that as soon as I leave the summit, this state of grace will disappear. I won't even be able to take a clear memory of it with me. It can only be experienced here.

All the works of humanity are reduced to their real importance: the only man-made things we can see in the distance are a few matchsticks which might be ski-lift towers at Superbagnères, and the town of Luchon, a miniscule smudge in a valley near the horizon.

Here nature is writ large. Which makes the artificial features of the summit – a curious collection of personal, religious and political statements – seem all the more pathetic. In the first category is the graffito spray-painted in red on a rock: 'Santos 22.06.2003'.

Religion makes its claim in triplicate. The first is a cross that I have seen in photographs although only the torn shreds of the aluminium base remain. The second is an absurdly dumpy aluminium pillar with, on top, a disproportionately small, black statue of Mary and the infant Jesus. The statue is encircled by ribbons, one red, white and blue – for France I suppose – the other red and gold – for Catalonia. There are a couple of tiny bunches of artificial flowers, a checked pink-and-white handkerchief, and a powder blue cotton baseball cap as well. The pillar is no longer vertical. A few more winters and it will go the same way as the cross. Finally, there is a trapezoidal aluminium box, like a small house, with, inside, a naïve wooden carving of Jesus on the cross. There was once a door, but only the hinges survive.

Politics is represented by the word '*Euskadi* – the Basque country' printed on the back of a tee-shirt which is draped over a concrete survey pillar, the only edifice which seems to be withstanding the elements. The mountain has been annexed by the Basques. But not for long.

'It'll be torn to shreds if it stays here,' says Pierre, stuffing the tee-shirt into his rucksack and sitting down.

'When I came here ten days ago,' he tells us, 'I found a kitten wandering around. It was exhausted. I took it down to the hostel.'

'How did it get here?' I ask.

'It could have followed someone,' suggests Pierre.

The High Pyrenees: Gabas–Luchon

'Across the glacier and the Pas de Mahomet? It's not possible.'

'Kittens have built in crampons, you know,' says Claude imaginatively.

We stay a long while, nibbling, recovering, and watching the unchanging scenery.

When we get back to our rucksacks after re-crossing the Pas de Mahomet, Pierre attaches us both to the rope without being asked, Claude at the front, me in the middle, and himself at the end. We head directly down the steepest slope, with Claude walking so fast that I have to monkey-skip to keep up with her. The surface is wet and in places there are rivers of water to be crossed. I have time to look down the slope. On the way up it was easy to restrict my thoughts and vision to a small zone where the next foot was going to fall. Now my vision keeps slipping.

In the car on the way back Claude asks if I want to stop for a tee-shirt.

'It wouldn't be right,' I reply. You can't represent bliss on something as trivial as a tee-shirt.

III

Luchon–Mérens: Ariège, *terre courage*

Non à l'ours

A year later I come back to Luchon for a short holiday at the end of April. Just outside the town there is a blockade across the road. Two tractors with digger buckets attached, a 200-hectolitre wooden barrel, half a dozen tree trunks and a significant number of bales of straw are there to back up a banner proclaiming defiantly: '*Non à l'ours*. No to the bears'. There are perhaps eight men and two women warming themselves around a small fire, inspecting every vehicle before letting it through.

I stop my car just short of the blockade and get out. Despite their evident numerical superiority, they huddle closer together at my approach.

'I saw your banner and thought you might be able to tell me more about what's going on,' I say. The protesters look visibly relieved. They tell me that they are from nearby St Béat, a few kilometres away, and Luchon. Between them, they have 2000 sheep in the *estives* around the Hospice de France, a little further up the valley. Although the government has reduced the projected number of new bears from 15 to five, they are not satisfied. They hope to stop the programme completely.

The first bear, baptised Palouma, was released in Arbas, four days ago. Nelly Ollin, the new environment minister, had wanted the event to be a celebration, but both she and the bear were greeted by a heavily mediatised chorus of bells, pots, and pans. She accused the protestors of 'having transformed a beautiful fairy tale into a nightmare.' The protesters replied that she was writing a horror story for them.

The next bear, Francka, arrived yesterday and, according to the *Dépêche du Midi* newspaper, the shepherds had the wool pulled over their eyes. Luchon was invaded by both protestors and policemen. The newspaper portrays the events as a clever bluff, with the police being deployed in Luchon to keep the protestors occupied whilst the bear was quietly being released at Bagnères de Bigorre, several valleys away.

'I don't think that that's what really happened,' says one man. 'Once the authorities realised the extent of the mobilisation they decided to go for their second choice. Next time round it will be different. On Friday [yesterday] we had 200 people here for lunch. But we have decided to split up, with spies along all the access roads. We'll know where they are going before they know themselves,' he claims.

A white van goes by slowly.

'That's the third time this morning,' explains the protester. 'They spy on us as well.'

'When do you expect the next convoy to arrive?' I ask.

'To get back to the mountains in Slovenia will take them 17 hours, but with a bear they will have to drive carefully on the return journey – about 22 hours. They could arrive as early as Tuesday.'

A mobile phone rings and there is a short conversation.

'France 3 [regional television] is coming at 13:30,' someone else announces. 'What are you doing here?' he asks me.

'Walking.'

'You know, in the future some areas will be out-of-bounds because of the bears, to stop them being disturbed.'

'But there have always been bears here and there weren't any reserves then.'

'The mountains aren't like they were 50 years ago. There are more people around. Just because there were bears here in the past doesn't mean to say that there should be in the future.'

'What do you think will happen next?'

'We know we can't stop them this time, but if we make enough fuss they'll think twice about trying again.'

Luchon to the Cabanes de Peyrehitte

Returning to the town six weeks later, the first thing I do is go shopping for food. I have some dehydrated provisions, but I want to keep them for when I am desperate. There are two criteria: weight and how well it will keep in a warm rucksack. I buy hunks of dried ham, good solid cheese, country bread, carrots, and apples – without thinking I have composed the kind of meals eaten in the mountains before the invention of refrigerators.

My rucksack is heavier than last year. I haven't got a tent but I have equipped myself for sleeping in huts… if they are open, and the shepherds don't mind. If not I will have to sleep *sous la belle étoile*, under the stars.

The next day I walk out of Luchon along the side of the river, past a fisherman hunched over the tranquil waters. The first village has flower beds at the side of a disciplined stream which runs next to its main street. The *lavoir* – where the women used to scrub their clothes – has been heavily renovated and planted with geraniums.

The path climbs through the forest and emerges two hours later into another world, at the village of Artigue. The name itself is significant. Artigue means *the* clearing. There are many Artigues coupled with qualifiers, like Bious Artigue – Bious' Clearing, but few which were so extensive that they became known simply as *the* clearing. In the middle of the 19th century when population pressure was at its maximum, creating new pastures from the forest was the last desperate attempt by younger disenfranchised sons to make a life for themselves locally, before they turned to emigration as the final solution.

There is holiday accommodation and even a restaurant, but this is a working community. Here, the barns smell of straw, and slurry dribbles out onto the road. I walk past the church and into the pastures where I am greeted by a row of home-made notices. Although polythene bags cover the paper, water has already penetrated and the letters have started to run; but the message is still clear.

Beware

You are in bear country. You can meet a bear at any moment. These new Slovenian bears are unpredictable. We cannot predict how they will behave when they meet humans. Be vigilant.

To our tourist friends
Do you want tidy mountains, maintained by sheep and cows?
Do you want mountains without farmers, with daily danger?
The undergrowth will take over, with all its associated disadvantages (fires, avalanches, impassable footpaths), knowing that the damage to the flocks isn't just a question of the sheep which has been devoured (when it is found). There is also the stress, the injuries, the miscarriages and, of course, the work of the shepherd!!!!
In conclusion, farmers abandoning their jobs will have more effect than bears on the environment and tourism, and soon!!!
A bear has been released a few hundred metres as the crow flies from our commune, to which we welcome you, hoping that your walk doesn't finish as a nightmare!!!
        Signed by the population of Artigue

We produce lambs of quality,
The best on all the markets.
Sheep are our trade.
They are our pride.
We bring them up.

Luchon to the Cabanes de Peyrehitte

We love them.
They are not bait
And we don't want
Them to be eaten
By a badly brought-up bear.

The population of Artigue was 168 in 1876; it had dropped to 34 in 1999. Evidently, all is not well.

Walking through the forest I was already thinking about bears. What would I do if I saw one? What would I do if one attacked me? If I whipped off my rucksack and put it on backwards, against my chest, would it afford me any protection? I tell myself that I am less likely to be killed by a bear than by a car accident – nobody has been killed by a bear for over a century. But logic has no power over emotions. I can't stop thinking about what *might* happen. My walk has become polluted by bears.

The path climbs inexorably. I overtake three people who tell me that they are just going to the top of the first hill and meet one man walking the Pyrenean Way in the opposite direction, and then nobody. I feel isolated.

The heat is building up but so are the clouds, so that when I arrive at the Cabanes de Peyrehitte, I decide to stay for the night. One of the huts is labelled *Cabane du berger*, shepherd's hut. The other, labelled *Refuge*, has a rudimentary stone bench outside it. There is a cheerful yellow sun painted on a beam above the bench, and a moon on the door, but no other instructions.

I open the door. There is no window but I can see that almost the whole floor surface of the hut is taken up by a rusty bunk-bed frame, with metal grilles to lie on. The floor itself is flagged; the walls are concrete. At the end of the bed, the chimney hosts a large amount of ash and a few sticks of wood. On the mantelpiece are two night-light candles, a broken jar, and several wine bottles, some intact, some broken, including a bottle of Taittinger, with the neck cleanly sliced off, as if someone had brought a sabre with them as well. I can also see a bottle of Chateau la Croix Mazerand, St Emilion Grand Cru 1987, a bottle of Fitou, Domaine les Mille Vignes and… hidden in the corner, what is it? … a very burnt saucepan. But the real discovery is two notebooks, filled in by walkers. Many of the entries thank the shepherd for his hospitality, exclaim at the beauty of the surroundings, or complain about the fog which makes the huts difficult to find. But some are much more poetic.

15 May 2005. There are moments when life takes a strange direction. Signs, people and places bringing us back to our destiny. This evening, in front of the fire, I know that I am not here by chance. I don't know where this is going to take me, but I know that I am on the right track. Outside the fog has lifted and the sun has appeared again. Thanks to Robert the Basque shepherd whom I met last week, and with whom I would greatly like to spend more time. Thanks to the shepherd who looks after this hut, absent, but to whom I transmit all my gratitude for the existence of this unique place of self rediscovery, and for the love that he puts into doing this work. From the bottom of my heart. Angeline de Saumur.

Tuesday 6 August 2002. The destination of the voyage doesn't matter, what counts is what one experiences here and now. You have stopped here. For a moment? To eat? For the night? This is the sign that one should not let encounters pass by. Step by step, mountain pass after mountain pass, I smile at my suffering. I appreciate the instant because it exists and don't propose to string the stages one after the other like pearls on a thread to make a necklace.

When I arrived I could see the central ridge of the Pyrenees. Now the clouds have closed in. Everything is grey. It is raining more or less continuously and there are claps of thunder from time to time, some near, some further away. I'm just sitting here, waiting, waiting. Sitting on my rucksack in the doorway of the hut.

Now I can hear the bells of sheep coming down the slope behind the hut. Now I can see the dog and the shepherd, who is actually a shepherdess. She says I can make myself at home, and then charges off down the valley after the sheep and the dog. The big flowery motifs on her ankle-length yellow dress fade into the clouds.

In the evening, after the storm – the painful labour – the valley is reborn in a mist which washes back and forth, softly lapping over the huts and then clearing again, under a sky of fast-moving cumulo-nimbus. The sun is timidly reappearing in the west; the grass sparkles, as if it too has been transformed by the lightning.

I inspect the shepherdess' hut from the outside. It is equipped with solar panels but the water heating consists of a black pouch hanging in the sun. There are troughs to collect the rainwater which falls on the roof. It has windows. Inside it looks cosy.

I'm feeling cold, so I retreat to my hut and eat morosely. It is getting gloomy when the dog nudges its way through the door. I feed it some scraps of ham and stroke it but the shepherdess soon returns and calls it home. So I light a fire and watch the endless flames into the dark.

Cabanes de Peyrehitte to Melles

The hillside here is covered in flowering rhododendrons, a gigantic purple bouquet which I traverse for the first hour of the new day. Lower down, shepherds' huts dot the slopes. Last night's shepherdess looks after 1280 animals: the ovine population here must run into several thousand. Indeed, higher up at the pass the grass is scored by a hundred *drailles*, parallel tracks ploughed by systematic sheep.

The last part of the descent into the next valley, down to the

Garonne river, should be a pleasant stroll between the trees to the sound of a cascading stream. The trees provide the necessary shade, the descent is only 1:5, and the path is well made, dry, and surfaced in stone. But I have been warned, so I extract my telescopic walking stick from my sack and proceed with caution. Even so, in the space of half an hour I fall down four times and slip but manage to avoid tumbling a further six times. Normally, in a week's walking I wouldn't fall over once. This innocent-looking passageway must be the most dangerous section of the Pyrenean Way.

Down by the river, at the side of the path there is a notice mirroring the one at Artigue, but here the reflection is different.

Welcome to Bear Country
Hello
I am a Pyrenean bear. With the ADET, I invite you to discover this walking country. In order to preserve our tranquillity and that of the herds, I ask you to keep your dog at your side and to stay on marked footpaths. Thank you. Have a good walk.

The text, picked out in yellow paint, is incised into a solid wooden board which is designed to last. At the bottom there are three logos. The first one is evidently based on the European Union flag, with twelve stars in a circle surrounding the word 'Life' (in English). The second is the logo of the Ministry for development and the environment. The third, a schematic drawing of a bear against a mountain background, is symbolically surrounded by a lifebelt, and sports the wording '*ADET, Pyrénées Centrales, Pays de l'Ours* – Association for Economic Development and Tourism, Central Pyrenees, Bear Country'.

In the village of Fos, the grocery shop shut definitively several years ago. There are no provisions to be had. For tonight it doesn't matter, but the nearest shop on the Pyrenean Way is several days into the future.

Cabanes de Peyrehitte to Melles

Walking along the main road I see a sign for a Bear Country exhibition, free entry. Naturally, there is an effigy of a bear outside, but not what I might have expected. Although he is a realistic size for an adult bear and is standing up, there is nothing scary about this teddy. He has a small head, a big smile, and the proportions of a 40-year-old man with a beer gut – his stuffing seems to have slumped. An average two-year-old wouldn't be afraid. I can just see the bear which would stand outside an exhibition organised by the village of Artigue on the other side of the watershed. If he had a big smile it would be because his teeth were clasped round the amputated leg of an unfortunate walker, blood dripping from his lips.

Inside, the exhibition is positive about the reintroductions but I come away with the impression that, in the crude market economics of the third millennium, even bears have to justify their existence. The issue is not whether the bear community can reproduce itself, nor whether it can withstand the harsh Pyrenean winter, but whether it can survive the rigours of a cost–benefit analysis. In 2006 the reintroduction programme cost the state 2,246,818€. Compensation has to be found for the dead sheep and destroyed beehives. Shepherds have to be paid to stay with the flocks in the *estives*; and shepherds are no longer satisfied with the *orrys*, the dry stone huts of their grandfathers. New huts will have to be built, with enclosures to protect the sheep if there is a bear in the vicinity. *Patous* need to be trained. Helicopters need to bring in supplies. Then, in addition, there are the costs of the teams, at the Ministry for the Environment and elsewhere, looking after the bears' interests.

Those are the financial costs. The financial benefits are much more difficult to define and slow to materialise. The ADET sees bears as a vital factor in the development of green tourism. It is developing the concept of a 'Bear Country' label for a range of tourist activities which conform to its ethos, and encouraging sheep farmers to reorganise their production methods so that they can afford to pay shepherds to stay with the flocks in the mountains.

There is also an on-off project to create an immense safari park for the bears, but it is unclear how this could work. If the park is supposed to provide a natural environment for the bears, surely visitors would have to be kept away from them, but if visitors are kept to one side, how would the park make its money?

One thing is clear: if bears insist on a first course of spring lamb followed by a dessert laced with honey, they will have to pay for their supper by attracting tourists to the region. They will not be allowed to live on state benefits indefinitely.

Despite the promise of the teddy bear at the door, there is nothing inside for kids. No, that's not quite true. Children can make casts of real bears' paw prints, a full-size one attributed to Pyros, 235kg, or a tiny one, no bigger than my thumbprint, from a newly born cub, 0.4kg. This reminds me that the bears which arrived earlier this summer were reported to be pregnant.

'Have they had their cubs?' I ask the woman behind the counter.

'No…' she replies. She sounds evasive.

'But they were pregnant weren't they?'

'Maybe. We'll only find out next spring. If they give birth.'

'Then why did all the papers say they were pregnant?'

'Because they probably *are* going to have cubs, but they are not like humans. They copulate in May but the pregnancy doesn't start until December, when the bear is in hibernation. And then it only starts if the bear has managed to eat enough in the summer to have a chance of surviving the birth and bringing up the cubs.'

Jean-Jacques Camarra, a specialist in the matter, points out that bears are implicated in the deaths of 100–200 sheep each year in the French Pyrenees. Yet dog attacks, disease, thunderstorms and other causes account for 10,000–20,000 fatalities.

On the other hand, although the list of attacks reads like an itinerary of the central part of the Pyrenean Way, they are not evenly distributed, as Violaine Berot writes:

27 September 2001… Gilbert has a herd of 138 sheep on the mountain. That day 44 will be killed by a bear, 20 will go missing. The beasts are scattered over more than 300m, lying on the soil, ripped open. Horrible vision, those massacred sheep, disembowelled. Unbearable vision for the farmer, however hardened he might be.

And what about global warming? Nobody seems to be addressing the issue, though it must have a significant impact on the viability of the bear population in the long term. Will it make life easier for them, or destroy their habitat?

With a question as complex as that surrounding the reintroduction of the bear, it is a pity that the answer has been reduced to the simple yes or no of the pros and antis which dominates the debate today.

I walk along the main road through the rest of Fos, clinging to the walls, hiding from the incandescent sun and the hulking lorries. This is the main cross-frontier road for the central Pyrenees. From here on eastwards there are no crossings for 90km as the vulture flies, until the other side of Andorra.

'*Vive l'ours!*' '*Non à l'ours!*' The battle for the future of the Pyrenees is being fought out in graffiti on the tarmac, within spitting distance of the customs post. Turning round I see an advert for Maya, *medium international, divination*. She has her offices here in Fos. Should I go and ask her what the outcome will be?

Instead I follow the track up the hill. Just outside the village of Melles I meet an old woman who is knitting, standing up, in a field where sheep are grazing.

'Is it your own wool?' I ask her.

'No,' she laughs, 'though I've got a room full at home. I can't sell it, but I still have to have the sheep sheared every year.'

'What about the bears?' I ask her. 'Do they cause you problems?'

'No, because the sheep go back to the farm at night. I'll be taking them down shortly,' she explains.

In the village a small ceremony is in preparation. Flowers are being placed round the war memorial and a loud-speaker is being unpacked. It is 18 June, the anniversary of General de Gaulle's rallying cry, broadcast from London after the occupation of France in 1940, calling for continued resistance. After the ceremony I talk to André Rigoni, the mayor, and ask him about the few bears resisting extermination.

It was here that Ziva was released in 1996, at Rigoni's suggestion, in the first wave of reintroductions. Later he was to be followed by Mellba and Pyros. A recent book recounts the events:

> That morning the Pyrenees changed era… The French state decided to reinforce the Pyrenean bear population, at the initiative of five communes in the Haute-Garonne. And thus the Pandora's box was opened…

It won Rigoni many political enemies, with cynics claiming that he knew the bears would soon leave his commune and that he wouldn't have to live with the consequences.

Today, Rigoni is a dapper man, wearing a broad-striped shirt and a light-coloured suit. I take him to be in his 50s but later learn he is 74. For him 'bears are part of our national heritage just like the Eiffel Tower or the Louvre'.

'I have been elected six, or is it seven times, and have been promoting the existence of bears since 1989. So if a majority of local people were against it, I would have been replaced long ago. There are shepherds in the commune who are in favour. What you see in the media is a well-orchestrated campaign by a few determined individuals.'

A poster on the town hall shows a picture of a bear with the caption:

Mellba died on 27 September 1997, killed by a 7.64mm bullet. Coming from Slovenia, she was brought to the Pyrenees on 6 June 1996. She had given birth to three cubs… The death of Mellba is the death of an idea. Intolerance sometimes brings men to kill bears as they kill ideas.

The Auberge du Crabère, where I am staying for the night, is opposite the war memorial. An elegant building with a decorative façade and ironwork balconies, it looks out of place amidst its bucolic neighbours. Inside, the furniture also looks out of place but for a different reason. The double doors leading to my bedroom, the windows, and the wardrobe all look as though they were intended for a full-size chateau although the building itself is quite modestly proportioned.

While drinking an aperitif, I talk to the proprietor and chef, Patrick Beauchet. He evidently enjoys eating – never trust a thin chef is a well-known French expression – and has a jovial manner and a bushy moustache. Although he is quite small, in his youth he played rugby against England. He then went to sea, as a ship's cook, working on the legendary *Le France*, the French equivalent of the *Queen Elizabeth*.

'I gave it up because I couldn't stand everything rolling about in the Bay of Biscay,' he tells me. 'We've been here 16 years now. At first we used to be full all the time, but now it's hard to make a living. There are only two of you tonight.'

'What's changed?'

'I'm not sure. Breathalysers partly. Also people think that self-catering accommodation is cheaper – it isn't. And then they don't like simple hotels anymore. They want televisions in the rooms.'

The inn doesn't have any stars, but is perfectly comfortable. And it is homely, unlike those antiseptic modern hotels which do have stars. Bed, breakfast, and evening meal for 32€ must be difficult to beat.

'I used to do gastronomic meals, which worked well, but I'm not sure if I'll do any more,' he adds.

He passes me a book of press cuttings and menus. It includes 'A tribute to Bocuse', a reproduction of one of the great chef's meals, faithful in every detail except the price.

He has written several books of recipes and has been commissioned to write one about his life on board ship. He asks me if I know anybody who can rescue it: his computer has just been struck by lightning.

Annie, his wife, comes in with a *patou*. Tammy is as big as the dog I saw near the Granges d'Astau, but a pet. She barks suspiciously at me, once, before lying down under the table, her head sticking out at one end and her legs at the other. She needs a full-size chateau. Annie disappears.

'That's Annie,' says Patrick. 'Annie looks after the guests. I do the cooking.' He changes the subject: 'You're walking on your own, aren't you? It's not a good idea you know.'

'You see more, and you can think about things,' I reply.

'You think *too much*. I wouldn't like to do it. Walking in company could be good fun, but I wouldn't like to walk on my own. No.'

Sitting at the next table is a gorilla of a man, the other guest, who introduces himself as Maurice. *'Comment tu t'appelles?'* he asks me. He is big, very big, with sequoia legs. There is hair sprouting out of the back of his tee-shirt collar, but less on his head. He is wearing thin-rimmed glasses. His face, his eyes, look solid, uncomplicated. He is also walking the Pyrenean Way; 20kg; Hendaye; four weeks. A retired engineer, he is due to meet some friends in Mérens in two weeks' time.

Patrick serves us a meal that is both copious and tasty. It starts with a tureen of *soupe ancestrale*, a soup that has been progressively redefined, but never quite eaten up. On its own this could constitute a meal but there are four more courses. Maurice downs everything put in front of him and a whole bottle of wine without any noticeable side-effects.

Melles to the Lac d'Araing

I leave the *Alice in Wonderland* inn with a packed lunch, wondering if eating it will shrink me or make me grow. It is still hot from yesterday and I am wearing only shorts and a tee-shirt. I can feel – but not see – spiders' webs breaking on my arms and face as I slip through the forest. Back in the open air, I sit down for a second breakfast next to a stately – and highly poisonous – common monkshood, flowering blue amongst the rhododendrons which, here, have finished their summer display.

I detect a movement on the slope nearby – an animal which looks like a fat *isard*. But it isn't an *isard*. It has long, thick, curved horns arching backwards, virtually sticking into the brown fleece on its neck. It must be a *bouquetin*. No, it can't be a *bouquetin* because they no longer exist in the Pyrenees – the last one died in 2000. There had been *bouquetins* in the Pyrenees for over 12,000 years, as witnessed by a magnificent Magdalenian cave painting in the Grotte de Niaux in the Ariège. But by 1980, of the 22 species or zoological genera identifiable in the Palaeolithic caves of the Pyrenees, only eight survived. And then there were seven.

Yet nobody is kicking up a fuss, even though *bouquetins* are an ideal candidate for reintroduction. They are inoffensive herbivores. They could even serve to nourish the bears if there were ever enough of the two species for them to have the chance – or bad luck, depending on your point of view – of meeting up. There are some further south in Spain but the Spanish are not interested in letting them go. After all, the French record with bears is not encouraging.

No, it must be a *mouflon*. These are wild sheep reintroduced some 50 years ago from Corsica by hunters, after having been exterminated by shepherds jealous of their pastures.

Are there any truly wild animals in the Pyrenees? Any which Pygmalion hands have not tried to resuscitate from the raw rocks of the mountains, or tried to crush against them; in the face of such complacent beauty, unable or unwilling to control their obsession with power?

On the plateau, sheep are everywhere, 6-month-old lambs and their mothers, two flocks mingling, stars for some, hearts for others, but unified by their distinctive coiffure: long back-and-sides with a razor-cut belly.

This is where the Haute-Garonne *département* becomes the Ariège. Walkers whom I have met coming the other way describe the Ariège as the most difficult section of the Pyrenean Way. Although the mountains are less dramatic, there is a distinct lack of facilities for hikers. The rare beds or meals are not to be sniffed at.

A blue emergency-services helicopter passes overhead as it descends towards the Lac d'Araing, scattering sheep in its wake. By the time I arrive at the hostel on the shores of the reservoir, it has flown off. It came for a man who had a minor accident yesterday, knocking his head, I am told. He appeared to have recovered, but in the night he started vomiting repeatedly.

The hostel looks like a big slab of milk chocolate with a small entrance made by nibbling mice. Officially it is run by Anoura Barre but there are half a dozen friends involved and I can't quite make out who does what, or indeed which one Anoura might be. I eat lunch in the sunshine and then go to take a siesta. Less than an hour later the sound of thunder and torrential rain beating on the aluminium structure gets me out of bed. Maurice is here, having arrived just before the storm. The door opens and an elderly woman comes in, dripping.

'Hello Julie. You're not a moment too early!' says Maurice, helping her to remove her rucksack.

'No. It's a long way from Fos,' she replies, grumpily.

'You stayed in Fos! I wondered why you didn't show up at the Auberge du Crabère.'

'I did. But when I arrived, the woman said that it was fully booked for the night. She didn't look too pleased to see me. I think I must have disturbed her siesta. So I had to go down to Fos again and climb back up this morning. I hope it's not like this tomorrow.'

'Don't worry, the storm will stop soon,' Maurice reassures her.

Julie is from Quebec. Retired, she is walking the Pyrenean Way, but is travelling light, with neither sleeping bag nor cooking equipment, so she has to stay under a roof each night. She is going to skip the rest of the Ariège and rejoin the path at Mérens. Maurice has met her *en route* on various occasions.

The door opens again. This time it is a fat man wearing nothing but a spare tyre and a pair of shorts, soaked to the skin, with a poodle. He mutters something to himself in German, drags a towel out of his rucksack, and dries the dog. We ask him the standard question. 'Melles,' he replies.

'I suppose you are walking, too?' Maurice asks another young man.

'No, I came by plane. We don't all have the same ideas,' he replies.

'Really! What sport do you do then?'

'I was joking. I work here. But every day I get asked where I have come from. I don't *even* have time to go walking.'

'That's a pity. But you could have arrived by plane. I'm a parachutist,' Maurice explains.

He does precision jumping. You leap out of the plane at 4000 metres. All you can see is the aerodrome. As you descend you look out for the yellow target. You open your parachute. You aim for the black bull's-eye, 1 metre across, in the centre of the yellow target. If you get it right, you land with one heel on an electronic pad three centimetres in diameter in the centre of the bull's-eye. He also does artistic jumping, where the competitors, in threes, have to execute six acrobatic figures –accordion, viper, diamond, propeller, marquis, and snowflake, for example – whilst descending in free fall at 240km/h. He started at the age of 38. Maurice is evidently pleased to have found an audience.

'The rain will stop soon,' he repeats. 'It will clear up soon.'

He is right. After the storm I go to sit on the bluff behind the hostel. The last of the thunderclouds are being chased down the valley by the wind. At the bottom of the slope, somewhere way out of view in the forest, must be the road. Above it vast swathes of rhododendrons lap over the pastures. An unchanging landscape, it seems, indifferent to the tempests which shake humans to their core. And yet, the landscape is changing. While it was raining outside, I read a dissertation written by Anoura for his Mountain Guide Diploma. The rhododendrons are colonising the hills. As sheep disappear, the pastures become flowerbeds, to disappear in turn under scrub and then forest. The flowerbeds have doubled in size over the last 30 years. The mountains are not immutable, changing only to the rhythm of some geological metronome, but in continuous flux, and the changes can be seen within a shepherd's lifetime.

Anoura also reports the reflections of Yves Garel, his predecessor. When Yves first started working in isolated mountain hostels, every drop of hot water was precious, an unexpected pleasure to be savoured. Now walkers expect free hot showers, although the hostels haven't moved any nearer to the pylons. The evenings were convivial, with the remote situation and the common experience of walking bringing people together, creating exchanges which wouldn't happen in a city hotel. Now, walkers increasingly want private space, to retire to their own room. In the common room, increasingly they keep to themselves, Yves regrets.

Lac d'Araing to the Cabane de l'Arech

I climb up to the pass, where a few metres of rusty railway and an electricity pylon betray the former presence of industry: the top end of the Bentaillou mine. Changing valley, way below me on the ragged scarp slope, I can see the decaying remains of the workers' accommodation and mine buildings clinging to a rocky knoll, in a windy Machu Picchu setting. Around the mine, the entrails of the mountain have been vomited over the grassy carpet, the sterile spoil tips staining it irrecoverably.

For Roman authors 2000 years ago at the heart of the empire, the distant Pyrenean rivers ran with silver, and gold was just as easily extracted. The rediscovery of ancient mines at Aulus in the Ariège in 1600 contributed to the reputation in a Europe about to embark on an Industrial Revolution. But the miners' rush of enthusiasm at the exposure of each new seam was often dissipated when they were confronted with the dislocated geology of the mountains.

By the middle of the 19th century the Biros valley here was overcrowded and emigration was the only future for many youngsters, so the new mine was a welcome alternative. But it was to bring problems in its wake: the extraction of zinc, lead, and silver, from 1853 onwards, was to be financed by capital from Bordeaux.

The scene was set. As in many valleys, the opening up of the mines was the first act in a tragedy which would eventually deprive the valley, first of its independence, and then of its population. Initially, the farmer-workers combined their pastoral activities with occasional employment in the mines, a day here, a day there – a kind of multi-activity before its time. But workers from outside were brought in, and through a series of strikes, closures, and take-overs, control of the mines passed from Bordeaux to Paris and then to England. By now the owners would only take on full-time staff. This was the end of the first act.

Then in 1879 a technological innovation was to transform the economics of the mine: a cableway was installed. This simple idea eradicated one of the major problems: the relief. The production increased dramatically. This was the beginning of the second act. (Incidentally, throughout the Pyrenees, cableways enabled the extraction of minerals and timber on a new scale and, with the arrival of winter sports, they became a vital part in the exploitation of that other emerging resource: snow.)

Back in the Biros valley the roads were being metalled. New sites were being opened up. By 1904, the mines were employing 400 people, but the ore was becoming progressively more elusive. Bentaillou went through a series of owners until it was finally closed down in the 1950s: 600,000 tonnes of ore had been extracted. The valley had been transformed both physically and socially. It couldn't return to its former autarchy. Nor did it have the resources to develop in a new direction. It didn't even have the resources to clean up the mess left behind by a century of colonial exploitation. The population dwindled. The commune, Sentein, had 1362 inhabitants in 1856, 716 in 1946 and just 150 in 2004. This is the final act of the tragedy.

A small marble monument by the side of the path is a reminder of another drama which took place here.

> In memory of
> Anglade, Fortuné
> Perissé, Alphonse
> Seube, Henri
> Electricity Board workers
> 29 December 1960

There is no other explanation.

The path heads for Eylie d'en Haut, a pleasant village, with a refreshing stream and buddleia bushes, only locally defaced by the remains of the mining industry. It is here that the ore was crushed before being transported down to the plain.

Going up again amongst ferns and flowers, the sun is intense, and although I filled up with water in Eylie I am consuming it rapidly. Opposite me, the pastures are parcelled up by hedges grown up into trees, each parcel with a postage stamp barn in the corner, testimony to the density of the habitation and the need to extract a maximum from the lower slopes in summer whilst the sheep were in the *estives*.

The hostel has prepared me a packed meal. Although the sandwiches are dry as only *pain de campagne* can be, I have to eat every crumb of them. It will be two days before I reach the next hostel and I only just have enough food. Pour water on one side, says the recipe. Turn the sandwich over and repeat. Leave for five minutes. Accompany with a bottle of tepid water.

Anoura has also sold me a large lump of *pain de campagne* and some local cheese.

'We don't really do provisions,' he told me. 'We often get asked, because there is no alternative. But it all has to be brought up from the valley in a rucksack so it is very expensive. I'm always embarrassed at the price.'

The cheese is 30€ for a kilo, but I would have paid more. And it is good.

The clouds are building up so I cut my lunch short. Within a few minutes I have arrived at a bifurcation. To the right, the path continues to the Mail de Bullard, another high-level mine. The seam was rich but the access dangerous. The owners called it *La reine des Pyrénées* – the queen of the Pyrenees, the workers called it *La mangeuse d'hommes* – the man-eater.

My path, however, turns to the left and descends a little, to the Cabane de l'Arech, five minutes' walk from the ridge. The shepherd has priority, a notice says. I knock, and then try the door. It isn't locked. Inside, the ash in the hearth is still warm but there is no other sign of recent occupation. There is the usual collection of bottles – though none of the quality of the Cabanes de Peyrehitte – but at least there is a table. *And* it is covered with a checked pink-and-white oilcloth. There is a single bed on the ground floor. *And* it has a mattress; *but* it is decorated by a series of circular stains. Upstairs, under the eaves, the three mattresses are clean, and there are some slippers which fit me. But for the moment the attic is stiflingly hot.

I am thirsty, and my water has run out. After many years of struggling under the weight of three, four, or even five litres of water, I have finally discovered the solution. Dehydrated water. It can be bought in most pharmacies around here. It comes in little white tablets. You find a spring. You add the liquid to the tablets, and there it is – water.

Of course, it is marketed as water *purifying* tablets. But the idea never appealed to me. You can't take water from a pure mountain spring and then disinfect it by adding chemicals. All the same, you don't want to drink from a spring which might have been contaminated by a suppurating dead sheep somewhere upstream. So I always carried a large quantity of water. It was only when I realised that the tablets were really dehydrated water that they started to interest me.

The spring marked on my map is dry and there are no others in the vicinity, but I discover a sheep trough with a black plastic pipe leading into it and fill up my bottles. The angry clouds have now dissipated so I lie down and sunbathe: a contented baby taking his afternoon nap, nestling down into the thick grass, dozing from time to time, in a grandiose natural cradle.

The uncoordinated sheep on the slopes above me graze from pasture to pasture, but as the sun descends one group falls into line behind a leader. Another group does the same, and they start to come down the hill, lines coalescing like fleece on a spinning wheel, until they form a single yarn, returning to the salt cakes strewn around the hut.

I get dressed and am just sorting out which food dust I am going to eat when Maurice arrives, waving his hands, showing the purple-stained palms.

'Bilberries,' he says. 'I've also got some mushrooms,' he adds, waving two plastic bags in front of me. 'Did you see the raspberries near the mine?' he asks.

'No. I saw the bilberry bushes in the forest but I didn't see any fruit on them.'

'You shouldn't walk with your eyes on the ground all the time. To really appreciate the walking you've got to stop and look around.'

He unfolds his tent, explaining: 'I snore, and I don't want to keep us both awake all night. I'd keep you awake when I snore, and myself awake trying to avoid keeping you awake.'

'Are there any hunters here?' he asks me, unexpectedly.

I look at the empty hillside: 'No, I can't see any. Why?'

'When I told my friends I was coming here, they said that I'd better be careful,' he says, taking his tee-shirt off and turning round. His back is covered with a mat of black hair.

'I don't want be mistaken for a bear.'

We each prepare our meal, Maurice sharing what he says are girolles – they look rather odd to me – and the bilberries.

'Why are you walking the Pyrenean Way?' I ask him. I am half way along it and I still don't know what my answer would be.

'*Parce que c'est mythique* – it's mythical. It was my wife who introduced me to walking – and the Pyrenees. She's left, but the walking has stayed. It's a challenge and I wanted to see if I was up to it. I've been walking 80km a week in preparation but it isn't just strength. It is a question of the head and the mule. Divided at the neck. You need both, of course. But if the head leads the mule will follow… And there's the muscular exhilaration. It's like a drug, I think.'

He spots a couple of walkers coming down the path. A thin young woman bouncing along in front. A man trudging along after her, carrying a rucksack which extends out behind him in all directions.

'Have you seen the size of the rucksack!' Maurice exclaims. 'They must have one of those instant tents you can get from Decathlon. They weigh a ton.'

'The head and the mule?' I suggest.

It isn't a Decathlon tent. Theirs is smaller, but the rucksack is still overflowing.

'We are camping,' Martin tells me in English. 'We are students so we don't have much money, but we do have plenty of holidays.'

They started at Luchon this year, having walked there from the Atlantic two years ago. They camped near the Lac d'Araing last night, though I didn't notice them. Martin has just graduated. Sylvia graduated last year, has taken a year off, and is going to do an MA in September.

'I'm hungry,' Martin complains. 'She won't let me eat, except at lunch time.'

'I don't want you to get any fatter,' Sylvia chides.

'It's true that I've put on weight. I'm finding it much more difficult than the last time. I'm exhausted at the end of the day,' he explains.

Martin goes off to wash at the sheep trough, shouting joyously as he splashes himself.

'If I had no clothes on, I wouldn't go announcing it to the world,' comments Sylvia.

She goes and washes more discreetly. It is getting late so I light them a fire to cook on.

'What would you like to eat?' Sylvia asks Martin. 'Tomato soup or vegetable soup?'

'Whatever you like,' he replies.

'I asked you what you wanted. I don't mind.'

'Tomato then, but we can have the vegetable if you like.'

'Ok. Let's have that.'

They eat the vegetable soup, reconstituted with a minimum of liquid to give it a thicker consistency, and finish off the meal with a bit of cake. Then they have a bowl of tomato soup. We all sit around the fire chatting, with Sylvia and me translating.

'I want to see a bear,' she insists.

'I don't. I don't want to be attacked,' says Martin. 'I think they should be exterminated. The government should get rid of them.'

Sylvia and Martin have just reached the edge of their map and are going to have to rely on a guidebook which covers all the major Pyrenean paths in a pocket-sized volume, with maps drawn by a spider which has just climbed out of an ink bottle.

'He walks so slowly,' complains Sylvia.

'So you carry the food, like a carrot, to make him walk faster?' I ask.

'Oh, no. He has the food.'

'But if you carried more then he could walk faster.'

Neither of them thinks this is a reasonable idea.

Having seen the mattresses upstairs, they decide to spend the night in the hut. I sleep downstairs.

Cabane de l'Arech to the Cabane d'Aouen

I want to walk as much as possible in the shade, while the sun is still hidden behind the mountains, so I get up first. The path follows a track for a few minutes before it leaps head-first into the valley, only slowing down when it hits the edge of the forest. Although the sun has officially risen by now, under the tree cover it is still sombre, indeed sinister.

The winter here must have been very dry as last autumn's leaves have not decayed, rustling with every step. Normally, I like walking along kicking at the leaves, but today I feel uneasy. Can I hear another noise? Another rustling? I stop. Nothing. I try to walk quietly. I'm sure there is a rustling noise somewhere ahead. I stop again. It stops. There is something there. Watching me. But I can't see it. I walk a few wary paces further and the rustling recommences, then develops into a frightening crescendo, a noise like the vapour escaping from the pistons of a steam train as it gains speed, faster and faster. And then it stops dead. Silence. But my eyes have followed the sound. At first all I can make out is a white backside, but then it moves into a patch of light. It is only an *isard* running away from me up the slope.

The path crosses the river and then cruelly climbs up again on the other side. Then, on the ridge I get lost, following a path perfectly marked with red and white waymarks, but not the Pyrenean Way. By the time I have retraced my steps, the sun has turned into an instrument of torture. I hide from it in one of the many huts which mark this part of the route, enjoying the chance to lie down in the dark with my eyes shut.

The path crosses a second valley, the Ribérot, and climbs again, back into the forest, but by now even the trees are sweating. At every stream I slop water over my head. At every spring I refill my bottles.

A small collie dog scurries up to me, gives me a quick sniff and then continues on its downhill trajectory. It is followed by a young woman in sports shorts and an elastic top, running, taking all the short cuts in the loops, using her long stick like a rudder behind her, *à la ramasse*, to steady her descent.

The Cabane d'Aouen is already occupied by a man from Bayonne who offers me some freshly brewed tea, in a choice of several varieties. 22 kg; Eylie d'en Haut. The shepherdess, he tells me, has just left. I would have seen her on my way up. She has two-thirds of the hut. There is still space for me in the separate room reserved for walkers.

The double bed takes up practically the entire space so I unpack my rucksack outside, and then go off in search of the spring. There are no sheep and the grass has grown high, perfumed like a flower shop by the wild carnations, there are so many of them. Opposite me, determinedly vertical but unusually stunted pine trees cling by their toenails to the cliff face. Further away, I can make out patches of snow on the slopes of the Valier mountain.

Maurice arrives later and pitches his tent, but Martin and Sylvia haven't got this far. Fearing neither sun nor lightning, they prefer a morning lie in.

Maurice and I agree that the next stop has to be Esbints. It is a real hostel, but more importantly, it sells provisions. I thought I had packed too much food, but I calculate that I will only have sugar cubes and coffee left after tomorrow's wild raspberry and reconstituted dust breakfast.

Cabane d'Aouen to Esbints

I am walking along a path high above the valley of the Ribérot. Below, clouds slopping from shore to shore push up from the Toulouse sea, the liquid surface glistening in the low light. To the east, the Pic de Crabère – named after the female *isard* – casts a witch-black shadow, dominating the horizon. Above, the heavens are empty, translucent but not yet transparent, the sun still struggling to disperse the night's damp legacy. The pastures are being tended by horses, cows, and sheep, in separate battalions, advancing one after the other across the vegetation.

On the shores of the Étang d'Ayes I scoop up the lake water with my hands and pour it over my hair. Then I plaster my face with sun cream and search out the spring marked on my map. The sun has captured the mountain tops, but I soon discover that it has not yet captured the slopes. Passing onto the northern side of the hill, I am suddenly enveloped in cold fog, with visibility down to a few paces, the air so thick that I can stick out my tongue and lick it.

Back in the forest, the clearings are covered with St John's Wort and *geranium des Alpes*, yellow and purple five-petalled flowers intermingled as far as the eye can see, which is not very far. Nearby, shallow scoops in the ground signal the recent presence of wild boar looking for roots.

By the time I arrive at the Col de la Core I am frozen through. I hide behind an abandoned caravan, which in better weather might have served me a snack, and light my gas stove to make some coffee. Maurice materialises with Jean-Michel, a walker he has just met. 12 kg; Hendaye; 22 days ago. We set off together down the hill.

We are soon below the clouds and, although the sun is still invisible, we heat up, going faster and faster in one of those puerile games favoured by men who have just met in the context of a sporting activity. There is also the incentive of lunch. If we are too late we will have to starve for another seven hours until the evening meal. We stop to take our anoraks off.

'Ow!' cries Maurice, slapping his thigh.

'*Merde*. What's that?' asks Jean-Michel, scraping a squashed brown insect off his arm.

'A horsefly,' I reply, brushing one off the back of my neck.

A swarm of them is chasing after us. We put our rucksacks back on and start running, cursing. Three men with big rucksacks running down the mountain, madly jumping and skipping for no apparent reason. Slapping themselves and each other, shouting loudly, occasionally yelping.

We hammer desperately on the door of the hostel but there is no answer. I lie on the grass, reasoning that at least my back won't get bitten. Then a car arrives and somebody gets out.

The woman who comes up the steps is fair-haired, tanned, and smiling. She introduces herself as Gila.

'I don't do hot meals at lunch time,' she tells us, with a slight German accent, 'but I can put something cold together, if that would be alright. Go and have a shower first if you want. Would you like to sit outside or inside?'

We opt for outside.

She fetches tomatoes, with basil and garlic cloves to spread on top of them; melon, pâté, cheese, yoghurt and fruit; wine and beer; and homemade rye bread.

'It's burnt on the bottom, because that's the way my grandmother used to make it and I like the caramelised taste, but I advise you to cut it off.'

She brings us tea and coffee afterwards and Maurice invites her to sit down and have a cup for herself.

'Did you have any trouble finding your way in the fog?' Gila asks.

'No. The only point where I hesitated was at the Col d'Auèdole,' replied Maurice.

'There were signs pointing in every direction except towards Esbints,' I add.

'Since the *département* has taken over, things have gone downhill,' says Gila. 'What about the path?'

'It was fine. Just after Eylie d'en Haut, somebody had recently cleared the undergrowth.'

'So the council *has* taken some notice of our complaints.' Gila continues: 'They are not very keen on maintaining existing paths. They are more interested in creating new ones, because they can have grants for that. But even the new ones are not always very well thought out. Last year two people were killed on a path near here, so they've had to improve it... We're very reliant on the Pyrenean Way but the number of visitors has decreased. Walkers by-pass the Ariège because there aren't enough hostels and the council does nothing to encourage new ones.'

She continues: 'Or they get lost, stupidly. Recently two walkers arrived at my door, asking to use the phone. Their friend was ill, they said. I told them that the police wouldn't do anything unless he couldn't move, and sent them back. They reappeared later with the friend. The next day I found out the real story from the man himself. He hadn't been ill. He was just extremely tired and got left behind. He had been following the path when he found that it was barred by a blue string. Assuming it was the end of the path, he went off across the *garrigue* and got himself into a thorough mess, so he decided to pitch his tent. Then he got down on his knees and prayed. God's reply was thunder and lightning. Even more worried, he packed up his tent and went back to the blue string, which is where his friends found him. The blue string was an electric fence to keep the cows in!'

A hen suddenly starts clucking.

'She's singing,' says Gila. 'I will have to go to find the egg. Feed the scraps to the pig.'

The pig is waiting on the other side of a wooden gate. She is Vietnamese, very black, and very pot-bellied.

'When are you going to eat her?' I ask.

'Never. My husband and my son would like to. But Zita is my pig so we are not going to eat her.'

It's like bears, I think. Giving them a name protects them; makes killing them less acceptable.

Maurice and Jean-Michel put up their tents and I go for a siesta in the building reserved for walkers. When I wake up, Gila's son, Mathias, is coming back down from the meadow with a haystack on his back. I can hear the sound of an accordion being played in the house.

Martin and Sylvia have arrived.

'There is somebody lost on the mountains in the fog. But they heard the accordion music and somebody is going to search for them. I think,' Martin tells me.

I am sitting at the table in the corner of the kitchen in the main house. The table is not a piece of furniture, it is part of the structure. Although, theoretically, it could be moved it seems improbable that this has happened since it was built in this very room some lifetimes ago. It is square and could comfortably seat four on each side, though there are only eleven of us eating. It is piled with food, dominated by dishes holding the various elements of a *couscous*. The rest of the kitchen is in keeping: the hearth and neighbouring bread oven; the beams which span the width of the room; even Gila's more modern kitchen which runs the length of the room.

'What happened about the person who was lost?' someone asks Gila. 'Did they find her?'

'Yes. It was Christine,' Gila replies, indicating a thin, pretty, young woman with curly red hair.

'I think I've worked out what happened now,' Christine tells us. 'Gila gave me instructions from the Col de la Core but as I was walking up the road somebody stopped to give me a lift. They thought they knew where I should go, so they dropped me off at a path. But it was the wrong path so I was lost from the start.'

'Where were you when you heard the music?' I ask.

'I didn't hear any music,' replies Christine, doubtfully.

'I was playing the accordion this afternoon to calm myself down,' clarifies Gila. 'If she had continued she could have fallen off a cliff. But she couldn't have heard me where she was.'

'How did you get back then?'

'I kept on trying to ring up on my mobile but it couldn't find the network. Then finally it worked. Mathias came to fetch me.'

Christine was going up to see Gila's husband, Francis, in the *estive* on the Valier, and intended to stay there for some weeks. She wants to see what life would be like as a shepherdess.

'But I'm not going up into the mountains again on my own,' she says, emphatically.

'You'll have to wait until Wednesday, when my son can take you,' says Gila. Today is Saturday. 'I'm too busy at present, but you can see how the farm works in the meantime.'

Christine tells me that she had tried all over before she found someone who would take her on. Eventually she found Francis on the Internet.

'It's difficult if you are a woman, and not from round here, to find an opening,' explains Gila. 'I know that from when I first came here 28 years ago. When I did my training I was the only woman. There were no shepherdesses then. The only women who went up into the *estives* were prostitutes. You should have heard the tales they told about me at the fair in Foix. Horrible things! But I had a different life then. I used to walk bare-foot.'

She tells another story: 'One morning I was bathing in a stream a little way from my hut and I saw the helicopter from the *gendarmerie* circling overhead. It just kept on circling round and round. All my clothes were in the hut. *Hallucinant!*'

Maurice recounts our descent from the Col de la Core pursued by horseflies.

'I killed three of them with one swipe,' he boasts.

'I don't kill them,' says Christine. 'I like insects. There are so many you could never kill them all, so it doesn't help to kill them. I just brush them off.'

She shows me her bulging wrist where she was a little slow in reacting.

'How long have you been here?' I ask Gila.

'Ten years. It was a hostel already but we have done lots of restoration. We needed something to supplement our income from the sheep. Multi-activity. The idea was that we would share the time in the *estive*, with one of us in the mountains and the other here. But Francis isn't renowned for his cooking so I asked him how he was going to cope. "I'll open a few cans", he said. I told him that it wasn't good enough. So he is up there with the animals and I am here with the walkers.'

Francis is a rare breed – an owner-shepherd. Most pastoralists are either sheep farmers who employ shepherds, or shepherds working for one or more owners. Francis is looking after 800 sheep, of which only 80 actually belong to him. For each of the four months in the *estives* he receives 1€ per sheep. He also cares for about 25 cows which are paid a little better. Naturally, he has a *patou*.

He is also a rare breed in another sense. A shepherd who sees bears as part of the Pyrenean landscape. On a pro-bear website he is quoted as saying:

> Fundamentally, profoundly, as a human being and a Pyrenean I believe that our mountains will no longer be the same [if the bears disappear]; that they lose a little of their splendour every time a bear dies. The bear is a legendary symbol of our region, he has always been an integral part of it. More concretely, he is also the proof that our countryside remains natural. Here biodiversity is still possible. The countryside is not simply a semblance of nature made for and by man.

Unlike many pastoralists, Francis and Gila are trying to adapt to the new economic and social conditions. Consumers are prepared to pay for quality but also demand certified organic labelling. So the farm went organic in 2000. To increase their margins, they sell directly to the consumers. And they produce *broutards* – grazers – lambs fattened in the *estives*.

Most of the sheep in the French Pyrenees are raised for their meat. In general the lambs are sold soon after birth for a low price to Spanish farmers who fatten them up. The *broutards* are more work but the shepherd receives more at market. I ask Gila if the system is economic.

'Not without the subsidies, no,' she replies.

Gila advises the seven of us who are heading east to follow the main path up to the Cabane d'Aula even though it is a long way round.

'It's beautiful up there, and the short-cut is dull.'

The over-riding advantage of the short-cut, however, is that it passes through Seix, where there is a shop. In the end, only two of us, Maurice and I, decide to go the long way round.

Esbints to the Cabane d'Aula

Breakfast is at the same table. While I am eating Gila prepares me a packed lunch and provisions for the next two days. Four hens come in through the open door.

'They've come to ask for their breakfast as well,' says Gila.

Seeing them I ask: 'Could I have some boiled eggs to take with me? It would be nice to have some really fresh eggs.'

'You can have some boiled eggs but they will be from the supermarket. The fox attacked our hens so I'm trying to build up the flock again.'

Later, when finally the road stops and becomes a path, I see a multilingual sign inciting walkers to take their rubbish home. It is covered in red paint, graffiti: 'Keep walking. Alaric, see you at cabin. Happy 17th. Luv H+J xx'. The graffiti is written in English, though Alaric is a French name.

Further along I read: *'Mort aux écolos de l'ours* – Death to the bear-loving ecologists'. Francis has his *estive* higher up the valley. Is this graffiti aimed at him?

Luchon–Mérens: Ariège, terre courage

An hour later, I come upon a clearing which smells of wood smoke. A barn by the side of the path is so chock-a-block with timber that it is falling out of the window under the eaves. The building next to it is being renovated. Two workmen and an old man, whom I take to be the owner, are standing outside, so I say hello. The old man looks at me suspiciously. A younger woman rushes out of the door with an Alsatian on a lead. The Alsatian doesn't like me either. I say goodbye.

In the middle of the woods there is a huge block of stone perched precariously above the path. Under it there is a flower pot with a few very dried-up flowers, and a plaque.

> Eric Garcia 1971–1994. Your life was full of nature and mountains, the object of all your studies. Your passion for life was stronger than yours.

An arrow points up at the block of stone.

The head of the valley is filled with clouds. I can't see, but I can guess where Francis has his sheep, to my right, beyond the forest, way above me on the valley side. It can't be much fun up there today. But as I climb, the clouds climb too and I arrive at the Cabane d'Aula at the same time as the first sun of the day.

The hut is at the very end of the valley, on the last flat pasture. To my right, the ragged summit of the Valier is breaking up like a rotten eye tooth exposed to the extremes of heat and cold, shedding unwanted enamel on the slopes. In front of me, the frontier ridge has long since buried its feet under still-mobile scree. To my left, the pass which the Pyrenean Way traverses seems hardly lower than the mountains on either side of it. But that is for tomorrow.

I inspect the inside of the hut. Rough concrete walls, a corrugated iron roof. An old notice complains about vandalism and asks walkers to respect the building. But the remains of the facilities are now ash in the chimney. The only surviving furniture is made of metal: rusty bunk beds, a few wobbly stools, and a table. The window is broken.

Outside, the view down the valley is clearing, and I can see Maurice lumbering up.

'I've lost my hat,' he complains. 'I left it on a rock. When I realised, I went back, but by the time I got there it had gone. I've had it for 20 years.'

We construct a table outside from a flagstone and a couple of stools, and eat rye bread, cheese, sausage, and apples, for the second time today, surveying the empty landscape. Maurice points out the Valier, with its near-vertical cliffs tumbling into the valley.

'It must be somewhere there that she fell,' he says. He doesn't need to say more for me to understand.

Gila told us about a woman who nearly came to grief on the mountain. She was walking alone and became disorientated in the low clouds, but she kept on going down, until she reached their base. Way below her, she could see the shepherds' huts in the valley Maurice and I have just walked along. There wasn't much vegetation because the slopes were steep, so although there was no path she made good progress. Then she fell, breaking her pelvis. She had been trying to descend a face normally reserved for rock climbers with ropes. For four days she dragged herself through the rhododendrons, across scree and broken rocks. The mountain rescue helicopter flew overhead seven times without seeing her.

That might have been the end of the story, but one of the shepherds in his *estive* half-heard an unusual noise. Without knowing that there was someone missing, he had the feeling that something was wrong: shepherds need to pay attention to their senses. He went to investigate and noticed a patch of rhododendrons which had been compacted like a nest, so he continued searching until he found the woman. But he realised that his sheep were grazing on the slopes immediately above. They could easily create a landslide, he thought, and he went off immediately to move them to safety.

The woman, in her confused state, thought her chance of rescue had disappeared. When the shepherd returned he found that he couldn't move her so he went to the local police station – mobile telephones don't work over large areas of the Pyrenees. It was night and he was agitated. He rang the door phone and talked to the policeman inside. His tale seemed so unlikely that the police thought he was drunk or deranged and refused to open the door. Until the shepherd said: 'If you don't come out and do something, I will break the door down.' Finally convinced, the police set the rescue services in motion.

We clear our things off the table and leave the salt-loving cows to lick it clean. I light a fire in the hearth and we sit next to it, Maurice reciting the *FFRP Guide* in detail, calculating the number of hours walking from here to Mérens, and where to stay the night. At the moment when the last light disappears from the sky we hear peculiar squeaking noises coming from outside:

pwiiiu…pwu…pwiiiu… pwu… pwu… pwu

It is too dark to see anything but the sound is circling above us and then coming to rest on the cliffs. Two birds certainly; three, perhaps even four. They sound like bearded vultures – but I'm no expert – coming home to roost. One of the rarest carrion-eaters in Europe, the bearded vulture intervenes after all the others, nourishing itself on the bones, which its stomach juices can dissolve. The larger ones, it carries high into the sky and drops against rocks to break them. Are they really bearded vultures? We will never know. At first I feel frustrated but quickly realise that it doesn't matter. Whatever they are, they have enchanted us anyway with their twilight magic.

Cabane d'Aula to Rouze

The sky is beautifully blue, or would be if there were enough colour in it to be any colour at all. I think it is Monday morning, but I might be

Cabane d'Aula to Rouze

wrong. Down below, the valley is partially veiled, but the red band of sunrise is already showing. The wind is warm and my rucksack seems light, but the path up to the pass makes no concessions to the early hour and my legs are heavy.

It is 7:30am. Just beyond the pass, a bright blue van is parked at the end of a gravel track. The back door is swinging open but there is no sign of an occupant and neither humans nor animals in the vicinity. Two unopened bags of salt and a sleeping bag on the passenger seat are the only clues as to the owner.

Turning round, I can hear a faint metallic noise in the distance. I can see something now, at the top of the hill on the opposite side of the pass. A small white handkerchief coming towards me. Some black specks running around the hem, barking. A taller blob behind. There are some more specks hovering overhead.

I'm not sure if it is the birds, the dogs, or the shepherd which are encouraging them the most, but the sheep are now almost running down the ridge. Finally in the valley, the dogs corral them into a neat rectangle and sit down.

An hour later, the path surmounts a small hummock and heads in the direction of the sun. Blinded, I can hardly see anything, but there seems to be a helicopter, a large tent, a humming generator, and a white van in a temporary enclosure. There are several people milling about. Has there been an accident? I can't understand what is happening. Until I get closer and notice the cows. The shining dome is a refrigeration unit. The tent harbours a milking station.

'As far as I know we are the only people to work like this,' the man tells me. 'We have 39 cows. As they go up the hill in search of new pasture we follow them.'

'Where have you come from today ?' he asks me.

'The Cabane d'Aula.'

'Where's that? We've only been here since November.'

I explain. 'Where were you before you moved here, then?' I ask.

'Near Le Mans.'

He tells me that they were attracted by the subsidies, which are not available in northern France.

At the Col de Pause, I take a break, walking a little off the path, to find some shade. Much further down the valley, when the Pyrenean Way has joined a tarmac road, I meet a white-bearded Rumpelstiltskin with a rucksack even bigger than Martin's. He is hobbling, not because he has stamped on the ground in anger, but because his walking stick is too short. In fact it isn't a walking stick; it is a brand new ice axe which barely reaches up to his knee. In order to use it he has to bend over to one side. He looks decidedly unstable. We don't swap names.

Then I walk through a couple of chocolate box villages down to Couflens, a village – and a valley – which seems to have missed several opportunities. The port de Salau at the head of the valley is one of the lowest passes into Spain in the Ariège and attracted pilgrims and travellers from an early date. According to Joanne, writing in 1858, 26,000 people passed through the frontier here each year. There were even projects for a cross-frontier road and a railway in the 19th century but they came to nothing. Then there was the paper factory – which closed in the 1920s – and the tungsten mine – which closed in 1986. But now there is not even a shop.

Maurice is already here – he must have passed me at the Col de Pause – eating lunch in a *lavoir* which has been converted into a covered picnic area. A female cyclist is telling him the intimate details of her double hip replacement. Not wanting to disturb them, and scenting the proximity of the public toilets, I decide to race for Rouze in the hope of finding sustenance at the hostel.

The track up to Rouze is typical of the Ariège foothills. The path rises slowly through the trees – two-fifths of the Ariège is covered in forest – following a small stream. Although we are well into summer, the ground is squishy from recent storms. Underfoot, ferns and grass alternate with cow pats and horseflies. Former habitation is represented by remains ranging from nettle-covered mounds, through piles of stones, to ruins. Where the path approaches a road, the ruins have been renovated. The numerous electric fences have insulated handles to allow walkers to unhook the wire and pass through unscathed.

In Rouze I am supplied with a very large, very red, very juicy tomato – which soaks up the enormous quantities of salt and garlic I sprinkle onto it – some bread, and some goat's cheese, before being shooed away from the table on the terrace outside the house.

'There's one outside the dormitory just up there, which will be more convenient for you,' says Jean-Pierre, the farmer. 'I'm going away for the afternoon, but make yourself at home.'

Maurice arrives while I am eating. He had intended to go further but the heat and the lack of a hat have discouraged him. The heat intensifies but clouds start to arrive from Spain, billowing at first, then blackening. By 4 o'clock it is raining. Through the window of the hostel, we can see the lightning striking the Valier. Half an hour later the farm is awash, the lightning and thunder all around. *Ça pisse la vache*, it is raining like a cow pisses.

A voluminous, agitated mass runs up the steps outside, taking them two at a time. The door opens and the mass divests itself of its outer layers leaving rucksack, anorak, pullover, and boots in a sad, damp, inert pile on the floor, and a jumpy, shivering man in front of us. It is as if all the energy has been sucked out of the discarded shell and concentrated in the man himself.

'... twenty minutes from Couflens,' he gasps. It took *me* thirty and I thought I was doing well.

'Sit down and have a cup of tea,' I suggest.

'Yes,' he replies, but he remains standing up, jigging from one leg to the other, shaking his head, distributing droplets around him.

'I don't understand it,' he continues. 'I don't normally get shocked by electric fences. But every one of them between Couflens and here gave me a shock.'

'You did use the handles, didn't you?'

'Yes, but I don't understand it. There were nine fences. I counted them. Each with two wires. Eighteen shocks. By the time I saw the farm, I was dreading each new fence because I knew what was going to happen as soon as I gripped the handle.'

'It must be the rain. The handles were wet so they were conducting the electricity.'

'I don't understand it,' he repeats mechanically. 'I don't understand it.'

Yann has come from Seix this morning, doing the journey which took Maurice and me two days in eight and a half hours. He left Hendaye ten days after Maurice. This is his second time. Last time he had a heavy sack. This time he is relying on walking fast and short cuts to get him to a hostel each night.

In the evening Caroline, the farmer's wife, serves us a meal which includes goat, the unfortunate son of one of those bleating in the barn outside.

'Have you lost a hat?' she ask Maurice.

'Yes,' he replies, surprised.

'Gila has just rung me up. She has been given one which was found on the path. She recognised it. She will bring it to the shop in St Lizier d'Ustou for you tomorrow.'

We can hear distant rumblings but the storm is all but finished.

'There's one good thing about the thunderstorm,' she tells us. 'It will get rid of the horseflies. They used to be a real problem for us until we had the Pyrenean Way diverted. At first we thought it was a good thing to have it pass directly in front of our door. Walkers couldn't fail to notice us. But the walkers brought their horseflies with them – they are attracted by the sweat – and sat down at the table on our terrace just outside our front door. They either went on walking, or they stayed in the hostel, but in either case they left us their flies.'

While we are eating the pineapple and watermelon salad Maurice asks: 'Is it always like this or do you have more guests usually?'

'From next week we are full up for the rest of the season. But we are really handicapped by the Cabane d'Aula. Nobody wants to stay there. So they take the short cut and then don't come here. There has been money earmarked for renovation for the last ten years but one of the shepherds up there doesn't like tourists so it has never happened. Sometimes we are nearly empty,' she shrugs. 'One night last week there was only one person here. A man doing the Pyrenean Way like you. A nice chap, we had a good chat. A hunchback from...'

'What was he called?' I interrupt.

'I don't know. He was retired, with silver hair. Small.'

'It must be Paul.' I explain that know Paul from two years ago. 'Which night did he pass through?'

'Last Thursday.' Today is Monday. It is unlikely that I will catch up with him.

Rouze to Aulus

I have miscalculated. I have become so obsessed with avoiding the afternoon monsoon that I get up even earlier than yesterday. But the path dives directly into the forest darkness and I have to put on my head-torch for the first half hour. Although it is refreshingly cool to start with, by the time I arrive at St Lizier d'Ustou I am wilting.

I can see a Heineken sign. As I approach, my Pavlovian reaction is discouraged by the sight of a menu with prices still in francs, and eliminated when the door refuses to budge. On the other hand, the shop is open. The baskets outside are filled with fruit and vegetables and the smell of fresh bread fills the air. It is the first shop I have seen since Luchon.

According to the *FFRP Guide* this is the only shop actually *on* the Pyrenean Way for the whole of the Ariège. Indeed, with one or two notable exceptions, the Ariège mountains are where rural development stopped. To what extent is this deliberate? To what extent is it bad planning?

Certainly, the Ariège is *authentique* and it wants to stay that way. *Authentique* is a word which goes much further than its English equivalent. In the Ariège, it encompasses the landscape, the buildings, the people, and their ideas. Above all it means: leave us to make our own decisions. Paris is to be kept at a distance.

Three illustrations. Firstly, the medieval *lies et passeries*, like those of La Pierre-St Martin further west, demonstrate that local priorities could transcended national boundaries. Secondly, the *Guerre des demoiselles*, a 19th-century rebellion centred on the Ariège, contested a national law limiting pasture rights and wood gathering. Thirdly, Occitan, not French, was the local language until the second half of the 19th century. The battle of the bear is just the latest explosion in a long-running guerrilla war.

'*La montagne aux montagnards* – the mountains belong to those who live here' is the rallying cry, a slogan which is resuscitated for every social conflict in which local interests seem threatened. In 1979 it united the opposition to a project to create a National Park covering the area round the Valier. National Parks provide the administrative structure for protecting and managing a natural environment, an idea which at first sight might seem to be a guarantee of the future *authenticité* of the area. It was rejected by the vast majority of the 59 communes concerned.

In 2005 a new project was born: a Regional Natural Park. The name suggest that this too will be an instrument for preserving the natural environment, also possibly to the detriment of human activities. Yet the idea is popular, with 145 communes – over half the *département* – participating in its construction. Why? Partly because the initiative came from the Ariège and not from outside, but mainly I suspect because its primary aim is presented as sustainable economic development, not nature conservation.

I apply a litmus test to the Park's website. What is its position on the reintroduction of bears? The most telling document is a SWOT analysis where bears appear as a strength, a weakness, an opportunity, and a threat! The only thing which unites the protagonists it that they don't want to argue about the issue.

Nevertheless, with the right therapy for its schizophrenia, the Park could present a way forward for local development, and certainly an efficient milking machine for government and European subsidies.

I open the door of the shop and enter a realm where everyday items have acquired a different meaning. The cavern is just big enough for two aisles and a central reservation. The shelves are packed and the tunnels between them correspondingly narrow. Customers can circulate, as long as they keep their elbows strictly under control, and as long as they all go in the same direction. Feverishly, I stuff my basket with luxuries: a kilo of golden, honey-smelling grapes, two very large, very orange carrots, some slices of freshly cut ham, smelling of salt, a *pain au chocolat* oozing its soft treasure, three Mars bars, three Lion bars, three Nuts bars, a packet of biscuits, a packet of olives – dried Greek ones, nice and salty, and a large can of ice tea. I add several other items and then remove them. On my second time round, in the gloom at the back of the shop, I meet a blue woman. She wasn't there the first time and there are no doors through which she could have come. She is blue from foot to head: Blue toenails, blue jeans, a blue tee-shirt, blue lipstick, and blue hair.

In the ordinary insanity of the outside world, sitting on a bench in the car park, I consume a second breakfast. Half an hour later I am struggling up the slope with a bloated stomach and leaden feet. I calculate that my rucksack is 5kg heavier than it was before my shopping spree, taking into account the two litres of water I added. I stop and throw away the remaining grapes, all the olives, and the two carrots, and empty out half of my water. I eat a Mars and a Lion bar.

Still, it doesn't make much difference to my energy levels so I take off my tee-shirt. (Approximately half the energy consumed in mountain walking goes in keeping cool. So any other means of refrigeration helps.)

By the time I arrive at the Col d'Escots at the top of the Guzet-Neige ski slopes I have eaten two breakfasts, lunch, and several snacks. The weight which was once in my rucksack is now burdening my gurgling stomach. My feet are complaining as well. There is a restaurant here; it is open; I am furious. I push down a couple of ice teas for the sake of it.

Now well above the tree line, the path flanks the mountain and I walk progressively faster as the clouds gather, blacken, and start to relieve themselves of their load. Very exposed and still a long way from shelter, I speed up some more, hoping to reach the forest before the lightning strikes. Then, a long, long clap of thunder rolls from horizon to horizon and, although I don't see the lightning, I fear that the storm is about to start in earnest. But instead of announcing the end of the world, the celestial belch seems to have resolved the meteorological indigestion. A sudden wind, and the clouds begin to disintegrate.

In the forest – except for the victim of a previous cataclysm, its contorted, sea-washed-white branches piled up like flotsam around a vain stump – the trees also are reassured. But they have suffered over the years, and not just from natural forces.

From 1829 to 1832 this area was the epicentre of a battle over the right to use the forest and its products: the *Guerre des demoiselles*. A literal translation would be the War of the Damsels, but I prefer to call it the Fancy Dress War. The 'warriors' – men – didn't wear women's dresses as some literature claims. All they did was pull their shirts out of their trousers. But this was considered sufficiently outlandish that it became their defining characteristic.

In addition, to disguise themselves, they blacked-up their faces with charcoal or covered them with scarves or animal skins. Just as they might have done for the annual carnival, when the normal rules of society were relaxed, and minor transgressions went unpunished. But the transgressions were not minor, and the psychological consequences are still evident. For the inhabitants of the Ariège, the *Guerre des demoiselles* remains a victory for local pastoralists against Paris-imposed foresters. So much so that in 2006, in an anti-bear march in Luchon, some of the demonstrators dressed as *demoiselles*, perhaps partly to hide themselves from police cameras, but mainly to remind onlookers of their latent power: in the 19th century the *demoiselles* had delayed and in some cases stopped the government's plans for reforestation.

In 1827 the government, concerned by a degradation of the nation's forests, had passed a law restricting access to them. But the Pyrenees were suffering from the effects of a growing population – it doubled between 1741 and 1846 – and every scrap of land was vital. The woods has always been used by the peasants: for building, for firewood, for food, and even for pasture – they were often not very dense. They were part of the local economy to the extent that the peasants confused use with ownership. The fact that the forests didn't actually belong to them, the vital one-tenth of the law, was of no concern.

For the government, one of the bones of contention was the way the locals managed the forests. A few trees would be left to grow to maturity but the ones around them would be culled young, often damaging the remaining stands. Self-seeded trees would be left to grow wherever they sprouted. The state-trained foresters disparaged this as *jardinage*, gardening. For them, the only way to manage a forest was to plant a zone, let it grow to maturity, and then raze it all at one fell swoop.

In peasant eyes there were three enemies, the state, bourgeois landowners, and industrialists, the first two trying to protect the forests from intrusion and the last destroying the forest for charcoal production for their iron furnaces. On 27 January 1830, 400–500 demonstrators marched on Massat just down the valley from here, crying 'Death to the forest guards'. A month later there were twice as many. The month of May saw an assault on the house of a forest guard who killed one of the attackers in self defence. On 15 August the inhabitants of the Ustou valley, armed with axes and sticks, besieged the mayor's house and burnt it down.

The government capitulated, granting an amnesty and temporarily restoring grazing rights. But the dissatisfaction – and sporadic outbursts of violence – continued, with pastoralists sometimes going as far as to endanger their own communities, as in the village of Arac which suffered frequent winter avalanches. When, in 1908, the villagers petitioned the authorities for reforestation to protect them, it was refused on the grounds that it was a waste of time; local shepherds were still repeatedly burning the heath and the young forest which might have held the snow in place. The lessons of Barèges had still not been learned.

By the 1930s, peace had returned to the forests, but not as a result of a crushing victory for one side or the other. Quite simply, the human population had declined; there was no longer the need to exploit every pocket-handkerchief pasture. Paradoxically, although the forest was now largely managed by state-trained foresters, *jardinage* and related practices had been rehabilitated. As Tamara Whited says, they were now considered to be

> a remarkable way of allowing sufficient shade and protection for young beeches and firs, preventing erosion, and mitigating damage from livestock… [*Jardinage*] produces the impression of a devastation; and yet this method, practiced for centuries along the entire range of the Pyrenees has assured the conservation of beech forests.

A long-retired forester and a wiry old peasant are sitting side-by-side on a bench overlooking the valley. For a century they have been looking at the same landscape, but the forester saw the woods whilst the peasant saw the trees. Now, finally, they are beginning to see the same thing.

The Pyrenean Way turns right but, needing supplies, I head straight on for the village in the valley. The road sign proudly proclaims 'Aulus-les-Bains, the cholesterol spa'. Aulus, like most Pyrenean spas, has been reinventing itself. Before the discovery of penicillin the road signs at the entrance to the village read 'Aulus-les-Bains, the syphilis spa'. Probably not. But venereal diseases were a speciality, and the arrival of penicillin was one factor in the spa's temporary closure. With cholesterol it has found itself a new disease, and a new spa building opened in 1989. It has also found itself a new vocation: there is now a leisure pool and a sauna.

At the same time that the syphilitic patients were flocking to Aulus and the shepherds were fighting a rearguard action against the foresters, the village – along with neighbouring Ercé and Ustou – was also famous for another activity: bear taming. In the 1880s, with a burgeoning population, any source of income was welcomed, and bears were literally part of daily life for 200 households in the valley, practically living with the family. They were trained to dance and perform tricks, and then taken throughout Europe and across the Atlantic. In Central Park, New York, the Rock of Ercé is a reminder of the American connection. When there were no longer enough bears left in the Ariège they were imported as cubs from the Caucasus.

The village is pleasant – even in the rain, for the storm has returned – the hostel Le Presbytère excellent, and the company at table friendly. Apart from me, there are eight Dutch people and one Frenchman. I learn that in Amsterdam if you wish to hire a bicycle, and even if both you and the bicycle's owner are Dutch, you will conduct the transaction in English. Even so, I am told, the Dutch do not feel they are being swamped by American culture.

Julie, from the Lac d'Araing hostel, was here last night but went on this morning. Maurice, on the other hand, hasn't arrived.

Aulus to Marc

The graffito on the road out of town reads:

Mushrooms, wood, etc. Collect them on your own property.

A little higher up, just in case the reader is in any doubt as to the author, there is another graffito, reading 'Private property', with an arrow pointing to the right. I interpret this as an act of defiance aimed at latter-day *demoiselles*.

In the woods, still dark, I can hear a wild but distinctly human voice crying: 'Eyow, eyow,' repeated plaintively again and again. And behind it, a waterfall crashing down the hillside. The waterfall can't be the famous Cascade d'Ars because it is on the other side of the valley. No, the waterfall is in the same direction as the voice, its inarticulate sound confused by its passage through the branches. As I move, and the light begins to penetrate the woods, the waterfall and the voice seem to move as well. Then, without warning, the sound disintegrates into a hundred quivering bells intermingled with the sound of hooves on rock. Now I can see them. The cows are being brought back from their somnambulant wanderings to their daytime pasture. I arrive at the Coumebière at the same time as the herd, which spreads out, preparing the meadow for its morning shave.

In places the mountain's skin is pock marked, its bones exposed, not through an excessive zeal on the part of the cows, but as the result of old injuries, not yet quite healed, from the mines.

At the Port de Salcix, a few hundred metres above, the Pyrenean Way turns to the south, bouncing up and down across rocks seemingly claw-marked by giant eagles, the limestone also speckled with myriad tiny lakes. At each one I fill my hat and pour the water over my head, shivering deliciously for a few seconds.

As I approach the edge of the plateau, the limestone is replaced by red-brown schist and the silence penetrated by a pneumatic drill. Down below, the Bassiès hostel, isolated at the end of a long valley two hours' walk from the nearest road, is being attacked. A small mechanical digger and a trio of workers are laying waste to an area behind the building.

Once inside it, I sit down at a table. There is a printed menu! I have never before seen a menu in an isolated hostel. It is difficult enough to put together a set meal in these conditions, never mind trying to cater for individual whims. I am stunned.

The manager, a small, stiff man with short-cropped hair, marches up to me and asks:

'Your order, sir?'

'I'll have the sea bream, please'

'Yes, sir. Straight away.'

He barks at a thin, nervous-looking woman in the kitchen.

When I ask about the building works, he tells me that the hostel is being renovated.

'I've just taken it over, this year. Today's walkers demand better quality food and proper bedrooms. I'm replacing the dormitories with smaller rooms.'

He'll have to do something about the toilets, then. Yesterday's walkers can understand that they can be completely out of order, but today's walkers won't want to expose their backsides behind a bush.

Digesting comfortably, I squelch unhurriedly across the reedy lake shore back to the trail. The waymarks have been repainted with military precision but, apart from a couple of unobtrusive reservoirs, the valley remains unconquered. At the end of it, the path descends steeply and then strides along a mossy concrete-covered aqueduct which has been carved out of the hillside. From time to time, gaping tunnels at the side of the path exhale their refreshingly cool mountain breath, dribbling a few more drops of saliva into the channel.

The end of the aqueduct is marked by a road sign offering the delectable alternative directions of Les Toutous d'en Haut or Les Toutous d'en Bas – literally the High Doggies or the Low Doggies. I choose the Low Doggies and go down to Marc.

Marc is an old hamlet, but surrounded by thoroughly new chalets. Bikini-clad teenage girls are walking back from the swimming pool. On the other side of the road, boys of their age are milling around, studiously ignoring them. Neither group believes that there is a hostel here. A holiday village, yes. But nothing as down-market as a hostel. Eventually I find the holiday village reception and despite my incongruity, I am made to feel welcome. Yes, there is a hostel, just next door.

It was evidently built for the purpose. For those who are doing their own cooking, the kitchen has a fridge, cooking equipment, and Formica surfaces everywhere. 'Choose whichever bedroom you like,' I have been told, 'there is nobody else yet'. The establishment is spotless.

Later, a man and a woman of my age arrive and then flit out again, taking their microcosm with them. So I go down to the bar, where one of the staff is trying to break the ice with a general knowledge quiz. In the evening I am placed at a table on my own in the restaurant and served quickly.

The room fills up with families and small groups who keep themselves to themselves. They are all dressed in clean clothes, conspicuously ironed . From overheard conversations I gather that quite a few people are going walking. I have, indeed, seen posters for organised trips with guides – don't go walking on your own, it's not safe, they imply. These holidaymakers must be 'today's walkers'.

All the same, I am really looking forward to the bed with its wonderfully silky, laundry-fresh white sheets.

Marc to Goulier

I walk in the murky gloom to the hamlet of Mounicou, and then under a volcanic sky up through the forest ablaze with the first shafts of sunlight. Yet, as the morning advances, the clearing sky belies the dawn's humid prediction. It is going to be hot again.

After diving down to the postcard-village of Arties and then scaling the other side of the Vicdessos valley, the path discovers the languorous virtues of contours, snaking along a mule-track balcony. I think I hear a cicada. It is as if the Mediterranean has advanced inland along with the sun.

Down below, in Auzat the long red necks of mechanical vultures are stretching out over the concrete carcass of what was once an aluminium smelter. Their beaks tug at its entrails, extracting the last lifeblood from the valley. The industrial carnage marks the end of a long association with mining and metallurgy. This time, the fate of the valley was decided elsewhere, but even when control of the industry was in local hands the valley fared little better. There were significant mineral resources here: nearby Rancié was the biggest single iron ore mine in the whole of the Pyrenees.

> All the inhabitants of the Vicdessos valley have the right to work there but their job is not determined by their aptitudes but by their village of origin. Those from Sem, Olbier, and Goulier work at the face, while the nine other villages furnish the transport and organise the commercialisation. As with the sheep pasture, the valley council decides the number of baskets the miners are authorised to extract; it fixes the working hours, and the price.

Production had started before 1293, when the mine is first mentioned in a charter. But the operation was anarchic, resulting in much wastage and numerous accidents. Like Bentaillou, in its 19th-century heyday, the mine provided work for 400, but it closed definitively in 1929. One estimate suggests that up to six million tonnes of iron ore were extracted. In the process, immense areas of woods were destroyed for shoring and the production of charcoal for the smelters. Only a concerted effort by the ONF and its predecessors has managed to restore the forest cover. The village of Sem, next to the mine and once a thriving community, today has a population of 19.

Some French Pyrenean valleys have managed to take a resource and make a living out of it, a living which is still economically viable in the 20th century. The spas, because the resource is still there. Summer and winter tourism around a few exceptional sites. But mineral resources have only provided a passing wealth. Even hydroelectricity, the great hope for the valley of Vicdessos, has finally left it impoverished, with the departure of the aluminium smelter in 2003 and the loss of 270 jobs. Elsewhere, only Saint-Lary has managed better – again in the domain of hydroelectricity – capitalising on a short-term income to assure its long-term future.

I arrive at Goulier in the middle of the afternoon. The outskirts of the village are well kept, with neatly-mown grass and hollyhocks ranged in municipal flowerbeds, but the interior presents a different picture. A terraced row of two-storey houses seems to encapsulate it.

The first cottage is roofed with excruciatingly uniform, rectangular mechanical tiles. A modern window reflects the sun, drawing attention to itself. The walls are carefully rendered. The shutters, however, are firmly closed.

The next house is covered with small *lauzes*, traditional rounded tiles made of schist, in a multitude of shades of grey and brown. There are no obvious gaps but regular undulations suggest both the positions of the rafters and a collapse not too far into the future. The rendering is cracked and large parts of it are missing completely, exposing rough stonework.

The owner of the third house has obviously taken to heart the advice that any renovation work should begin with the roof. It is made of new, half-moon shaped mechanical tiles and has a gutter. But there is nothing below the gutter. Literally nothing: I can see through the house to the trees on the other side. A couple of rusty acrow props hold up the roof, themselves supported on the crumbling walls of the ground floor. The shutters are falling off their hinges.

The roof of the fourth house is rusty corrugated iron but the guttering is new and the rendering intact. A sun umbrella is leaning against the door.

Elsewhere in the village, carefully tended geraniums, ivy, and honeysuckle climb up the walls. Despite the heat, water is everywhere, trickling along the channels at the side of the narrow streets, pouring out of fountains. Although cars could theoretically pass through, albeit at the risk of scratching their bodywork, they are banned.

Frequently, the houses are pierced by cobbled *passarots* leading through to another street, each neatly labelled with a wooden plaque: one of them, the passarot Micoòu, was created in 1832. Although there are some passages through houses in other Pyrenean villages, Goulier has an exceptional number of them. I realise, eventually, that *passerot* is a misnomer. They are not so much passages dug through existing buildings, as the opening left when a neighbouring house was extended over the street at the height of the 19th-century mining-driven population boom.

In the 21st century the population is also changing: on the village notice board I read:

The 'Friends of Goulier' Association
Do you have a project for activities, exhibitions linked to our village? Would you like to publish an article or a photo in our 6-monthly journal? Don't hesitate to tell us about your ideas, by letter, email or when we meet in the streets of Goulier.

The address of the president is in *Toulouse*, 120km away. And then there is the mayor's New Year message:

Luchon–Mérens: Ariège, terre courage

The soil of our ancestors, though engraved in our hearts, does not belong to us. Wherever you may have been born, wherever you may have lived, if – respecting our traditions – you have decided to put down roots here, you have the right to do so. You have chosen Goulier, Vicdessos, and the Ariège and from now on, like us, with passion and affection, talk, write, be active: make them live.

In the evening Veronica, my wife, comes to join me, bringing dehydrated supplies and warm cuddles from the Corbières where we live. I decide to have a day's rest at the Relais d'Endron.

Goulier

In the morning after Veronica's departure, I meander lazily around the village, following the road which leads up to the ski resort. At the first bend there is an *orry*, the local equivalent of the Basque *cayolar*.

Orrys are dry-stone huts, occasionally rectangular, but usually circular. Built like igloos and covered with stone and turf, reeking of smoke, sweat, and lanolin, they provided shelter for shepherds in the *estives*. In the better class of *orry* a raised stone platform served as a bed; otherwise heather provided the only comfort. Their construction is so rudimentary that it is impossible to tell how old they are: dry-stone buildings like these first appeared in the Neolithic. Indeed, some of the surviving ones may have been in use, every summer, for centuries. Then husbandry practices changed: for the last 50 years they have remained empty.

Made of newly hewn stone, kept clean by designated staff, out of context at the edge of the village instead of lost on a mountain slope, this *orry* is a parody of its ancestors. Or perhaps I am missing its deeper artistic significance. Is it a subtle combination of performance art and sculpture, a critique of modern rural life? A reflection on the changing world of shepherds? There are still *patous* and sheep gathering around the *orry* but the new *patous* sit behind the steering wheels of excursion coaches, and the new sheep have two legs.

Meanwhile real *orrys* are decaying, neglected on the hillside.

Further up the road, two megaliths straddle a spring. A notice explains that they are cup and ring stones, each stone being marked by three hollows and a crudely incised ring which in themselves could be the work of nature – except that there are two of them and that they were found side by side. The notice also explains that they don't belong here. They probably come from a prehistoric site further up the valley know as the *camp de la breiches*, the wizards' field, where there are other cup-and-ring stones 'some of which have been, alas, destroyed during the construction of the road'.

There is a third tourist attraction a little further along. This too is out of context. But in this case the town council can't be blamed. The 'Roco de Goutelhe' is an enormous glacial erratic.

I sit down on a bench outside the Swiss-chalet-style town hall. On the gravel esplanade in front of it, four teams are playing *pétanque*: a second swallow-sign, after the cicadas. Maurice limps up and slumps down onto the bench. He has walked all the way from the hostel at Bassiès today, a stupendous feat. He is looking for somewhere to pitch his tent and, although I suggest that he sleeps in the *orry*, decides to camp outside the village.

I have booked Maurice in for dinner and we are both standing at the bar drinking mead when a local resident enters. Maurice is very good at striking up a conversation with strangers and when we sit down to eat he asks Arthur to join us.

I ask him to interpret the mayor's homily to newcomers 'The soil of our ancestors…'

'He has a poetic turn of phrase. But there is a problem with second homes. Not only do they put the prices up but the owners don't understand what is good for the village. They don't even understand village politics. It's not a matter of ideas. It's not even a matter of personalities. It's all a matter of clans. It is the same in all villages. They don't understand that.'

'House prices have gone up enormously,' he carries on. 'I reckon mine is worth eight times what I paid for it. But this isn't a good thing. Youngsters can no longer afford to buy property in the village where they were born.'

I ask him about another item on the village notice board:

Letter of support for the mayor, published in the *Dépeche du Midi* newspaper, May 2006.

The town councillors of Goulier, whatever their individual position on the reintroduction of bears in the Pyrenees, unanimously and unconditionally support its mayor, Claude Théron. They strongly condemn the insults and death threats made against him and his family in an anonymous letter from the group 'kill the bears'. The council considers that such methods are unacceptable in a democracy. It hopes that the writers will be identified rapidly and made to realise the gravity of their actions.

Arthur leans towards me, conspiratorially.

'I don't want to speak too loud, because I'm friendly with the people who run the hostel and I don't want to start an argument. The manager and his wife are outsiders, not only because the hostel is on the edge of the village, but also socially. So they don't cause any problems, and they don't have any problems. They are perfectly well accepted like that … as long as they don't talk about bears,' he whispers. 'I can't see how you can live in a village like this and be in favour of the reintroductions. My shepherd neighbours fear that they will discover a massacre each time they go up to the *estives*.'

I am reminded of the possibly apocryphal story of the death of Gaston Fébus as related by a guide at the Foix château, here in the Ariège. Gaston was one of the greatest Pyreneans of all time.

A renowned diplomat and a redoubtable warrior, he carved out a sphere of influence which spanned two-thirds of the length of the Pyrenees in the 14th century. He was also a passionate hunter, writing a hunting manual which still commands respect today. Unsurprisingly, perhaps, he died as the result of a hunting incident. But the manner of his death was unpredictable. He wasn't mauled by a bear or crushed in its unloving arms. He was simply startled by one appearing unexpectedly nearby, the fright provoking a cerebral haemorrhage. The bear left him untouched. Will Pyrenean sheep farming die like Gaston Fébus, I wonder, not because of the damage caused by the bears themselves, but from fear of them?

Arthur changes the subject, pointing out a small statue of a bear on the mantelpiece.

'Look carefully and you will see that it's made of two sorts of talc, one bluish, and the other pure white. I used to work in the quarry where the talc is dug up.' And so we talk about the quarry instead.

'When you get to the Plateau de Beille, you can't miss it,' he predicts.

Goulier to Col de Sasc

I walk for three and a half hours before I meet anybody, a typical early morning experience.

'I've seen lots of shepherd's huts but I didn't notice any for walkers,' a man coming the other way tells me.

The *FFRP Guide* says that there is a hut at the Col de Sasc: '1798m. Spring... shelter possible mid-slope, four places, without amenities.'

The clouds are low today. They almost touch the tops of the trees but the path is dry as it climbs up to the pass and down into the valley of Siguer. Just before the village, a large poster announces an all-day *pétanque* contest. Just after it, a hang glider circles on a thermal. The sun has melted the clouds and I am beginning to roast.

Then, approaching the Col de Sasc, I see a herd of cows, eying me up.

Yann, whom I met at Rouze, warned me about these very beasts, just here.

'We were walking along the path when the cows started to follow us, and then started to run after us. We started to run too. In the end, we only escaped by jumping into a ravine. The cows were at the very edge with their front hooves in the air! I was terrified but not half as much as my friend. She was brought up on a farm with cows. She couldn't believe that they could behave like that. Later, we met a local and explained what had happened. He asked me to turn round, and pointed to the black plastic bag for rubbish tied to my rucksack. "It's your bag," he said. "The cowhand has just gone down into the valley to get some salt because it has run out. Your bag makes a rustling sound like a sack of salt being opened. Cows go mad for it."'

Today, the cows must have already had their fix. They ignore me, and shortly afterwards I reach my destination. I have been guzzling water in anticipation of filling up at the spring but when I find it, the water is weeping rather than flowing out of the ground. Not only that, but the tears emerge at ground level. There is no way of putting my mouth, a bottle, or even my hands under it. After a few languid centimetres the water disappears into spongy, muddy peat. I get out my plastic spoon and start scraping to create a hollow.

From the Col de Sasc I can see, down below, what must be the hut described in the *FFRP Guide*.

The Cabane du Besset d'en Haut is as adequate as the spring. The size of a garden shed, it is built of breeze blocks and has gaping holes where there might once have been a door and a window. Inside, the walls are decorated with graffiti graphically evoking the pleasures of cannabis, or possibly the horrors of delirium tremens. The evidence of drug consumption, however, is limited to a single empty bottle of *vin de pays* and two beer bottles. The floor is concrete, with a stained

Goulier to Col de Sasc

piece of foam rubber pushed into one corner. Apart from a burnt-out Baby Belling and an empty gas cylinder, that's it. I unroll my sleeping bag and take a siesta.

I am woken up by Maurice.

'I'm going to camp a couple of hundred metres away. There's just a little bit of flat ground, next to the spring.'

'A real spring?'

'With a cistern and a tap.'

I pour out the brownish fluid in my bottle and go to fill it up.

Later, whilst waiting for my dehydrated rations to reconstitute, I look over the valley to the east. The grass and shrubs, the soft verdant contours nearby, give way to banks of black conifers spilling over into the gulf carved out by the river Ariège. Beyond, the sharp grey angles of the St Barthélemy mountain are accentuated by the low sunlight.

Every one minute and thirty seconds precisely an aircraft passes silently high overhead on its way to Barcelona. Two, three, four. My dinner must be ready by now. Tomorrow, at least I will be able to eat a proper meal in the restaurant on the Plateau de Beille.

The sun dips behind the ridge, although it won't set for several hours. Instantly the heat is sucked out of the air and the cooling process begins. I go to see Maurice, who is already in his sleeping bag in his tent. He shows me the video he has taken of a herd of *isards* – 30 or so – which he came across first thing this morning. His mobile phone rings. Near ski resorts, and rarely elsewhere, mobile phones work. Afterwards he says:

'To hide nothing from you, I will probably go to the Rulhe hostel tomorrow evening. So I will arrive at Mérens on Monday and have a chance to rest before my friends arrive.'

I go back to my cold-store hut telling myself that I will go up to the ridge to see the sunset, but by 8 o'clock I am shivering. I get into my sleeping bag and doze fitfully, woken up by aches in my feet spreading out from the blisters on toes and heels. I am also too hot – it *is* a good sleeping bag.

Luchon–Mérens: Ariège, terre courage

Col de Sasc to Plateau de Beille

The sun climbs over the horizon, at first cold, turning from purple through crimson and then melting, through orange to white hot, flowing down the slopes of St Barthélemy announcing the day to come. My shadow is as long as the mountain itself. The horses and cows are already at work but their foreman at the Cabane de Courtal Marti is still slumbering. Even his two barking dogs don't bring him out.

I steer well clear of his hut, its white van, and the dogs, but I see that there is a second hut. Opening its door reveals the mountain nest of my dreams. Clean mattresses, wood for a fire – clearly, it has recently been converted for walkers. Needless to say it doesn't feature in the *FFRP Guide*. It was empty last night: a spider has had the time to spin a web between the bedposts, now refracting radial rainbows in the crack of light coming through the door.

Down in the first valley of the day I struggle through ferns on a neglected section of the Pyrenean Way. At the top of the next hill, Maurice catches up with me and we walk a while together, getting lost and found again, until my right knee lets out a sharp pain, and I sit down to give it a rest.

Water is running out and I am correspondingly dried out when I start the final ascent to the Plateau de Beille, through the woods in the stifling heat. I don't appreciate the climb at all, even though the sun's ardour is diminished by the foliage. The path has become a multitude of possibilities, each as contrary as its neighbour, between waymarks spaced too far apart. When I emerge into the full sun at the edge of the plateau, the only thing I really want to do is to lie down with my eyes shut. I press on because the restaurant has promised me that I will be able to eat a proper meal at a real table, with cool beer, *if* I arrive before 14:00.

I have a few minutes to spare. Maurice is sitting at a table outside, and is just about to get up and go on.

'It's full. I've been here about half an hour but it was already too late. They might be persuaded to do you a sandwich.'

I eat several baguettes and drink many cans of ice tea. There are perhaps 20 people sitting at tables on the terrace, under red and yellow sun shades, nibbling sandwiches or sipping beer, sucking Coca-Cola through straws, mostly family groups. A cowhand ushers his herd in front of us and within seconds the terrace empties.

'*Regardez. Vaches sauvages* – Look. Wild cows,' says one woman.

I count 16 adults and children, cameras clicking, striding towards them.

I ask one of the waiters if I can sleep at the Cabane de Beille d'en Haut, which is a designated hut according to the *FFRP Guide*.

'Yes, there are three parts. One for the shepherd, one for walkers.' He doesn't specify the use of the third part.

Here I could buy postcards, knurled walking sticks, whistling *marmottes*, or sweets. But not food to take away. The Plateau de Beille is primarily a ski resort, doing its best to promote a summer season.

I waddle out of the building dragging my rucksack and then try to put it on. My stomach bulges out between the straps. I have just bought a litre and a half of bottled water to supplement the three litres that I took from the tap. With all this extra baggage, I am carrying eight kilos more than I was when I arrived. I walk past a hut labelled 'Base Angaka: dog sledding', pining for snow, a pack of willing huskies, and a sleigh to whisk me off comfortably up the hill to my hut.

An hour later, on a dirt track, I am passed by a white four-wheel drive vehicle, with three collies yelping in the back. When I arrive at the hut five minutes later, the car is parked next to it but there is no sign of the shepherd or dogs. I knock on the door.

'*Putain de merde* – fucking hell!' shouts the cowhand as he explodes through the door in his underwear, followed by his three growling dogs.

'I'm sorry to have disturbed you,' I reply, 'but I have been told there is a part for walkers.'

'No!' he spits at me. 'There isn't. In any case it is occupied. And it is only for when it is hailing.'

'It was the waiter at the restaurant who told me. If you don't want to be disturbed you'll have to see him.'

'That's bullshit. Bullshit. In any case, it will be fine this evening. Everyone under his own roof.'

He ushers the dogs back inside and slams the door.

I walk another two kilometres to an *orry* marked on the map. This is a step down from yesterday's accommodation. It is not a Goulier built-for-tourists high class *orry*. There is no shelf for a bed. The floor is a mixture of mud and sheep shit, and the roof doesn't look too stable. Its earth covering has washed away leaving gaps open to the elements. Until recently the motto of the *département* was *Ariège: terre courage* – land of courage. I am beginning to see why.

I decide to sleep in the open air and start cutting heather, still partly in flower, and sweet-smelling pine branches. Lighting a pine cone fire, I force down some re-hydrated mush, rinsing the pot with water to clean it and then drinking the swill, so that I don't waste any. Tomorrow, there are no springs until the Rulhe hostel according to the *FFRP Guide*, and the two that my map shows are marked as 'intermittent'.

Opposite me, the slopes of St Barthélemy are an open wound, the layers of skin showing white: the terracing of the Trimouns talc quarry. At this distance, set against the scale of the Pyrenees, it looks insignificant. Yet it produces 8% of the world's talc, for pharmaceuticals, for making paper, paint, plastics, and car tyres. At over 1700m above sea level, quarrying is only possible in summer but the refining takes place all year round, employing 300–400 workers. In short, it is the single biggest remaining extractive industry in the French Pyrenees.

Looking at the quarry reminds me that I have a problem. On a six-month old it would be called nappy rash, the result of dicey digestion. Despite the immense quantities of talcum powder visible on the opposite side of the valley, I only have two possibilities: sun cream or anti-inflammatory cream. Sun cream doesn't seem very appropriate since that area rarely sees the sun, so I try the anti-inflammatory cream, and regret it immediately. It stings like hell. Trousers still round my ankles, I jump up and down. I try rubbing it off. In desperation I try washing it off, wasting precious water. But it does no good and it takes ten minutes before the fire has settled down and I stop hyperventilating.

As the sun sets I spread my perfumed mattress out and get into my dew-damp sleeping bag. The plateau is completely empty, except for the animals. Nearby, cow bells are tinkling; in the valley the sheep are echoing them. Then I hear a helicopter far off. It approaches. Then the noise is all around me. It is not a helicopter, it is bees or wasps, hundreds of them, thousands perhaps. They are collecting something in the small pine trees which are protecting me from the breeze. They arrive with the dusk and depart with the dark as the first stars begin to appear.

The cows seem to be coming nearer. Will they lick my face in the middle of the night? At least their bells will warn me if any wild animal approaches. The sheep settle down and I drift off to sleep, but not for long. In my nightmare I am at home, upstairs in bed, and a burglar is trying to break in through the back door. I wake up with a start.

The bells are tinkling. Something is disturbing the cows. It isn't that they are very agitated but nor have they settled down to sleep. I sit up and look, but can see nothing. I listen for a long while, but I can't hear anything either. Eventually I realise that the cows are right. There *is* a strange animal in the vicinity. I'm not supposed to be here.

Dog sledding – a Winter interlude

I come back in the mid-winter to try out the dog sleigh ride I had so pined for.

Imagine sitting on the comfortable seat of a fairy-tale Christmas sleigh. The nodding reindeer glide across the gentle hills, only the quiet swish of the parting snow disturbing the winter calm. A red-and-white fur coat keeps out the chill.

No. It's not like that.

Imagine, instead, a top of the range Harley Davidson motorbike. Imagine also – I know that this is will be difficult – that this machine, for which you have paid thousands of pounds, has two major faults. The throttle is permanently stuck down; and the handlebars won't turn. Oh, and there is no seat either.

When I arrive at the Plateau de Beille it is surprisingly quiet: no wind, no cars, and almost no people. It is just a few degrees above zero. The road has been cleared since the last snowfall two weeks ago and the pine trees have lost their covering, but everywhere else is blindingly white.

David, one of the two mushers at the Base Angaka, opens the gate to the compound where the dogs are kept. They are individually attached to metal stakes by heavy chains, just long enough to allow them to rub noses and just short enough to prevent them from fighting. There are twenty-seven of them altogether; cross-bred huskies from Siberian and Greenland stock.

The snow on the ground has long since solidified into ice but the dogs seem indifferent to the cold. Most of them are jumping up and down excitedly, running in mad circles. A few are lying down, but only one or two are hiding in the rudimentary wooden kennels.

'We built them so that the visitors didn't think we were mistreating the dogs, but they hardly use them,' David explains.

These are quintessential dogs. Dog's dogs. They don't walk, they run – up to 25 km/h. They don't yap, they bark. And when they smell, they stink. The air is sickly sweet with the smell of wet hair, stale sweat, urine and excrement although, apart from the inevitable yellow stains in the ice, the compound and the dogs themselves look clean.

I go to stroke one of them but he leaps up at me. I have no choice

Dog sledding – a Winter interlude

but to take him in my arms and cuddle him, to let him lick my face. They can be affectionate, David tells me, but they have not sold their souls. Vivacious and powerful, they are quite capable of living in the wild. They are obedient – in some ways – but not slavish.

David points out the dogs I will have on my sledge. Onyx, brown and beige with a nose like an Alsatian, is thin, short-haired, and quiet. She will be my lead dog. Sam is mostly black, much more stocky and already trying to knock me off my feet. He is part of the power for the sledge.

'Start with Onyx and then work your way backwards along the traces,' David instructs me. I undo Onyx's collar from the chain and she pulls me across the compound to see a friend.

'Lift her up by the collar. You won't strangle her. Grip her between your knees and pass the harness over her head,' advises David. Onyx is easy enough but I soon discover that the other dogs can drag me wherever they want to go, even with only two legs on the ground.

The sledge is attached to a tree but the dogs make fitful attempts to free it. 'Stand on the brake *before* you unhook the rope. Otherwise they will disappear.' I unleash the rope and the dogs instantly drag on the sledge. I have to put all my weight on the brake to stop them.

I assume that David has grown up in the countryside with dogs from his earliest youth but he corrects me: 'No. My father is a dentist and he doesn't like them at all. When I was young I could have a lap dog at home but nothing bigger. He said that if I wanted a pack of dogs I would have to wait until I had my own house.'

'And now that you've got your own house?'

'We've got eight settees, but my wife and I only use one of them. Even the lazy ones and the fighters have a right to their share of affection.'

David is twenty-five, small and thin, with a girlish face and long golden brown hair. He has a disconcerting way of laughing at the end of every sentence, making me wonder if I have quite understood what he has said. He shows me his puny hairless arms to demonstrate that one doesn't need to be muscular to control a dog sledge.

The three of us are waiting in line. David, with six dogs, followed by me and then Guillaume, another neophyte, with four each. The two other people who had booked in have already chickened out.

The sledge is built around a glass-fibre baseboard with two skids running along its length and projecting out the back. If the snow is solid the skids glide over the top of it. If the snow is soft, the glass fibre base takes the weight. At the front of the sledge is a curved wooden bumper. 'When you hit a tree it will deflect the sledge to one side or the other,' says David. Strapped onto the base is a large blue waterproof kit bag for stowing provisions and, if necessary, injured dogs. For the moment the only thing in it is the anchor, a vicious looking device which serves as a handbrake. We are advised to stow it in the sack with the points facing down and away from us. Towards the back of the sledge is a vertical hoop, making the whole thing resemble a Victorian brass bedstead with the legs sawn off. This bendy wooden framework, described inaccurately as the 'handlebars' by David, seems rather flimsy for its purpose. Behind it, between the two projecting skids, is a small rectangular aluminium grid: the brake pedal.

The huskies decide that it is time to go. I lean back, as instructed, and release the brake slightly. The dog team surges forwards. My hands are welded to the 'handlebars'. My feet, on the other hand, are precariously balanced on top of the projecting skids. But only for an instant. As soon as I have recovered from the shock of the acceleration, I jump with two feet onto the brake pedal again. The grid forces two spikes deep into the snow. After several metres accompanied by annoyed growls, the sledge shudders to a halt.

Huskies can pull twice their own weight, happily, all day long. My four are capable of pulling 200kg – about twice the weight of me and the sledge put together. And they are fresh.

I lean into the first bend and swish round it, one foot on the brake, the other on the skid. Then the dogs charge down the hill on an icy slope between rows of pine trees. The sledge is catching up with the dogs and the traces are dangling dangerously between their legs. I hit the brake to avoid disaster.

The next bend is sharper. I lean into it but straighten up at the last moment to avoid attaching my head to a tree trunk. The sledge swerves wildly and nearly hits the trees on the opposite side of the track. After several more bends, my heart beating ferociously, David pulls up his sledge and we slam to a halt behind him. I remove four of the six layers of clothing I am wearing.

Off we go again. This time through the forest on a path which seems hardly wider than the sledge. These dogs live to run. At each corner David calls out '*gauche*' or '*droite*' and the lead dog starts tugging, almost walking sideways in her efforts to persuade the others to follow. Onyx mostly follows David's tracks but every so often she takes a short cut, dragging me into drifts and over bouncy snow-covered rhododendrons. The dogs run round cavities where the snow has partially melted. The sledge flops into them and then flops out again. Miraculously, I don't fall off, but by lunch time my arms are aching.

After eating, David, Guillaume, and I add one dog to each of the sledges.

'*La montagne va plumer l'oie* – The mountain is going to pluck the goose.' says David looking at the sky.

The dogs are beside themselves with excitement. This afternoon, the bends seem to be sharper and the dogs less disciplined. We leave the relatively smooth tracks of the morning and on the first serious bend I lose control of the sledge and it falls over on its side.

'Don't let go of the sledge, or the dogs will run away,' David has warned us. 'But don't feel that you have to go over the cliff with them, either' he adds comfortingly. So I cling on to the handlebars, shouting 'Stop', being dragged through the snow until the dogs decide to pull up. Still dizzy, I scramble to my feet and right the sledge. The dogs race off immediately, wrenching my shoulders out of their sockets. I

Luchon–Mérens: Ariège, terre courage

have to jump on the skids or leave go. We are off again. The next time, my coccyx finds something hard to land on. The time after, I decide to play dead. The dogs are not fooled and after a very short time they start tugging at the traces.

Meanwhile Guillaume has stamped so hard on his brake that it has broken in two. We find another abandoned sledge a few metres away and transfer his kit bag to it. Guillaume is approaching retirement but is as tough as the sea boots you can buy at his ships' chandlers and boat repair shop. His daughter has given him a weekend dog sledding as a Christmas present. He thinks it will make a change from snow shoeing, which he finds rather tame.

Scientifically speaking, the lower your centre of gravity, the more stable you are, or so I believed. So, as well as leaning back as far as possible, I bend my knees. The huskies charge down the hill. At the bottom, there is a hairpin left-hand bend with the obligatory pine tree and adverse camber. I navigate the bend somewhat shakily, but when I stand up again the sledge slithers sideways, one skid off the ground. I can see myself shooting over the low cliff on the outside of the bend so I lean in the opposite direction and the sledge falls over. Guillaume jumps on his brake to avoid me and is thrown over in turn. We are both pulled along the ground by our arms until the dogs decide they have had enough. After another three crashes I conclude that science can't explain everything. Standing up is better.

By now the clouds have come down the mountainside and visibility is about ten metres. It starts to snow. I have no idea which way David has gone, but it doesn't really matter. The dogs have no problem in following his tracks.

At five o'clock it is beginning to get dark and we make our way to the camp where we are going to spend the night. Guillaume and I intend to sleep in one of the igloos. David, who has done it all before, prefers the hut. The dogs prefer the stakeout. Attached to a rope stretched between two trees, they sprawl on the snow, panting. We fill their bowls with biscuits, pouring water onto them and leaving them to stand until most of it is soaked up. 'It's the only way to get them to drink,' explains David. Some of the more obstinate dogs tip their bowl over and leave the biscuits to drain before eating them.

Lifting up a straw bale to block one of the entrances to the igloo, Guillaume cries out in pain. Subsequent attempts to bend over make him gasp in agony. I wonder if he has cracked a rib but no, he thinks he has torn a chest muscle in the crash on the hairpin bend. Now that he has stopped moving, the muscle is seizing up. We prop him against the living pine tree which is the central structural element of the hut and pass him things as he needs them.

'I'm going to go to bed early. I think I will be better off in the cold,' he says. Getting into the igloo is not much fun because the low entrance tunnel forces him to bend over. I unlace his boots, take them off, and ease his legs into the sleeping bag. 'No, it's worse,' he gasps, 'and if I need to get up in the night I won't be able to get out.'

Guillaume follows me out of the igloo, literally screaming. Back in the hut he sits on a bench, hyperventilating, his eyes watering. We suggest calling the emergency services.

'No, it's alright. Just help me get into my sleeping bag. As long as I don't have to get up and go outside, I'll be fine.' I empty my plastic water bottle and cut its top off, in case he needs to use it in the night.

David, is stirring his cassoulet. 'What do you do with the dogs in the summer? How do you keep them in condition?' I ask.

'In summer they run wild around the prairie and then in September I start training them again. I have a sledge with three wheels which they can pull over the grass. When they get a bit stronger I have a Renault 4L. I've cut off the roof and most of the bodywork and I attach them to it. The advantage of the car is the brakes.'

Somewhat later the dogs start to howl and I go out to investigate. The sky has now cleared. A group of walkers with snowshoes is crunching through the forest in the bluish snow-refracted light of the full moon. They disappear over the hill and the dogs fall silent, leaving me to appreciate the *dépaysement*, the magic of being 'elsewhere'.

Opening the door to the hut, I overhear David talking quietly on his mobile: '*C'est la vie*'. Something bad has happened in the other world. His accountant has fallen 300m in the Alps; he is in hospital with broken ribs. He managed to stop himself just 'that far' – David spreads his arms apart – from the cliff edge. '*C'est la vie. C'est comme ça.*'

The morning is crisp and cloudless. A snowmobile comes to take Guillaume back to the base where a doctor will examine him. David and I attach the dogs to the sledges. '*Allez*,' he says, and we head off up the hill. He calls back to me: '*nous nous sommes réduits comme une peau de chagrin.*' I translate this – inaccurately – as: the group has shrivelled up like a dry chamois leather. Certainly I feel about as supple as one, still tired from the day before.

On the slope I push the brake a little too hard and the dogs stop momentarily. When I release it the sledge surges forward but, unnoticed by me, Sam has taken the opportunity to squat and relieve himself. The other dogs drag him forwards, waddling, legs akimbo, spraying indelicately. I jump on the brake and wait until he has finished before releasing it again. But the huskies have picked up the scent. At the slightest deceleration, one or other tries to squat down or to drag the sledge towards a tree. The dogs not involved in this activity seem to take a malicious pleasure in forcing the sledge forwards. In the Tour de France the cyclists haven't the time to stop and find a convenient bush. The difference is that the cyclists wait until there is nobody else in range. As my friend Francine says: '*Il faut laisser ses complexes à la maison* – You have to leave your hang-ups at home.'

David points to a hill: 'Let's go that way.' The hill isn't very high but the slope is steep, 40 degrees or more, and the snow loose and powdery, impossible on foot even with crampons and an ice axe. The dogs are soon up to their shoulders in it, forging their way through, their feet scrabbling to find a foothold. We hang on to the sledges, walking between the skids, being hoisted upwards. I feel as though my arms are only held in their sockets by my skin, the residual strength in my muscles having already been used up.

I tell David, and admit that I can't continue, so we head back to the base, well before the intended hour. Back in their compound, the dogs are disappointed. One of them shows his disgust by breaking the thick iron ring which attaches him to his stake.

I'm over 50. I think to myself that a red Ferrari would be much less effort on the muscles and perhaps wouldn't confirm quite so clearly that I am no longer 25.

Exciting? Yes. Exhilarating? Yes. Enjoyable? Hmm . . . most of the time. Will I do it again? Definitely. But next time I'll do press-ups for three months beforehand.

Plateau de Beille to the Rulhe hostel

In the mountains, winter and summer are two different experiences.

Today, at the Col des Finestres, where plateau turns into ridge, I strip down to shorts and tee-shirt and slather sun cream over all the exposed surfaces, working it into my ever-thinning hair. It is 7:30 am and I am already too hot. Either side of the ridge, the valleys are hidden in cloud but further away islands peek out.

The path temporarily leaves the ridge and descends the slope passing a hut and a spring, neither of which is mentioned on my map or in the *FFRP Guide*. Soon, it climbs sharply to the pass at the Col de Didorte, a strategic viewpoint. Back in the valley I have just left, a man is assembling his cows, aided by dogs. They are already in a tightly packed formation, complaining, tossing their heads, sounding their bells, but moving slowly towards the hut. On the ridge opposite me a long straggly line of sheep is making its way down, pushed by a shepherd and his two dogs. Behind me, on a different high ridge, another line of sheep, this one more disciplined, is outlined against the sky. Walking head to tail, this flock has another general behind it.

The route is well marked, but I am unaccountably nervous. The residues of last night are still lurking in some corner of my unconscious.

Heather is everywhere, still in pinkly lilac flower, criss-crossed by sheep tracks like the estuary of a river as the tide recedes, dividing into a hundred creeks. When I get to the top of the hill, I can see a third flock of sheep, in a different valley. Only about 50 of them this time, but tightly packed together. All is quiet. Then the shepherd says something. The flock moves a few steps to the left. Another order and the flock moves to the right. It becomes a triangle and moves resolutely forward only to stop abruptly, and then revert to a circle: in training for the next battle.

Finally I meet some walkers coming from the Rulhe hostel. A family. They tell me that there is a water crisis at the hostel and advise me to fill up my bottles if possible. A few hundred metres from the hostel I meet the manager digging with a pick and shovel at the side of a small stream.

'You can go in,' he tells me, 'but don't use the toilets.'

So I sit on the terrace, on the leeward side of the corrugated metal box, sunning myself, looking at the lakes and the broad glacial valley below, then up to the rocky heights of the Rulhe mountain.

By evening the hostel is bustling with walkers arriving from all directions. Like all isolated hostels, the Rulhe has a special conviviality. I am at a table with an oldish couple who have already completed the Pyrenean Way and a younger couple who have just overtaken me. We talk about weight, distances, times, and, inevitably, getting lost in the fog. Various methods of dealing with fog are mentioned: hitching a lift on a mechanical excavator, cowering in a sheepfold until the shepherd comes to tend his flock, or playing leapfrog with the waymarks (you need to be at least three to try this).

Rulhe hostel to Mérens

Paul, I discover, passed through here two nights ago. Tomorrow I will finish for this year, at Mérens, so I won't catch him up.

Rulhe hostel to Mérens

The waymarks are so close together that sometimes I can stretch my hands from one to another. Yet at every one I have to stop and look for the next. When I can't see it I strike out in one direction, hopefully, frequently to return to base a few seconds later. But it isn't foggy – the sky could hardly be clearer. It is the scree. Not just any scree. Not the sort of scree one can glide over. Here, the loose stones are a metre, two metres across and the path is nothing more than faint scratches on the surface of the blocks. There are cairns as well as waymarks but they too melt into the rusty unweathered moonscape, which reminds me of the summit of the Aneto. Jumping, slithering, stumbling, I am soon exhausted.

The map and the waymarks disagree but in the end I make it over the pass into the Mourguillou valley, frightening a bootlace-obsessed Spaniard on the way. The valley itself is home to several herds of Mérens horses, named after the village at its end.

Small, at just over 14 hands, they were originally considered as draught horses, then ponies. But since 1998, they have officially become horses again. Hardy and versatile, they are ebony black with a long mane and a Rasta fringe, for preference. They like nothing better than being left to fend for themselves all summer in the high pastures. Mérens stallions are selected at 3 years old and only those deemed 'fit to ride', currently about 100, are qualified as breeding stock.

Despite the name, the National Mérens Horse Centre is not in the valley but 50 km away at La Bastide de Sérou. Yet it was the communes of Mérens and neighbouring Le Hospitalet which took the first steps to save the breed from decline creating, in 1933, the Syndicat Hippique d'Élevage de la Race Chevaline Pyrénéenne Ariégeoise dite de Mérens – the Union of Breeders of the breed of Pyrenean horses from the Ariège called Mérens – SHERPA. It now has the snappier title: Association Française d'Élevage de la Race Pyrénéenne de Mérens. Like Pottoks, at the other end of the Pyrenees, they have been saved from extinction.

The village itself is grubby, from the passage of the thousands of cars which daily wind their way up to the tax-haven of Andorra. In the centre, a rotating advertising panel vaunts, in turn, the leather goods on sale at a boutique there, a motorbike accessory shop, and a supermarket. A train clatters through. But there *is* a bar for a celebratory drink.

The hostel, La Soula, well away from the main road, is quiet and I sit in the garden and wait patiently for it to open. At five o'clock the manager, Stéphane, drives up, and a Dutch couple and a Spanish man arrive seconds later. They are followed by an Irish couple, Veronica, who has come to pick me up, and Maurice who has decided to quit the campsite and stay in the hostel for the night. His friends are late and he is going to continue alone.

Later, Stéphane tells me that Paul left this morning, on his way to Banyuls.

'He tired himself out on the rocks after the Rulhe, so he stayed two nights to recover.'

'I saw him yesterday,' says Maurice, 'but I didn't have a chance to talk to him. I was in the grocers and he was walking along the street. By the time I had finished, he had disappeared.'

'When you catch up to him, say hello from me,' I request.

Stéphane invites everyone to sit down at a table in the wood-panelled dining room with a massive bay window overlooking the valley. The conversation meanders between English and French.

The Irish couple, Aileen and Patrick, are here by chance, because petrol is 20% cheaper over the border.

'A year ago, going to Andorra, our car ran out of petrol so we were obliged to stay in the village. We only stayed overnight,' Aileen explains, 'but we liked it so much we came back. Short walks only, though. We're wimps.'

I go over to the bar and ask Stéphane to suggest an aperitif. He proposes Banyuls. This naturally sweet wine is made from over-ripe grapes grown in tiny vineyards at the end of the Pyrenean Way. It seems appropriate to me and I order a bottle to share.

Back at the table, I ask Maurice, who hasn't heard me ordering: 'Would you like some Banyuls?'

'Thanks but I've being promising myself a bottle when I get to the Mediterranean, as a kind of incentive and I don't want to drink any before I get there. It wouldn't be right.'

'What can I get you then?' I ask. But before Maurice has had the time to reply Stéphane reappears.

'Here's your bottle,' he announces, presenting me with one.

'Oh, never mind,' says Maurice. 'I can still buy myself a bottle when I get to the coast. I didn't buy this one so it is all right. Cheers.'

The Spanish man, David, is walking the GR 107, le chemin des Bonshommes, which most people do from north to south. It takes twelve days from near Foix in the Ariège to Berga in Spain, traversing the Pyrenees. Only, he is doing it the wrong way round.

'I meet people coming in the other direction, but I never see them again. There was one couple who were walking in the same direction as me but they walked much more slowly and after the first night I never saw them again. I'd hoped walking would be more sociable,' he tells me. 'I'm not really enjoying it but I'm nearly there now,' he adds wearily.

The Dutch couple, two days into their abbreviated Chemin des Bonshommes, are going in the right direction, and enjoying themselves. Their baggage is being transported from hostel to hostel, so they are walking light.

Maurice has dumped his rucksack on the floor nearby. I pick it up to see how much it weighs and then invite the others to do the same. It isn't 22kg. It must be at least 25kg.

Picking up the sack has a dramatic effect on everyone who tries it.

'You carried that from Hendaye!' exclaims Veronica, examining him carefully. 'He's got muscles on his muscles,' she whispers to me, admiringly. I ask him about the journey from the Col de Sasc to the Rulhe hostel.

'I was knackered at the end. I can do 450m of climbing in an hour but still it took me 12 hours altogether.'

'You walked for 12 hours!' is the chorus. Like me, the other walkers can rarely sustain more than six or seven.

'And he does parachuting,' I add, consciously stoking the fever. Maurice explains that he will be taking part in a national championship in September. He has his own parachute. Out of 800 jumps it only failed to open three times.

'What's the attraction?' I ask.

'The weightlessness. In freefall you drop from 4000m to 1000m in a minute.'

David interrupts: 'If you can descend 3000m in one minute, how come you can only go up 450m in an hour?'

Aileen turns to me: 'What's it really like, the Pyrenean Way? Can wimps do it? Or do you have to be a hero, like Maurice?'

'What counts is the head,' I reply.

At home, two weeks later I receive two postcards, one from Maurice, who has arrived at Banyuls nine days after he left Mérens, making 51 in total. Paul, however, has given up for this year:

> I had to stop at Batère. I slipped in the shower of the hostel, cut my head open, and was taken to hospital. Nothing serious but still a bit dazed. Fatal imprudence: never take your boots off!

IV

Chez les Catalans – Mérens to the Mediterranean

Mérens to the Bésines hostel

Back in Mérens, we stroll up the peaceful valley under the grey cool of the mid-morning clouds as I explain the *pas de Mahomet* to Veronica. Not the ridge which guards the summit of the Aneto, but a way of walking all day long without needing to rest.

'Lift your foot off the ground and hold it in the air for a fraction of a second before putting it down again. Don't push too hard. Alice learned it from an Arab guide who took her up the Toubkal, last summer.'

Before I have finished we stumble into a war zone. The roof has gone and the interior has been gutted, but the four walls are still intact and the bell-tower is still standing. The ruined Romanesque church in Mérens d'en Haut is another reminder that the Pyrenees were not always as peaceful as they are now. It was burnt by the Spanish on 29 October 1811 in one of the last aftershocks of the Franco-Spanish skirmishes which had shaken the mountains for centuries. The church and the village which surrounded it have never recovered. The village gravitated down the slope into the valley, and was renamed Mérens-les-Vals.

In the forest, higher up, heavy, sulphurous fumes cling to the trees. At the spring, acrid water trickles out of the hillside into the first of two pools, mere hollows in the rock, with a few roughly hewn stones garnishing the surroundings. The top pool is just a little too hot but the lower one is a more reasonable temperature and we dangle our hands in it, swirling the water between our fingers.

I kiss Veronica goodbye and she goes back down to the car in search of a Mérens to ride. Now in mist, I can hear water crashing down the mountain side, but of the nearby river I can see nothing. Brushing through the ferns, the legs of my trousers are soon sodden.

A jagged dark green mountain ridge has sawn its way through the cotton wool, exposing an intensely blue sky, but the water in the lake is icy cold and the frogs prefer to bask on the shore.

From the Porteille des Bésines, the highest point on the walk today, I can see down into the valleys, still partly hidden. So I decide to slow down, let the sun dry out my trousers, and have lunch in a mountain meadow, watching the clouds billowing below me.

It is mid-afternoon when I arrive at the hostel, having seen nobody else all day. The Refuge des Bésines is still enveloped in cloud. Benjamin is already there.

'*La finlandaise*, the Finnish woman, passed through an hour ago. She's going to camp somewhere further on in the wilderness,' he explains. 'She was still looking stressed. I don't think she has managed to relax yet... I got here at 10:30. Have you seen the sun?'

We all stayed at the La Soula hostel in Mérens yesterday evening and have the same destination – Banyuls – and roughly the same timetable. *La finlandaise* has come for a soothing holiday, away from the stresses of work, but she still can't sleep properly.

The Bésines hostel is one of those space stations which the Club Alpin Français (CAF) has dropped on to some of the most natural and isolated mountains of France. Its corrugated metal cladding would not look out of place on a city industrial estate. Les Bésines is well hidden by the forest but some of the others – at Ilhéou, Araing, the Rulhe, and elsewhere – are visible from a great distance. Yet the CAF is not completely insensitive. The first refuges, much more in harmony with their surroundings, were largely constructed in wood and stone but had a limited life in the harsh climate. The new hostels are comfortable, clean, energy efficient and, above all, affordable because they can be made in kit form in the valley and then assembled on site. Solar panels, radio-telephones, and helicopters are part of the way of life of the modern hostel manager.

At the Refuge des Bésines there is a warm welcome and a considerable selection of herb teas. We hear a helicopter coming up the valley but, unable to land, it flies on over the clouds to supply shepherds' huts higher up in the mountains. It will try again tomorrow.

Later on the mist clears, unveiling a sumptuous view over the lake towards L'Hospitalet. This evening, there are four of us. Glancing out of the window, I see two roe deer calmly walking along a path on the other side of the valley. They are not usually so high at this time of year.

Bésines hostel to Bolquère

By common agreement we breakfast early. We all leave at the same time but Benjamin quickly outdistances me and the others take a different route. I spot his pink tee-shirt against the snow drift blocking the path up the side of the valley ahead of me. He is trying to cross it horizontally some distance above the valley floor. If he slips he won't be able to stop on the icy slope. He is nervous and not making much progress.

I decide on a different approach and start at the bottom of the snow and climb upwards, laboriously hacking footholds with a stick and enlarging them by kicking violently at the hole until I can get a purchase on the ice-covered snow. I get to within stretching distance of the top edge of the snow but my dead branch no longer penetrates the hard crust. I look across. Benjamin has disappeared. I look down. I descend ignominiously backwards down the steps I have created. Regretting having left my ice axe at home, I spend the next half hour circumventing the problem, clambering over giant granite blocks which, like those between the Rulhe and Mérens, have not moved since the last Ice Age.

Going on up the valley and across more drifts, without any difficulty, I catch up with the others. Together we form a mutual safety net and tackle a huge sloping snowfield together. Alone, I would have walked around it. But once the difficulty is behind us, we split up again.

A few minutes later I step out of winter and into spring: near the Étang de Lanoux the wild daffodils and blue gentian are in flower. But I hear thunder, though the clear cloudless sky gives no indication of its origin.

The Portella de la Grava in the shadow of the Carlit, reached soon after, marks the watershed which separates the Atlantic-bound rivers of the Ariège from the headwaters of the Têt, which flows through Perpignan to the Mediterranean. It also marks the beginning of the Pyrénées-Orientales *département* and the unofficial border of Catalonia.

Catalonia is the modern name of the medieval kingdom which spanned the eastern end of the Pyrenees, ignoring the logic of theoretical geography, like the Basque country at the other end. Three-quarters of it is in Spain, one-quarter in France. Since the death of Franco in 1975, southern Catalonia has also been reasserting its independence. Barcelona, its capital, is a flashy modern city. Northern Catalonia – effectively the Pyrénées-Orientales – is noticeably less dynamic. Only a surrealist painter – Dali – could claim that Perpignan railway station was the centre of the world.

The blood-red and gold stripes of the Catalan flag are reproduced in innumerable ways, including on major footpaths. According to the FFRP, yellow and red waymarks are only supposed to be used on secondary routes, but from time to time I notice the familiar white and red of the Pyrenean Way repainted in the local team colours.

On the long descent to the Lac des Bouillouses I see cows eating the first grasses exposed to the sun by the melting of the last of the winter snows. For the moment the grass is rather short and not very green but the flowers are increasingly abundant, yellow broom sweeping across the northern side of the valley. The southern side is yellow and purple, the broom alternating with clumps of rhododendron. It is getting increasingly hot. In the space of a morning's walking, winter has melted into summer.

The Lac des Bouillouses itself is a startling electric blue, reflecting an increasingly Mediterranean sky. The water drives turbines which provide the power for the *petit train jaune*, the little yellow train which runs in the valley below.

Like the rack railway at Luchon, this one had its share of problems. The line was about to be inaugurated in 1909 when the brakes failed on a steep downhill slope and six people were killed, including the engineer who had built it. An extra brake had to be added before the official opening a year later. It is not strictly a rack railway as the third rail doesn't have teeth: the adhesion is magnetic, hence the need for megawatts of electric power. This also means that the rail is a live conductor: the nickname for the railway in Catalan is the 'dog killer'.

Spectacular bridges span the river Têt giving vertiginous views as the line wiggles from one side of the valley to the other. It no longer transports goods – minerals and cattle were important earners at first – but tourists now fill the wagons painted in what pass for Catalan colours.

After the lake, the last few kilometres before arriving at Bolquère turn out to be a monotonous trudge, relieved only by escaped lupins and the screaming sirens of a squadron of police motorbikes. A helicopter descends to look at me. Not knowing what is going on, I signal that I don't need any assistance and it swerves away.

Veronica arrives later and drives me to a hostel in nearby Odeillo.

'The advantage of riding a horse in the mountains,' she says, 'is that the horse looks where to put its feet so that you can look at the countryside.'

Chez les Catalans – Mérens to the Mediterranean

The hostel is a huge building let into the hillside which keeps it cool in summer and warm in winter. It is run by a couple who have exchanged the claustrophobia of Paris for the wide open landscapes of the Cerdagne. Sylvie used to be in charge of the positioning of road signs in the north of France, spending her time meeting city councillors. At the Cariolettes – named after the edible mushrooms which grow in the garden – she and her husband Francis eat at the same table as their guests and talk about the area with an easy familiarity which belies the fact that they have only lived here for a few years.

Sleep in a comfortable bed is interrupted by aching feet. I bought some expensive new boots six months ago and have been breaking them in ever since. My old pair leaked and the soles had worn smooth, but they were wonderfully comfortable. Now, every time I go out, I come home with sore feet and blisters. One pair of socks – as advised by Aimé – two pairs, double-layered, thin, thick, it makes no difference. It is too late to buy different boots; I will just have to put up with them until I get to Banyuls. When I arrive I will walk into the Mediterranean, unlace them, and leave them there.

Already, my big toes are tender from kicking at the ice and the toe nails are just beginning to colour. I predict that they will fall off in three months' time. The blisters have burst and don't cause too much trouble but the bones feel a lot older than they did at Mérens, two days ago.

Planes to the Ras de la Carança

When I get out of bed, the legs are raring to go but the feet are somewhat less willing. Veronica drives me to Planes, skipping an hour of dull walking along roads and across flat meadows. Above the village the shamrock-shaped church is shut so we content ourselves with walking around the three lobes which make up this unusual structure.

Middle-eastern, mosque-influenced Father, Son, and Holy Ghost can wait for another day. Veronica goes to look at the solar furnace in Font Romeu, 'the sunniest town in France'. I head off up the hill, on a familiar path: our Corbières home is two hours' drive away and I have already walked several stretches of the Pyrenean Way between here and the sea.

Veronica, not being a walker, is following me in the car this time, spending lazy days seeing the tourist sights, meeting me from time to time when the path crosses a road or descends into a village. Our next rendezvous is in two day's time, in the village of Py.

In the forest, Benjamin catches up with me. He started early and didn't cheat. He promises to reserve a place for me tonight at the hostel.

At the Refuge de l'Ori I meet a young man walking with a donkey.

'It takes me about one-third longer than it would if I were alone,' he says, looking at the donkey, 'because he needs to stop and eat. So I walk eight or nine hours a day instead of six.'

He asks me about Bésines and I confirm that a donkey wouldn't be able to cross the snow.

'Apparently, even without the snow a donkey wouldn't be able to get through. I have been told that I can use another pass, to the north. I'll ask when I get a bit nearer.'

Fresh puffball mushrooms are waiting to be picked by the side of the path, but I leave them to grow some more as I have no way of cooking them.

Finally, I descend to the hostel at the Ras de la Carança, surrounded by cows bells-a-tinkling, gorging themselves on the pasture; also a colony of flies attracted by the new season's cow pats.

Benjamin leaps up to tell me that he has spotted *la finlandaise*. She was just leaving when he arrived. She had camped in splendid isolation at the Étang de Lanoux two nights ago and is pressing on this afternoon at a feverish pace. He has also seen a family of *isards* licking at a salt cake put down for the cows. He is making notes.

'I did the walk fifteen years ago, and I can hardly remember anything about it. That's why I'm doing it again,' he explains.

Petit Pois nuzzles up to me and sniffs at my sack. Today, he is lazing around but normally it is Petit Pois' job to transport fresh bread and other necessities from the nearest road, a six-hour return trip. The helicopter only visits at the beginning and the end of the season. Donkeys are cheap to run and a necessity for isolated hostels, and yet like so many Pyrenean breeds they are in danger of extinction. The Pyrenean Donkey Association was set up in 1995 to define what qualifies as a Pyrenean breed and to encourage better breeding practices. It claims that a well-bred adult should keep its hair short in summer, its ears pricked up, its nostrils wide open, and stand up straight.

This evening, there is an empty place at our table. The hostel manager explains that a young scientist who has come to look at the plants and animals will arrive shortly. We are told not to wait for him, so we share out his soup. We even share the dry, tasteless spaghetti carbonara. One of my favourite dishes normally, and ideal walking food, this version was conspicuously without eggs, basil, or cream. Plenty of bacon, however, and at 22€ half-board one shouldn't complain.

I've had some really bad meals in the Carança valley over the years, mostly my own fault. Once I brought a dried beef stroganoff with me. The cardboard packaging smelled more appetising than the food and looked considerably less tough. Another time, I was preparing spaghetti with a tomato sauce. I tasted it and realised that the vital ingredient, left at home, was salt. I had passed a salt cake half an hour before stopping to camp but wasn't even sure I could find it again. The answer to my problem was at the bottom of my rucksack: peanuts.

There are two approaches to this extraordinary valley from the French side: walking along the Pyrenean Way, or climbing up from Thues-entre-Vals, one of the stops of the *petit train jaune*. Between

Thues-entre-Vals and the hostel, the river has cut a 150m-deep slice into the mountain. The beginning is a deceptively ordinary walk by the side of the river, like the Gorges de Kakouéta. But the path then climbs steeply up the hillside, incised into the vertical side of the cliff, winding giddily between river and sky. Further on, rope bridges swing wildly between metal walkways stapled onto the rock face. Once you have learnt how to cope with the vertigo, it is great fun.

We are just finishing the last helping of chocolate mousse as I look out of the window into the dusky half-light. A flash of blue and yellow is bounding down the hillside. As it comes nearer I can distinguish a man, his arms flapping wildly as he tries to keep balance. No rucksack; he has a waistband stuffed with canisters and technical equipment. I tell the others, 'I think our young scientist has just come back.' We look sheepishly at each other. When he crashes through the door, panting, the hostel manager doesn't even give him time to catch his breath. 'You said you'd be back in time for dinner, an hour ago. If you hadn't arrived shortly I'd have had to call out the rescue services.' Nevertheless he scrapes together some more food and we all relax a little.

Before turning in for the night, I walk the fifty metres to the toilet shed. As I approach, I hear the noise of a braying donkey coming from inside it but only a man comes out. There is no sign of the donkey as I open the door and the décor is clean and surprisingly under-perfumed, a novelty as far as mountain-side toilets are concerned. The secret of this innovation is to separate the solids from the liquids, which is where the donkey comes in. The braying comes from the wooden plank which scrapes the metal sheet and sends one's digestive extracts into well-earned oblivion. Operate it three (crossed out), five times please.

The dormitory, taking up the whole of the first floor of the hostel, contains just two large bunk beds. There are 28 unwashed walkers already sardined into them but still a few spaces left, so I position myself where the body count is less dense. Luckily the quadraphonic snoring is drowned out by the sound of the nearby river.

Chez les Catalans – Mérens to the Mediterranean

Ras de la Carança to Py

I grab a plastic bag out of Petit Pois' mouth, pat him on the back, and stride off across the river and up the hillside into the woods. A rustling in the undergrowth startles me. A bird flies off cawing its warning. A few steps further on there is another rustling and an unmistakable snort tells me that I have just missed a close encounter with a wild boar.

Boars can be dangerous and people are regularly killed by them. A couple of years ago, an old woman from a village near to mine was walking her grandchild in the vineyards when she saw a boar at the end of the row. It had been injured by hunters. Dripping blood, it charged her. She tried to escape with her grandchild by slipping into the next row but the vines were too close together and she was gored to death.

There are around 700,000 wild boar in France and where I live is one of the main concentrations. Yet I have never seen one in the wild, though I have seen many dead ones being cut up by hunters. They weigh up to 130kg, and look ferocious, but somehow, I have never been apprehensive about meeting one in a vineyard or on a narrow track. They are almost familiar. Bears, on the other hand, represent the unknown, and the unknown is always more terrifying.

At the top of the hill, the pine forest gives way to pasture and I can see the characteristic double peak of Mount Canigou clearly for the first time. Looking back, the Carlit stands out against the sky.

At the Refuge de l'Alemany I fill my water bottles from the spring. In the Second World War, this was the headquarters for a German patrol which controlled access to the Spanish frontier, an hour's walk away. Customs officers are said to still keep a discreet eye on the mountain passes. I have never seen any, but then, if I notice them they aren't doing their job properly.

My knees tell me to walk more slowly and I pick my way carefully down to Mantet where the path fords the river and clambers up to this little paradise-in-waiting, clinging lovingly to the steep hillside. Flat pasture is a valuable resource in the Pyrenees – too valuable to be used for human habitation – so the houses are dug into the slope, with the grey slate sliding down the back of the roofs almost to ground level. On the exposed side of the buildings, the stonework is flattened by the intense sun. The streets are paved with large irregular stone blocks. Flowers, more or less domesticated, vie for attention with the harsh breeze blocks and steel mesh of unfinished restorations. Heaps of worn stone rubble await their turn.

Below the village, the river banks are the preserve of goats. Mottled brown-and-white, black, or long-haired Angora, the goats are owned by Richard, one of the two dozen permanent residents. Although he looks as if he has always lived in the mountains, he was brought up on the plain and spent ten years working in a Social Security office before leaving Perpignan. When I was last here, his white hair and full beard were long and straggly but he has recently had them shorn. He is short but stocky, with strong legs. In the daytime he has a quiet measured voice. But in the evening he talks passionately and knowledgeably about local political and financial scandals, village intrigues, and life in the valleys in general. He looks after the animals. His wife, Angeline, looks after the hostel. When she smiles there is a curious shyness to it, but she smiles a lot. She frowns when she disagrees with what Richard is saying, but doesn't interrupt. She busies herself in the garden and the kitchen. The food is excellent but I won't be able to eat here today because they can only serve food to people who are staying overnight. In small villages with precarious economies the town council lays down the law about who can provide which services. If there are too many restaurants fishing for the same customers none of them will net a decent living. Mantet is not a place for free-market liberals.

In 1901 the village was a thriving community with 157 inhabitants, but in the Second World War the Germans suspected the residents of helping the Resistance and evicted them. The village remained deserted, apart from a few shepherds with their flocks in summer, until the 1960s. The difficult access over the pass and rising expectations discouraged newcomers. The old track, suitable only for donkeys, was replaced with a tarmac road in 1964 but it wasn't until the 1980s that electricity was installed. Even now Mantet is a 30-minute drive from its nearest neighbour.

When Richard and Angeline moved there at the end of the 1970s, Mantet was just beginning to revive. Making a living still isn't easy. The hostel and the livestock have been through several permutations. Each time there are new skills to be learned, new challenges to be faced.

'The only predator in this valley is humans,' Richard complains. 'I've lost four goats in recent years because people have let their dogs off the lead. Last year I heard a commotion outside and looked down from the terrace. There was a dog chasing my goats. One of them jumped off the cliff. My son picked up his gun and rushed out and caught up with the walkers. "Don't worry, we are insured," they said. They didn't give a damn. But it isn't just a matter of money. My son aimed his gun at the dog and pointed out that he had the right to kill it. It was only then that they started to look concerned. "You can't do that!" they said. "Don't worry," he replied, "I'm insured."'

'But I'm still learning myself. I managed to kill one of my own goats because I didn't know what I was doing. I was coming back down from tending to the horses on the Col del Pal. When I got to the Refuge de l'Alemany I saw that the herd was working its way up the valley, in the wrong direction. I wanted to bring them in for the night but the closer I got the higher they went. Normally I wouldn't let the dogs out of my sight but I was tired and it was getting late. So I sent the dogs off to round them up.'

Richard has two dogs, a male and a female.

'When I caught up to them, one of the goats was dead. The bitch had attacked it. I couldn't understand why because she is normally so well behaved. The male dog had gone round the herd and brought most of them back, no problem. But there were six of them which were a bit wilder than the others. They were born on the mountains and it was several weeks before I brought them home. They would never keep together with the rest. We were always having trouble with them. They had climbed up onto a bluff and the bitch had grabbed one of them by the leg.'

'It was much later before I discovered why. You know the shepherd who did that turn at Olympia, in Paris?'

'Yes,' I replied. He had previously told me how the shepherd had come to Mantet to prepare his sheep and dogs for their Parisian début.

'He told me that you should never use a couple – male and female – for herding. Two males or two females but not a couple. In the wild, when a dog and a bitch go hunting together she waits, hidden, whilst the dog goes round the prey and brings it back for her to kill.'

'Will she do it again? Did you have to get rid of her?'

'No. She pays for the winter hay for the goats ... I'm just more careful and I never let them out of my sight. My son has another technique. You can tell when he is bringing the goats home. First you see a cloud of dust in the distance. The ground starts to vibrate and then you hear the sound of pounding hooves, getting louder and louder. Finally the goats appear, charging down the valley at a furious pace. It's like the Alamo. I don't really like it, but he is my son. What can I do? He has to do things his own way.'

I wonder how the bitch pays for the winter hay.

'She had nine puppies this year. At 300€ each I sometimes think I should go into breeding seriously.'

Since I can't eat with Richard and Angeline, I go up to the restaurant at the top of the village. I am tired, and looking at the map I see that the second half of the path to the village of Py and my rendezvous with Veronica is on a tarmac road. This is not an inviting prospect so I settle down to eat a hearty meal. I know I'm going to regret it later but my only concession to the crushing heat is not to drink the cool refreshing beer that I had promised myself.

Even without the dehydrating alcohol – it may well refresh at first, but the effect is rapidly eliminated – and despite my efforts to pace myself, I feel rather faint at the end of the climb up to the Col de Mantet.

However, for once I am pleased that the map is wrong. The Pyrenean Way does *not* follow the now-melting road which bootlaces its way down from the Col de Mantet to Py. Instead I find myself on the old cobbled track which was abandoned when donkeys gave way to motor cars. It is steeper but shorter and shaded by trees. A lizard darts across from one dry stone wall to the other. A few steps later another stops abruptly, trying unsuccessfully to melt into the rock. These are browner than their cousins in the Corbières. Suntan?

I pass abandoned gardens and reach up to collect the just-ripe cherries overhanging the path. Today is 21 June. In the nearby valley of the Tech the cherries are famously ripe from the beginning of May, but at 1600m above sea level everything is later.

Between the Col de Mantet and Py there is a plaque which marks the *méridienne verte*. I arrive there just after the solar mid-day on the day of the solar mid-year, by pure chance.

Since time immemorial, man has constructed monuments to mark the cycle of the seasons, frequently endowing them with mystical significance. Stonehenge is aligned on the mid-summer sunrise. On mid-winter's day, the last light of the setting sun filters down the long, narrow entrance passage to illuminate the cold central chamber of the tomb of Maeshowe in Orkney. Discovering the *méridienne verte* is not quite as moving as sitting quietly a 4,700 year-old stone tomb just before dusk, waiting for the sun's annual renewal, but it is a pleasing coincidence.

The *méridienne verte* is France's answer to the London Dome. It is remarkable for its simplicity and the idea behind it, and also for its cost. Britain spent over £800m on the Dome. The French government spent £5m on the *méridienne verte*. In the run-up to the start of the new millennium, the government put together a 60-member committee to tell it how to celebrate the event. The larger the committee, the longer it takes for everyone to have their say, so a 60-member committee sounds like a recipe for disaster. Nonetheless, the committee chose a project presented by the architect Paul Chemetov, a line of 10,000 trees stretching 1000km from Dunkirk on the Channel to the Spanish border, passing by way of Paris. And there was to be a giant picnic – billed as the biggest picnic in the world – to celebrate planting the trees, at different points all along the line. Thankfully, the 60 wise men and women didn't insist on celebrating the millennium on 1 January with the rest of the world, but left it to 14 July, the French national holiday. 'Above all, I didn't want something fixed, nor a kind of Eiffel tower 3000m high dreamed up by architects in need of Viagra.' explained Chemetov.

If the idea caught the public imagination it was partly because it united 337 different towns and villages in its execution. It wasn't something created by Parisians for Parisians. Also the *méridienne verte* has a considerable historical significance. It follows the line of the Paris meridian, an imaginary line running from the north pole via the French capital to the south pole. Like its ultimately more successful cousin, the Greenwich meridian, it was the starting point for measuring longitude, the zero degrees for French sailors. In addition the basic unit of length, the metre, was defined using the Paris meridian.

The French Academy of Science had come up with a revolutionary idea. Their new unit of measurement was to be not just for France, but for 'all men and for all time'. It was to be something *universally* acceptable: 1/10,000,000 of the distance from the poles to the equator. Unfortunately this is rather difficult to measure but messieurs Delambre and Méchain were asked to do their best. They decided that it was not necessary to leave mainland Europe to do the work. So instead of setting out for the North Pole they headed for Dunkirk, France's nearest equivalent. Striking a line due south they passed through Paris and Py and ended up in Barcelona. Thus, although the Greenwich meridian became the standard for seafarers, it is the Paris meridian which shapes modern scientific measurement.

I arrive at Py soon after, feet aching, knees wobbling. As in Mantet, the stone-built houses crowd the narrow streets. Here, in contrast, they are capped with red-orange clay tiles brought up from the Roussillon plain.

In the distance I see two people waving at me. As I approach I recognise one of them as Veronica. *La finlandaise* is also there. She explains that she has blisters on her 'pinky toes'. I suggest glibly that she cuts them off.

'It's not really a very good idea. I've done it once and I don't want to do it again. I made a complete mess of it.'

'What?'

'I'm a surgeon. The bloke had frostbite. But I can tell you, amputation hasn't advanced greatly since butchers used to do it with a saw borrowed from the carpenter down the road.'

Tomorrow she will go to a bookshop in Perpignan, followed by a beach on the Mediterranean. She will come back and finish the Pyrenean Way another time. We never did discover her name.

Veronica drives me to Vernet-les-Bains. Although the town only has 1400 permanent inhabitants, it has seven doctors (including three specialists), eight nurses, a chiropodist, two masseurs, and a dentist. In the 19th century and early 20th century it was a genteel spa town, much favoured by the English. Rudyard Kipling called it the 'Paradise of the Pyrenees'. It is no longer genteel. In summer the population swells to 10,000.

We are staying in a hotel named, confusingly, *Le* Princess, though as far as I know princesses are required to be feminine. Like *le* vache, and *le grande randonnée 10*, the name seems to be designed to trip up foreigners. The hidden words, which determine the gender are, respectively, *hôtel, fromage de* and *sentier de*.

In the bathroom I remove my socks and gently ease off the remains of the plasters. Second skin it calls itself, and as long as it stays in place, that is what it is. In the mornings I have the impression that my heels are baby-soft. But after a few hours the plasters begin to slip, leaving a disgusting semi-liquid goo on my socks. I put on new plasters every lunch time.

I examine my feet under the harsh illumination of the light above the bathroom mirror. There are no longer any blisters, just tender suppurating red patches covering half of each heel. A yellowish liquid drips into the wash basin. Tomorrow, I must see if something can be done.

This evening the town is making an effort to provide some entertainment for the annual national musical festival. A local rock band is rehearsing, deafeningly, on the square. We search for a restaurant out of earshot and eat on a terrace carved out of the castle rock. Canigou is lit up by the sinking sun.

Py to Mariailles

The next day, Py to Mariailles is an easy 3-hour stroll along a natural balcony overlooking the valley, then up through the forest. Veronica arrives in the car just before me and I book us in for breakfast at the hostel at Mariailles tomorrow morning, though we are staying down in the valley in Vernet again for the night.

I telephone around and discover that the only pharmacy open today, a Sunday, is in Font Romeu. As well as housing the experimental solar furnace, the town is a lively ski resort in winter and a high-altitude training centre for high-level athletes all year round. It is full of shops, hotels, and cafés, but on a summer Sunday has the air of a superheated ghost town.

Finally the lights come on in the pharmacy, though it appears to be completely empty. We look longingly through the plate glass windows at the cool imitation-marble, the gleaming white emphasised by a scattering of colourful publicity. We open the door and walk in. Instantly, music starts playing – jazz music, swing, Mildred Bailey singing with the Red Norvo ensemble. We glide across the floor and stand timidly by the counter expecting the pharmacist to emerge from behind a curtain, arms in the air, crooning, as in the wonderful 1964 French umbrella-shop musical film *Les Parapluies de Cherbourg* which helped to launch the career of Catherine Deneuve.

The pharmacist tells me that he has seen worse. He floats around the shop, selecting spray-on antiseptic, something he describes as 'dry water', lint eye pads, especially big second-skin plasters, and sticky elastic bandages. According to the instructions the 'water' is designed to clean out babies' noses. According to the pharmacist it will dry up the antiseptic. This, in turn, is removed by the absorbent eye pads. The plasters are held on by the bandages. He throws in some liquid soap samples to wash my socks.

Mariailles to the Chalet des Cortalets

After breakfast at Mariailles Veronica drives back down to Vernet for a rendezvous with a four-wheel drive which will take her up to the Chalet des Cortalets on the upper slopes of the Canigou.

The track descends at first, climbs steeply through a mixed forest, then gives way to rough grass. Below, half way up a steep ravine, I can see the terracotta roofs of the abbey of St Martin de Canigou, which I have visited in the past. Founded in the 11th century, this Benedictine monastery has had a mixed history but since 1988 the buildings have been occupied by the Catholic community of the blessings, dubiously described as a 'private association of the faithful', but nevertheless a fully-fledged arm of the Catholic church.

The abbey's treasure, for me, is the cloister with its decorated capitals. Wild roaring beasts, and an abbot roasting in the fires of hell, but also parables told in miniature: the dance of Salomé, for example. This capital shows an underdressed Salomé dancing lasciviously while musicians strum their instruments. The price of this, Salomé's most seductive, salacious dance, was John the Baptist's head on a platter. The moral of the story isn't shown, but would have been well known to the monks. Not only would Salomé suffer eternal damnation but also she would die a cruelly appropriate death. The Bible relates that she was crossing the frozen river Sikoris when she fell through the ice. Her head remained above the water, but she could not haul herself out. She tried to escape, her arms and legs thrashing wildly in a grim parody of her famous dance, but she was trapped as the sharp ice closed in around her. Her body was never found, but the head was recovered and taken back to the palace.

John the Baptist is an important figure in Catalonia and, indirectly, the reason I am climbing Canigou today. Tomorrow, 24 June, is his feast day and tonight a bonfire will be lit on the summit to celebrate this event.

On the mountainside it is hard going. The rough grass has given way to a barren rock-strewn slope, dotted with *joubarbe*, with its star-shaped purple flowers, and the exuberant yellow sunburst spikes of gentian flowers.

I drink from my water bottle spilling some on the stones. They sizzle. The cairns which mark the passage are indistinguishable amongst all the other boulders and soon there is no sign of the path. The ferns and brambles, initially knee-high are now waist-high as I force my way through into the forest. In a small clearing I extract the GPS from my rucksack. It tells me that I really am on the path. So I strike off, following the contours until I come to a larger clearing and see the path only a few paces away, plainly visible now that there are no trees obscuring it.

I am pleased with the results of my visit to the pharmacy. My feet still ache but a lunch-time inspection shows that the layers of bandages are still in place.

After lunch, however, my feet decide that if they don't do something I will simply continue to punish them. So instead of the constant dull ache that they have been putting out since the beginning, my left foot comes up with a sudden stupefying pain which stops me dead in my tracks. Tendonitis again. I sit down and curse. I tentatively try a few more steps – with the same result. I get out my collapsible stick without much faith and step gingerly forward, putting all my weight onto it, persuading myself that it is less painful.

A man striding down the path greets me. '*¡Hola!*' he says, continuing without stopping. A few minutes later it is '*Bonjour,*' again with a heavy Catalan accent. I am approaching the top of *their* mountain.

I can see the hostel at the other side of a couple of lakes, girdled by Swiss mountain pine. The Chalet des Cortalets consists of two blockhouses – made in local stone, it is true, but still unremittingly, heavily, rectangular. In front is a circular arena defined by ranch style fencing. Four-wheel drive vehicles chase each other around the periphery, snarling. For them this is the end of a gruelling 90-minute drive from Prades, only 9km away as the crow flies.

In front of the main building there is a covered terrace where the manager serves me a beer. He is in his fifties, solid, and no-nonsense, like the building. Yes, Veronica has arrived – at 9 o'clock in the morning. No, he doesn't know where she is.

On the terrace a plaque records that Les Cortalets was burned to the ground by the Nazis in July 1944 – Henri Barbusse, a Resistance fighter, had sheltered here. Also during the war, the peak was officially renamed Pic Pétain, an incident not mentioned in any of the numerous French books and articles I have read.

Today, a good-natured nationalism fills the air. More and more groups of people appear, some on foot, but most in four-wheel drives. They are Catalans, southern Catalans, identifiable – even before I can distinguish the words – by the babble of voices competing with each other, all talking at once.

A flickering paraffin lamp sits on a blood-and-gold flag draped over one of the tables on the terrace. A Catalan brings his own lamp, lights it and then returns to his car and drives off. The paraffin lamp on the table goes out. Unconcerned by this symbolic disaster, somebody relights it with a cigarette lighter.

I wander through the woods and pastures. There are tents pitched all over the place but none of the usual cows are present. Apparently, they became ill and had to be taken down to the plain. Eventually I discover Veronica. She has been reading, wandering around, eating lunch, reading, drinking an occasional beer, and reading. We snuggle up together on a bed of pine needles cushioned by spare clothing, in a small clearing padded with flowering rhododendrons. Veronica picks up her book. I look up at the light sparkling through the tree tops, and doze.

The menu this evening is lettuce and onion salad, *escudella* with macaroni, cheese, and *crema catalana*. *Escudella* is a local version of *garbure*, with ham on the bone, blood sausages, meatballs, potatoes, carrots, cabbage, chick peas, leeks, Swiss chard, onions, and anything else which happens to be handy, plus a good dose of salt. *Crema catalana* is a kind of *crème brûlée* thickened with cornflour and flavoured with cinnamon, the latter being a classic Catalan ingredient. Perfect walking food with regional overtones. Lots of liquid for rehydration, carbohydrates for sustained effort tomorrow and the day after tomorrow, minerals and vitamins in the salt and vegetables. I sip parsimoniously at my glass of wine; Veronica finishes the jug.

I like the Chalet des Cortalets. Despite its size and the number of people who arrive in motor cars, its entire ethos is geared towards walkers, as indeed it should be at a hostel run by the Club Alpin Français. When I ask for breakfast at 5:30, the waitress simply takes note and asks me where I am going.

I had intended to climb up to see the fire but I just don't have enough energy so I go to bed at 9 o'clock. In any case, I tell myself, I was there exactly two years ago.

Bonfire on Canigou

On that occasion I walked over from Mariailles in the afternoon and up the last bit of the slope in the evening to see the fire, *the* celebration of Catalan identity. Fires are lit simultaneously throughout the region and beyond, metaphorically reflecting Canigou's glory as the highest peak at the western end of the Pyrenees. But what might now seem an ancient rite was only invented in 1955.

From the summit you can see: to the east, a golden arc of sand curving into the distance, separating the dark Mediterranean from the silver coastal lagoons and the regimented vineyards. From the summit you can see: to the north, the rolling heath of the Corbières stretching almost to the turreted walls of the medieval city of Carcassonne, 100km away. From the summit you can see: to the west, the Madres, the Carlit, and a long inventory of the Pyrenean peaks. From the summit you can see: nothing. You can hardly even make out your feet. It depends.

I arrive at sunset. This evening, I can see the top of the Carlit but its base and the plain are hidden in haze. Although theoretically at the height of its powers, this evening the sun dissolves ignominiously into the murky grey, hardly colouring it.

Tomorrow, 24 June, is the traditional midsummer's day, three days after the true solstice on the 21st. It has always been a time of festivals and magic to mark the apogee of the sun, a time of bonfires to keep it burning. Enrolled by the Catholic church, the festival became the saint day of John the Baptist.

The crucial moment in John's life was when he passed his spiritual leadership on to Christ by baptising him, saying, 'He must become greater; I must become less.' Just as the sun begins to decline after midsummer's day, from then on John's authority was waning. This, at least, is one explanation for the choice of 24 June as his feast day.

This is the first reason for the celebrations. The second lies in another tradition, equally old, of collecting herbs on the slopes of the mountain on midsummer's eve. Herbs are at their most pungent at this time of year and folklore and chemistry combined to endow them with special powers. In the Vallespir, the valley to the south, carline thistles with their sun-drenched flowers were collected and nailed to the door to protect against evil spirits. Elsewhere St John's Wort was favoured for its medicinal properties.

The summit of Canigou is a jumble of rocks. The area that might be called flat is about the size of a large living room. At one end of the living room is an orientation table. At this time of night it is useless for showing local landmarks but it nevertheless indicates the orientation of the evening: bottles of *blanquette* (a sparkling wine from the next *département*), whisky, and other drinks and snacks are being pulled out of rucksacks and placed on top of it. At the other end of the room a large metal cross, constructed like an electricity pylon, is surrounded by a pile of combustibles brought here over the last few weeks. Instead of walls, the room has cliffs dropping away into the growing blackness.

Sixty people have been invited, or invited themselves to the party. Being a *gavatch*, a non-Catalan – I qualify as a gate crasher. But nobody cares. We move the wood from around the cross to the middle of the room. Helmuth and Yvonne, 11-05, have bound their bundle of neatly cut chipboard together with black wire – it looks like a gigantic wine bottle cork. But the rest of the faggots are vine trimmings tied into bundles with Catalan ribbons. The pile is draped with Catalan flags and a home-made pennant with a sketch of a donkey, another Catalan icon. The labels on the faggots name nearby villages like Sahore, ones from further away, and other organisations: the Narbonne Natural Park, for example, has sent a faggot even though it lies outside Catalonia.

'Good evening everybody,' says a man in a blue anorak, standing up. 'For those who don't know me, my name is Daniel. Today is special for me, because I am going to light the fire for the twentieth time.'

Night is closing in around us. The feeling of being on a summit fades at the same time as the distances disappear. We are floating in space. An increasingly windy, increasingly cold space. Progressively, I empty my rucksack and add protective layers.

'The first time,' Daniel continues, 'everything went well. The second time everything went well. The third time everything went well... The tenth time, we were about to leave the Chalet des Cortalets when it started to snow. We said to ourselves, are we going or not? Then I saw the Catalan flag. We must be up there for the fire! So we set out and the further we advanced the more it snowed. We were within five minutes of the top when we were forced to turn around. We came back the following Saturday and lit it in the middle of the day... And now it is the twentieth time.'

He is given a present, a tee-shirt, and reads out the motif, in Catalan.

'Tell us what it says. Translate,' demands a woman behind me.

The speech was entirely in French as is nearly all the conversation around me. I can identify only three people who are exclusively speaking Catalan and they are patently from Spain. Of the others, some slip into Catalan for a few words but soon revert to a language in which they are more comfortable.

'The first fire was organised by François Pujade,' Daniel continues. 'He decided to light the fire on the summit of Canigou because, on the one hand it was his birthday and at the same time it was to celebrate the victory of the Perpignan rugby team. A group of friends. Just like that. That lasted several years.'

The fire was seen in the neighbouring villages and the tradition was born. In subsequent years wood was stacked near ancient watchtowers and at other high points in the area. The lighting of the Canigou bonfire became a signal which was to be passed from fire to fire. One year, a radio link was established with Perpignan, and the Catalan song *Muntanyes regalades* was sung at the summit to commemorate the event.

Muntanyes regalades	Bountiful mountains
són les del Canigó	Are those of the Canigou,
que tot l'estiu floreixen,	Covered in flowers all summer,
primavera i tardor.	Spring and autumn, too

Bonfire on Canigou

Jo que no l'aimo gaire,	And I, who don't like it much
jo que no l'aimo, no.	I, who don't like it, no.
Jo que no l'aimo gaire,	I who don't like it much
la vida del pastor.	The life of a shepherd.
El pare m'ha casada,	My father has married me,
m'ha donada a un pastor,	Given me to a shepherd.
ell se'n va a la muntanya,	He goes off up the mountain,
jo resto al Rosselló.	and leaves me on the plain.
Jo que . . .	*I, who...*
Ell beu de l'aigua clara,	He drinks the clear water,
jo bec vi del millor;	I drink the best of wines;
ell dorm damunt la palla,	He sleeps on straw,
jo en llençols de cotó.	And I, on cotton sheets.
Jo que . . .	*I, who...*
El menja pa moreno,	He eats coarse bread,
jo em menjo del flecó;	I eat from the bakery;
ell cull brotets de menta,	He picks sprigs of mint,
jo floretes d'olor.	I, scented flowers.

In 1958 more than 50 singers from the association A Cœur Joie clambered up the slopes.

But by 1962 interest was flagging. The weather was not always clement and fire on the summit not always visible. And if the mountain was not visible, the necessary symbolic link was lost. The problem was that the flame had to come from the mountain *and* all the bonfires had to be lit at the same time on midsummer's eve. It required a feat of physical and intellectual gymnastics to resolve it.

Jean Iglésis, president of the Perpignan *Cercle des jeunes* (Young people's club) thought up the idea which would ensure the future of the event.

Daniel explains: 'In 1964 an old lady, Marguerite Mestre-Grando, captured the sun with a magnifying glass and lit a fire in the kitchen of the house where she had spent her youth.'

'By that time, the kitchen was in the Catalan museum in Perpignan. This flame has become the Canigou flame. It burns all year in the museum. At 10 o'clock on the morning of 22 June it is taken by three members of the *Cercle des jeunes*, who bring it to the summit of Canigou. That was yesterday. Just after midnight, they regenerate the flame: they take the flame out of the lamp and light a faggot. And from that moment on, the flame is shared. There are lots of Catalans from the south who come for the flame and distribute it. The three walkers then bring the flame down to the Chalet des Cortalets and leave it for me to bring back up to the summit.'

So the flame which lights the fire on the summit on the evning of 23 June can simultaneously light fires on the plain, in Perpignan, and further away: in Paris, in Japan even. Thousands of fires. The technical problem had been solved and the centre of the celebrations displaced from an inaccessible summit to Perpignan where the festivities last well into the night.

'You have the text of the song? Pass the photocopies around,' Daniel instructs.

A few words in Catalan, the fire is lit, and we sing from the song sheets – *Muntanyes regalades, Canigou, Se canto, Les montagnards sont là, La Santa Espina* – in Catalan, French, and Occitan. The bottles are passed round, as we toast.

There are many odd things about this celebration of Catalan identity. It was invented to celebrate a rugby victory and a birthday. It is mostly conducted in French for a French audience. The lighting of the fire has been sidelined in the sequence of events, which mainly take place elsewhere. Even the fizz is French *blanquette* rather than Catalan *cava*. But all the same it makes for an enjoyable evening.

The fire burns rapidly down to glowing embers and people start to make their way back, the glow-worm trail stretching down the slope. For those who remain there are grilled sausages and melted camembert.

Finally I am alone. Away from the fire, to avoid the sparks, I move a few rocks to make a v-shaped slot and wedge my sleeping bag into it. The wind has cleared the sky and I can see the lights of Perpignan and the coastal villages. The stars are here too. I am no longer enclosed by the night but part of it.

Chalet des Cortalets to Arles

Back on the Pyrenean Way it is just light when I fill up my water bottles at the spring outside the hostel. It is going to be a long hot day but for the present the air is coolish. I warm up carefully, avoiding straining my muscles. The path climbs steadily. I trip over a lump of metal. A little further on, the path is strewn with the tangled skin and dismembered sinews of an aircraft: aluminium sheets and spars, all that remains of a Dakota travelling from London to Perpignan with 31 passengers and three crew on 7 October 1961. There were no survivors. At the time, the magnetic influence of the mountain, long mined for its iron ore, was blamed for upsetting the plane's instruments but in reality the problem was that the radio transmitter in Toulouse was too far away and too weak to work properly.

Strolling comfortably along the Balcon du Canigou, everything seems to be on schedule for arrival in Arles-sur-Tech this afternoon. In the thick of the woods, I meet a young man, his tangled hair exploding around an unwashed face, two sparklingly clean collie dogs scampering around his grubby trousers. No rucksack. He is living in a hut, though he is not a shepherd, he tells me.

The path winds down through the ONF-managed forest and up

again to the Col de la Cirère, the watershed between the valleys of the Têt and the Tech. I emerge into the open pasture overlooking a strangely irregular landscape. Below me, where there was once an industrial ant heap, nature is again reclaiming her rights, smoothing the contours, pencilling in the hillside.

The mines, the last on the Canigou massif, closed in 1977. The company itself limped on selling its stockpiles for a few years until it finally collapsed in 1987. The mines had been worked through the millennia, but the distance from the main markets made them uneconomic. The workers' hostel at Batère was taken over by the Club Alpin Français, and the cable system which transported the ore to Arles-sur-Tech was dismantled. In 2001 the mines were sold for one franc to the Arles town council.

One by one the industries of the Pyrenees have closed down over the last century, and not just the mines. St Laurent de Cerdans is a striking example. Tucked away in the folds of the mountains, in the shade of the frontier ridge just south of here, the town relied on the products of the mountains – iron and wood – for many centuries before taking up the manufacture of *espadrilles*, cloth and rope sandals, in the mid-19th century. By 1911 the population had grown to 3022, with the vast majority of the adult population involved. But tastes changed and following the Second World War *espadrilles* were no longer in vogue. The industry declined. After a brief flirt with fashion shoes, it finally succumbed in the 1970s.

The valleys are changing. With the exception of talc, the mineral resources are either exhausted or uneconomic. The timber industry still exists, but wood is no longer the primary resource that it once was. Hydroelectricity, though important, employs few workers. Tourism is hardly an *industry*, in any real meaning of the term. Pastoralism is a sideline. The Pyrenees are no longer *productive*.

I stride down the slope from the pass, full of energy, but within a few paces the mechanism judders sharply to a halt. My left knee has given way. I experiment. Every time I take a step forward it sends out a sharp pain. I take off my rucksack and pull up my foot behind me, stretching and twisting my muscles. I straighten my leg against a rock and tension other muscles. This works for a few steps and then the pain comes back again. I try walking like a duck; I try turning my feet inwards. I use my stick in my left hand, then my right. Nothing seems to make any difference. I turn round and try walking uphill and discover that here lies the solution. If I can just walk uphill, I can keep going for as long as I like. The only problem is that my destination, Arles-sur-Tech, is 1500m lower down. Eventually I discover that the pain is bearable if I do not bend my leg more than a few degrees and stop every few minutes.

A herd of sheep huddles under the overhanging cliff, hiding from the sun. I stumble awkwardly down past the concrete platforms, avoiding the holes left by subsidence, tripping over the sprawling steel hawsers, through the ruins of the abandoned mine.

I limp on to the hostel taking two hours for a section which should have been done in less than one. The hostel is closed and knocking on the door fails to produce any reaction. But it looks as though it might be open at lunch time so I sit at a long wooden table in the shade of an umbrella.

A notice defiantly proclaims, 'No water, we don't have any to spare.' Nobody appears, so I can't even buy a can of sickly brown bubbles. Instead, I sip carefully at my remaining litre of tepid liquid and gobble down a melted Mars bar. By 11 o'clock I am feeling sufficiently restored and decide to attempt the three-hour walk into Arles. The first section along the almost flat tarmac road flanked by pine forest is easy enough. Then the path turns off into a luxurious grassy green cleavage between two ferny hillocks. A small stream feeds shady pools, but there are sheep and cows around and I don't dare take the risk of drinking polluted water: 'purifying' tablets have their limits. The grass gives way to heath, small kermes oaks, waist high bushes, broom, brambles, cistus, an uneven path, and an extremely painful knee. Two hours later I am still less that two kilometres from the hostel. I sit on a concrete block which once supported the aerial cable transporting ore down to the valley, and cry. I try to rationalise my situation. There will come a point when I cannot move at all. I have only seen two people on the path all day and I would be surprised if anyone was foolish enough to be climbing up from Arles in the heat of the early afternoon sun. My mobile phone can't find the network.

The nearest road is not too far away. Even though this will mean a much longer haul down to Arles, at least it will be less steep, and it is better to be crippled and incapable on a road than in the middle of the heath. A track leading to the road swings around the contours without slipping down the hillside and I arrive without too much difficulty.

Sitting at a bright blue folding picnic table where the track meets the road is a prim young couple just starting lunch. He is unfolding the sunshade, she is opening a bottle of wine. There are real glasses and china plates on the table, and a new wicker picnic basket displaying enticing foodstuffs.

I analyse the situation. They have a shiny new car. This road doesn't go anywhere apart from the hostel and they don't look as if they are going to stay there. There must be no more than half a dozen cars a day. The road winds sinuously. And Arles is 14km away.

I straighten my back, swing my arms nonchalantly, smile radiantly, and say my best '*bon appétit*'. Do I look wholesome enough, the kind of person you would be happy to have in your brand new car? Have I managed to disguise the dribbling, sweat-stained, limping tramp, with smelly feet oozing pus and probably a beard full of lice and yesterday's food? The longer I stay in their vicinity, the more likely they are to realise that they would prefer not to get to know me in the intimacy of a small metal box.

I continue on down the road, feeling wobbly from the effects of the sun. I have now completely run out of water, so I decide to try the Captain Bligh method of rehydration. The stream trickling down the hillside is only a thin reminder of what it must be in winter so I cannot possibly submerge myself in it. Instead, I dunk my tee-shirt in the none-too-clean liquid and put it back on without wringing it out.

Arles to Moulin de la Palette

Then I fill my hat and pour it over my head. I drip, deliciously. There is no possibility of hitching a lift now, so I eat lunch by the side of the road.

Although the road isn't steep, the hard tarmac jars my knee. I carve a second stick out of a branch. At the first farm, I knock on the door. Five bushy men come rushing to the door and glare at me, but one of them takes my bottles and fills them up, chatting pleasantly, if a little nervously. Back on the road, dry by now, I am making slow progress when a Dutch car drives by, ignoring me. Much later, I hear a second car. I take my hat off, smooth my hair down, and ... the car stops. It is the couple who were eating lunch earlier. I arrive in Arles on schedule, but rather less smug than I was this morning.

I check into the only hotel in town, the Glycines, named after the wisteria which covers its magnificent wrought iron terrace. The thermometer on the pharmacy says 31°; the doctor says, 'Inflamed tendon. I'll give you some anti-inflammatory tablets, which will get you to Banyuls.' Veronica will be there waiting for me. Tired of chasing up and down mountains, she is spending the rest of her holiday lazing on the shores of the Mediterranean.

Here in the Vallespir, the last major dip on the Pyrenean Way before it tumbles into the Mediterranean, I am beginning to see the mountains more clearly. The range is not just a long spine — albeit distorted and cloven longitudinally — with ribs sticking out. Certainly the rocky structure is important. But it is not just the bones which count, there are also the spaces between them: the valleys, with their histories, their communities, their individuals. The Pyrenees are mountains *and* valleys. Mineral, vegetable, and animal, of course. But above all human.

Arles to Moulin de la Palette

This morning I put the *pas de Mahomet* into practice, with a light day's walking. The climb up to the Col de Paracolls is unrelentingly steep and although the sun is now veiled behind a haze, the temperature does not seem to have dropped at all overnight, and the humidity has increased. Half way up I wring out the handkerchief I have been using to mop my brow. The vegetation is increasingly Mediterranean: sweet chestnuts, kermes oak, and spiky-leaved holm oak, fig, and rosemary. The sweet chestnut is garlanded with starbursts of white flowers.

I amble along but the navigation is tricky as the path no longer follows the route marked on the map. The owners of Can Soler, a large farm, have decided that they no longer want walkers passing by their door, although the path has been there for many years and follows a traditional route through the woods. A few years ago they put a notice saying 'Private' at the edge of their property and forced walkers to make a long detour. By May 2003 the courts had ruled the action illegal and a new route with a much smaller detour was set up, leading directly to the hostel. But the gangrene had already spread and two other owners in the area have put up similar signs.

I arrive at the hostel at the Moulin de la Palette with a few twinges but nothing show-stopping, and spend much of the afternoon paddling in the river. I am the only guest and eat alone at a long wooden table outside. A heavy, slightly sickly perfume fills the air: the hostel manager, Roger Chinaud, is also a bee keeper.

Later, I sit on the terrace, alone, feeling melancholy.

Moulin de la Palette to the Salines

Following Roger's advice, I turn right instead of left to head straight for the frontier and the Roc de France, avoiding the 'official' detour.

I have been walking slowly and trying to avoid jarring my knee but as soon as I start to descend from the Roc de France I rediscover my inflamed tendon. However I walk, whatever I do, every step is painful. Even an unusual waymark in the form of a pink pig fails to lift my spirits. At 10:30 I stumble down to the Col du Puits de la Neige. I don't even bother to look for the ice house after which the pass is named. I ring up Veronica.

'I'm in the aquarium. The fish are fantastic. All kinds of colours, it's like a painting. The more you look at it the more you discover. And the hotel is superb. Wonderful food,' Veronica exclaims.

'Come and sweep me up. I need a *voiture balai*. I'm giving up. It's no fun any more.'

We arrange to meet at Les Salines, a chapel on the Spanish side of the border. The chapel is a short distance away through the forest but twice as far on the track. I choose the track. It is less steep, but above all it allows me to walk backwards, tricking my knee into thinking that I am walking uphill. An hour later I am at the chapel, defeated.

On the map there is a white dotted road leading from the nearest village to the chapel. In reality, as Veronica discovers, this is a dirt track roughly hewn through solid rock. Five hours after my phone call we arrive in Banyuls.

The next day I look regretfully at the plaque on the town hall at Banyuls marking the end of the walk.

Las Illas to Col de Ullat

Two weeks later Veronica drives me back to the mountains. We stop in Céret in the foothills to eat and are immediately swept up by the bacchanal surrounding the annual bullfighting. Yesterday's victim is being served up on today's plates at the improvised restaurants which line the streets. On the edges of the *féria*, the air smells of spilt wine and other semi-liquid offerings. In the centre, frying *churros* and fresh sweat create a distinctive atmosphere. Every stall seems to have its own pulsating sound system, with marching bands adding to the cacophony.

As an appetiser to this afternoon's entertainment in the arena, young bulls are raced up and down the main street by a man on horseback.

Their human equivalents, a red bandana tied round their necks or ankles, try to wrestle the bullocks to the ground. When one is brought to its knees the crowd roars its approval. The scene could come from a Minoan bas-relief. But we have evolved in the last 3500 years; there are now barriers to protect the crowds.

I pick up the baton at Las Illas, on the French side of the frontier and much more accessible than Les Salines. In the enchanted wood above the village I trail my fingers in the still, cool ponds which punctuate the cascading stream. Here, under the tree cover, everything is still dark green despite the continuing heat wave. Water is in its element.

Veronica has abandoned me. I will have to get to Banyuls under my own steam this time. As yet, I am the only person at the hostel in Las Illas but the owner tells me that a group of Belgians rang up from Arles-sur-Tech at 10 o'clock booking in for the night. Neither she nor I believe that they will make it.

By 9 o'clock in the evening, the restaurant at the top of the village is full despite the half-hour drive up the windy road from Céret, and many of the customers appear to be regulars. The food is *correct*, reasonable value for money but nothing special. I can not work out where the clients have all come from, certainly not from the huddle of houses which makes up the hamlet.

Back in the hostel dormitory, the beds are now covered with sleeping bags and rucksacks but their owners are nowhere to be seen. A tall angular man leaps out from the shadows, frightening me.

He has come from Arles-sur-Tech today; 20 kilos, Mérens.

'I left at seven this morning and I arrived just five minutes ago,' he looks at his watch. 'Nine o'clock. Twelve hours on my feet and only two hours' rest. I'm done for.'

I am suitably impressed.

'The path goes all over the place. The guide book is useless.'

No, he has not seen any Belgians.

'Not a single blister,' he insists. 'You must try this anti-burn cream.

Las Illas to Col de Ullat

I put it on every day before setting out. It's not actually supposed to be for blisters. It is for putting on burns, but blisters are just like burns really.'

He is visibly shaking from the effort of the day, his muscles unable to relax properly. Leaving his wife and family in the Ariège, he started a week ago. 'I've got to eat something,' he mumbles and disappears into the growing darkness. I get into my bed and finally doze off after the other fourteen hikers have flopped into theirs two hours later.

Stealing quietly out of the dormitory at dawn, I sit on the terrace, easily warm enough in shorts and a tee-shirt, eating a very skimpy breakfast. The hostel doesn't provide food and the hotel-restaurant isn't yet open. I slather both knees with anti-inflammatory gel and take two anti-inflammatory tablets but refuse the *ariégeois*' offer of anti-burn cream. He is agitated, muttering that he intended to be underway already.

I am a long way down the street when I hear shouting and see him waving his arms wildly. He has found a soap bag in the shower and thinks that it might be mine. He seems excessively disappointed when I tell him that it isn't.

The road passes under umbrella pines, immense villas widely spaced on either side. The houses are numbered with figures which jump by fives or tens or more up to 175, as if the village plans to destroy the green isolation which has attracted these first new residents. This does, however, explain the popularity of the restaurant yesterday evening.

A sign of the climate: fig trees can grow here at 700m above sea level and in sufficient quantity for a small plateau to be named after them – the Col del Figuier. Occasional wild asparagus and more frequent cork oaks add their confirmation: the sea is not far away.

A notice on the path tells me that I am about to enter a reserve and warns me not to disturb the human inhabitants, who have their summer quarters here during July and August. They appear to be living in some kind of symbiotic relationship with a flock of geese.

Cackling a warning, the birds chase me away as I approach too close to the nesting area. The inhabitants must still be curled up, asleep. A pity. I would have liked to have seen them in their natural state. A few minutes later, at the other boundary of the reserve, another notice indicates that I can put my clothes back on again.

Further on, I come across a plantation where the cork has been stripped off the oaks, leaving their newly exposed trunks to tan in the sun. Piles of bark wait to be collected, stacked against the trees, reminiscent of the rounded tiles which have covered local roofs since the Roman era.

Cork oaks belong here, on the edges of the Mediterranean. Natural forests are know from earliest antiquity but it was only in the early 1800s that they began to be managed commercially. The trees can live for centuries but they are highly susceptible to frost and can only be harvested once every twenty years. In certain circumstances they can be prolific. One exceptional tree near here had a recorded circumference of 5.65m, and produced 368kg of cork in 1926. But specimens of this kind of size no longer exist: the forests have been in slow decline since the beginning of the 20th century. Competition from the big producers in Spain, Portugal, and North Africa, the introduction of plastic substitutes, and forest fires have ravaged the industry. Nowadays, although there are roughly 10,000 hectares of cork oak in the region, much of it is overgrown. In total about twenty workers process 700 tonnes of cork a year, mostly for wine bottles.

At a turning in the path I discover frontier post no 565. Only another 30 or so to go. The frontier here has always been porous, like the bark of the forest which covers it. Over the centuries the *trabucaires*, smugglers, took advantage of the ease of access to Spain, and during the Second World War the French Resistance followed in their footsteps.

Officially 33,000 people – French refugees, Jews, and British and American pilots shot down by the Nazis – passed across the frontier during the war. Jean-Claude Billes, from Pézilla near Perpignan, was one of them. Too young to be called up in 1939, he continued to work on his father's farm until the war caught up with him: on 7 October 1943 he was ordered to report to Toulouse to start work in a factory. When he arrived he was horrified to discover that instead of making fertiliser he was going to be producing shells for the German military. He was even forced to wear a uniform. He decided to leave at the first opportunity. One evening two weeks later, he and two friends jumped onto a train just as it was leaving the station. They managed to avoid being caught by the patrols on the train but at Perpignan station a German officer was checking all the arrivals and, of course, they didn't have the correct papers. They hung back but there was no way of avoiding the situation. They were the last people to approach the barrier.

'Ah, you're on leave. That's great. Have a good time,' exclaimed the officer, tapping them on the shoulders. He had seen their uniforms and didn't bother to enquire any further.

The choice was Spain or the *maquis*, hiding in the mountains. Jean-Claude opted for Spain and used family contacts to get in touch with the Resistance. With a guide, he hiked across the fields and scrambled through the forest to the Puig Neulos, a little further along the Pyrenean Way. A German patrol caught wind of them but a liberal sprinkling of pepper put the dogs off the scent.

In Spain he was soon arrested and like most escapees spent several months in prisons. He was then packed off to Casablanca to join the Free French.

Curiously, after the Second World War the situation was reversed for a while. Many Spanish men had left their homes, fleeing Franco at the end of the civil war in 1939, and the only way for their families to rejoin them was to pass across the mountains.

At Panissars, I climb up from the path to frontier post no 567. The trees have been cut back here and the view encompasses both the French and the Spanish sides of the watershed. To the north, badly maintained stone terracing cuts through the pale green rows of vines.

The historic fortress of Bellegarde on a promontory dominates the scene, hiding the modern frontier town of Le Perthus from view. To the south, the Mediterranean oaks and pines cascade down the hillside towards the coast and disappear into the haze.

The hillcrest itself is an astonishing memorial to the passage of time. The most immediately obvious remains are those of an 11th-century priory, but underneath them archaeological excavations in the 1980s discovered the base of a massive stone structure. It is here that the Roman general Pompey decided to commemorate the capture of 876 Spanish towns in the 1st century BC by erecting a monument. Known as the Trophée de Pompée and mentioned by many classical authors, only the foundations now remain. But the most impressive vestige of the past is neither the priory nor the monument. It is the ruts engraved into the solid rock by the passage of thousands of wooden cartwheels over tens of centuries.

It is little quirks of circumstance like this which make archaeology meaningful for me nowadays. I spent twenty years as a field archaeologist, mostly directing excavations on Roman sites in Britain. I slowly discovered that I was no longer interested in the minutiae, nor in academics' overarching conclusions. Above all, I was tired of the words 'probably' and 'ritual'.

It is fifteen years since I decided that archaeology was a thing of the past. No more reports which detail the exact colour, texture, and inclusions of each layer of soil on the site. No more earnest discussions about the classification of trituration grits. Looking at this dig confirms to me that I have become a rank amateur.

Like William Golding I am 'digging for pictures'. Professional archaeologists, he wrote: 'are very efficient. Their published minds never run away with them. They are austerely proof against the perils of exercising an imagination which might assume too much.'

But now I can see carts laden with stone crawling up the slope, the reluctant oxen wheezing from the effort. Masons are trimming the blocks to shape and the more skilled among them are carving the hundreds of names which will feature on the sides of the monument. Roman soldiers, stationed at the checkpoint between the two provinces, look on indifferently, bored. Their thoughts stray to the potential delights of Narbo Martius, the capital of southern Gaul, LXV miles away. Well-dressed merchants on horseback make out that they really have paid all the necessary dues, then canter down the slope, destination Tarragona. As yet there are no ruts in the rock surface.

Continuing along the Pyrenean Way, within a few hundred paces I have changed centuries. The watershed has taken on another meaning. It has become a barrier. The physical evidence of communication and common identity is replaced by evidence of discord. A watchtower stares defiantly at the enemy to the south. Forlorn ironwork crosses in the 17th-century military cemetery record individual destinies caught up in the storm. And the nearby fortress of Bellegarde, dominating the hilltop, commands respect for the French government and the burgeoning power of the increasingly centralised state.

It is 1688. After eleven years, the work on the fortress has just finished. The medieval castle which stood in the way of the new structure has been demolished. The priory at Panissars has been robbed for its stone. The watchtower remains to be built, but the essential work has been done. The 1659 Treaty of the Pyrenees, defining the possessions of the kings of France and Spain, now has a solid foundation.

Vauban, the king's military commissioner, has done his job well. The multiple walls will withstand the worst assaults of modern flintlocks and cannons. The well, 65m deep and 6m across, will provide water during a siege. The projecting towers on the outer defences may look like decorative ornamentation but they provide for raking fire along the outside of the walls.

Vauban's solid, forbidding, spiky pentagon finds its echo wherever there was a frontier to be defended. In the Pyrenees he constructed or improved forts in Prats-de-Mollo, Villefranche-de-Conflent, Mont-Louis, and St Jean-Pied-de-Port, not to mention the coastal ports.

Even so, the treaty failed to put an end to war between France and Spain. Several disputes broke out over the next century and a half, with Spanish possessions in the Netherlands being one of the prizes at stake. The French revolution of 1789 destabilised an already fragile peace and four years later France declared war on Spain. Bellegarde was taken by Spanish troops and it was only recaptured after a four-month siege. The church and village in Mérens were later victims.

Leaving the fort behind me, I suddenly realise that the mysterious clap of thunder I had heard on the path down to the Lac de Bouillouses was artillery fire from Mont-Louis, the one Vauban fort still in military hands.

I can hear the insistent sst … sst … sst … of the cicadas for the first time this year. Doomed to compete with the roar of the motorway linking France and Spain, they seem to be making little headway in their amorous quest.

Ten minutes' walking has taken me away from the artefacts of military defiance and hostility and back into a frontier zone of feverish contact. The relationship between France and Spain is turning full circle. Two thousand years after the first carts began to etch their passage into the exposed bedrock at Panissars, the A9 motorway carries more than 50,000 vehicles a day over the Pyrenees. The European Union has replaced the Roman Empire.

Until the 19th century the aim of the treaties between France and Spain was to reduce conflict by defining areas of influence. Since the Madrid Convention of 1980 the aim has been to increase cross-border cooperation. The 1995 Treaty of Bayonne is revolutionary. Previously, local agreements between French and Spanish villages on the border, the *lies et passeries*, were treated as potential diplomatic incidents and needed the approval of Paris. Now, local councils can cooperate with their equivalents across the border in a wide range of areas. This is not just cooperation between rural village councils immediately on the border. Eighteen million people in three French regions and four Spanish autonomous communities are involved. The projects range from the prosaic – rubbish collection at the Atlantic end of the Pyrenees – to the monumental – the high speed train which in 2009 will link Perpignan to Barcelona.

The motorway sweeps up the valley and over the pass, swerving wildly at the last moment to avoid crushing the little town of Le Perthus. The town (population 626) is overlooked by huge car parks (with space for 3000 cars) for French shoppers desperate for Spanish prices. Le Perthus is the Basque Col d'Ibardin writ large. This is not ordinary shopping. This is seven-day-a-week consumer worship. Today being Sunday, the church is full. Cigarettes are exceptionally cheap. Overweight couch potatoes struggle to push trolley loads of lung cancer back up the hill to their cars.

Yet the town council is evidently not rich. On my way to the town centre I pass through a flaking council housing estate worthy of some of the depressed suburbs of Paris. I try to phone Veronica but the phone box has been vandalised. Graffiti asserts *'sem catalans'*, we are Catalans, and *'Catalunya lliure'*, free Catalonia.

I wander down the high street. The contrast between the thriving commercial centre and poor housing estates seems inexplicable at first and it takes me some time to understand the schizophrenic personality of this wild-west town. All the big supermarkets are on the left hand side of the high street and all the staff are chattering in Spanish or Catalan. On the other side, from the open windows of private houses and small cafés come the unmistakable nasal vowel sounds of the language of Molière. The customs post is plainly visible at the bottom of the high street at the very edge of the town, but this is misleading. One side of the high street is in Spain, a part of the commune of La Jonquera, and the other side is in France. The shops are all in Spain. The French town council gets little benefit from the pilgrimage to Our Lady of the Consumer, even though there are many believers.

Coming out of the town, I pass under the motorway stilts. Above me, a monstrous pyramid topped by a post-modern evocation of a classical temple marks the frontier. The work of Catalan architect Ricardo Bofill, this is architecture for architecture's sake. The heavy handed geometry makes references to the ancient civilisations of Egypt, Mexico, Rome, and Athens, and only the use of red and yellow bricks vaguely evokes the Catalan flag. The pyramid makes no attempt to integrate itself. Like the motorway, it simply asserts its right to be there.

I trudge along the tarmac for the next hour, climbing slowly, crossing over the road at each bend to stay in the shade of the trees. The cicadas are soon left behind. The motorway too, but convoys of cars pass me every few minutes. Looking at the map I can see a series of cart tracks parallel to the road. It is a pity that the Pyrenean Way doesn't follow them. I fill up my water bottles at the Font del Molinas, the Spring of the Mills. At the Font Sant August I kneel down in the grotto and let the water dribble into my hair and over my shirt. The Font Santa Maria, I pass without stopping. The Font Miqueta, the Driblet of a Spring, is dry. Finally the route leaves the road, and tunnels into the forest. This is the beginning of the Albères, where the Pyrenees tumble into the Mediterranean. The name is derived from the pre-Roman *alp*, meaning mountain or mountainside, but they have no resemblance to their namesakes.

Picnic tables, cows, and cedar trees mark my passage through St Martin de l'Albère, where there is another diversion from the official route. I struggle up through the rough pasture hiding under the few trees, suffering from the relentless sun. At least my knees are holding out.

The hostel at the Col de Ullat would look more at home in the Alps. A chalet made mostly of wood, at least it is appropriate to its setting. The surrounding park is occupied by families out for the day, picnicking, their cars waiting patiently. Inside, a giant television screen is showing the Tour de France cycle race, on its second day in the real Alps. Life-size cyclists drip sweat into the bar but few people are paying any attention.

Although the couple who run the chalet have been there for several years, they don't seem to understand the needs of walkers. The evening meal has several varieties of grilled meat but little in the way of carbohydrates. When I say that I want to leave at half past five in the morning they are visibly shocked.

'But the sun won't have risen,' they protest. Perhaps they could get up for half past six, they suggest. I propose that they leave me breakfast and a packed lunch somewhere with a thermos of coffee.

At least the rising sun will wake me up, I think, leaving the shutters open in case I don't hear my alarm clock. But I sleep badly in any case. During the night, I am woken up by the full moon shining through the shutters. I look at the clock, anxious not to sleep through its signal. Not only would I miss the cool of the early morning but also I would have to face the scorn of the owners. I dream that my left knee collapses as I am walking along and I fall sideways over a cliff. In the end, my stomach knotted, I am thoroughly awake well before five.

Col de Ullat to Banyuls

I push on the door of the room opposite, where my breakfast is waiting for me. It seems to be stuck. I push harder but it is locked.

Outside, the moon casts a reddish light over the chalet; the terrace, where I ate yesterday, is eerily abandoned. I can't bring myself to wake the owners up but I can't leave without provisions for the day.

I finish packing my rucksack grumpily and come across the tiny bottle of Atlantic seawater, now nearly empty: the water must have permeated through the polythene. Then I wander around the chalet again looking for any signs of life. Finally I realise that they must have left my breakfast in a different room. Wolfing it down, I attach my lamp to my forehead. Outside, I trip over the tangled roots of giant Corsican pines, as I clamber up the hill. The moon is setting to the west as I enter the beech plantation. Soon, I can see the first signs of the new day beginning to appear.

At the top of the hill, I slip surreptitiously through the bars of a gate which marks the frontier, and meander through the yellowing ferns to the *pou del glaç*. A large cairn with loose iron bars vaguely protecting the opening marks the top of the structure. The entrance is further down the slope. I switch my lamp on again and squeeze through the tunnel which leads into the flank of the mountain, narrowly avoiding falling into the pit at the end. In England this would be called an ice house but the Catalan translates literally as ice well. Like an iceberg, it is mostly submerged below the surface of the mountain. In winter, ice and snow were shovelled through the hole in the top, and in summer ice was extracted from the tunnel at the bottom. The ice house is 400 years old, a pretty good age for a refrigerator still in perfect working order.

At the Puig Neulos I can see the Mediterranean even though it is hidden behind a television transmitter and an ugly mesh of barbed wire.

At the Refuge de Tanyareda, a hut for walkers, a head pokes out of the door. I recognise the *ariégeois*. He complains about the number of wine bottles littering the floor. When he arrived yesterday evening a clutter of young people was already in residence. A few minutes later they were falling into their car, visibly displeased that they couldn't smoke their joints in peace anymore.

We set off together but the *ariégeois* soon outdistances me. My phone has packed in and I have six hours of walking before I reach the next road. Most of the route is downhill, unfortunately. I realise that if my knee decides it has had enough there is little hope of immediate rescue.

Col de Ullat to Banyuls

As yet, the sun is still timid and low mist obscures the Spanish foothills as I follow the ill-defined frontier ridge. At the Puig des Quatre Termes where I catch up with him the *ariégeois* is drinking greedily from his water bottle.

'There's a spring marked on the map just down the hill, at 970m above sea level' he says, getting out his digital altimeter. 'Look, I've climbed 6,517m since I set off.'

We agree to search together but he races on ahead and when I reach the spring he is nowhere to be seen. Half an hour later I catch up with him, still searching the undergrowth, still hoping to find the water. I offer him some of my liquid wealth but he declines; his frenetic manner is beginning to irritate me. I would like to walk quietly, alone, but he keeps on waiting for me to catch up.

At the final pass before the long descent to Banyuls there is a small crèche tucked into a niche in the rock. In a small Perspex box, the pottery *santons* play out the Nativity scene once again. The inscription reads 'Happy Christmas 2000. Peace – wisdom – love for the third millennium.'

Halfway down the rocky ridge I meet the first person coming from Banyuls, soaked in sweat from the climbing to get to this point. My right knee begins to hurt and I decide to stop for an early lunch. An enormous ham sandwich seems to solve the problem – sympathetic magic, perhaps.

Finally, I can really see the Mediterranean. The yellow-brown strand of Argelès Plage stretches out northwards before curling up for its afternoon siesta. I was there last year. Argelès has an unforgettable ambiance, full of sound and fury. The gaudy colours of the shops cry despairingly for attention. Families huddle together, afraid of losing each other. Everything screams 'enjoy yourself'.

The hillside is much quieter but I am not yet capable of relaxing. The heath is waiting, dry, for the thunderstorm which would normally punctuate the afternoon. But it has been waiting for two months now. Earth, wind, fire, and water in a nervous equilibrium, almost smouldering, are waiting for the slightest spark. There are no more trees to provide passing shade and the sun is still rising, but the first signs of civilisation appear in the distance: the healthy vivid green of a vineyard stands out against the dull grey-brown of the surrounding heath.

Gradually I become aware of the sound of gurgling water, although there are no streams here. At first I think that I am suffering from some kind of audible mirage, as the sound ebbs and flows, but then I notice a loose rough stone pad by the side of the path. I lift it up and see water flowing below it. There is an underground conduit following the line of the path, with intermittent access holes for cleaning. It is not clear where all this water is going but even 'purification' couldn't make it drinkable.

Finally, I reach the road and the Tour de Madaloc on the hill watching over the coastal plain. A young couple sitting at the pass ostentatiously waits for me to pass by so they can continue with whatever they were doing before I appeared. The heath has been replaced by vines, cultivated cactuses, and flowers. The cicadas are stage-whispering again. Artfully trained olive trees decorate onetime farmyards, now populated by impeccable four-wheeled ruminants, driven down from the north for the quality of the summer pasture. The houses have new windows, the shutters open, letting in the afternoon heat, betraying the presence of *gavatch*.

Below, Banyuls sprawls along the coast with modern tower blocks guarding its flanks but it still manages to look attractive. The end is in sight. My maps tell me I have walked almost 1000km, including 50km up and 50km down. I can't quite believe it. It has taken me 62 days, including rest days and extras.

Why did I do it? Amongst the many valid suggestions made by fellow walkers, have I discovered one over riding reason why I *need* to walk? Perhaps, but not in the Pyrenees. Before I set out this year I went on a walk in the Calanques, near Marseille. One of the participants, Michèle, said: 'Walking is a primitive activity. Not only have we been doing it since childhood, but it has also been programmed into us genetically. We spend so much of our lives thinking, analysing, and coping with new situations that it is good to return to doing something instinctive.'

Yes, that's it.

The *ariégeois* is waiting for me in his underwear at a spring just before the town.

'It's too hot.' he says. 'This is the first drinkable water I have found. I tried drinking from the underground conduit but it was disgusting. I'll just finish my lunch, then I'll be with you.'

'Don't hurry. I'm sure you'll catch up with me anyway. You walk much faster than me,' I say, and I take the opportunity to escape. Now that I am within sight of my goal, I speed up, virtually sprinting the last few kilometres.

In the town centre, my first objective is a clothes shop. The only one which is open has racks of tie-dyed skirts outside, with mock-designer tee-shirts crowding the doorway. Inside, it is small and dark, with tiny electric lamps highlighting brightly coloured cottons. My rucksack brushes against the hangers on either side. The main clientele must be young women in their twenties but there are some men's swimming trunks on one of the shelves. The assistant emerges from the background of which she was part – she is wearing the same garments as are on display in the shop. Slim, with long black hair, elegant and poised, I expect her to recoil at my visibly unwashed state but she treats me as if I am exactly the kind of customer she was hoping for. She asks me if I would like to try on the trunks, but I feel that this is taking politeness too far. I hold a promising pair in front of me and ask if she thinks they would fit. As I am leaving the shop, she fishes a paper bag out from behind the counter and insists that I take a plum. I'm not quite sure why.

My next objective is a bar. I choose the darkest and quietest I can find and hide myself in a corner. Two beers and a quick change in the toilets and I feel almost respectable. I see my reflection in a mirror, wide-eyed, disbelieving. I have done it.

On the beach, I open the pocket of my rucksack to look for my talisman, the tiny bottle of seawater from the Atlantic, but it isn't there. I empty the pocket and then the rucksack onto the beach, carefully sifting through my belongings, turning the rucksack upside down and shaking it. The bottle has vanished: perhaps I lost it when I filled up at the spring. There is nothing to be done.

Removing my boots, I stow them carefully with my clothes. I am not going to throw them into the sea. We get along just fine, now. Either they have worn my feet down or I have broken them in.

The swimming trunks are somewhat skimpy but I don't care; I walk into the sea as if it wasn't there, only stopping when it is up to my chest. Turning round, I see another rucksack next to mine. The *ariégeois* has rediscovered me. He comes down to the shore, takes out his mobile phone, and rings his wife, putting the mouthpiece to the waves so that she can hear the sea. Finally, we shake hands and swap names. Christian and I take each other's photos in front of the plaque on the town hall marking the end of the Pyrenean Way and settle down for a large beer. I am really pleased to see him. We are both grinning like Cheshire cats.

Afterword

A few days after I arrive home, it rains during the night leaving the morning sky clear and the air dry, so I climb the hill behind our house to get a good look at the Pyrenees. Canigou seems closer than usual, with a slightly purple tinge, I fancy, but apart from that it hasn't changed. I put my binoculars to my eyes and can distinguish the outlines of the Madres, the Carlit, and perhaps the Rulhe. The mountains seem solid, natural, eternal… at least at this distance.

But I have also seen them in close-up. Close enough to distinguish every blade of grass. And I have been able to listen to their uneven heartbeat through my Pyrenean Way stethoscope.

No, they are not eternal. They are not even natural. We humans have constructed them both physically and in our minds. And now they are changing rapidly.

The process started two centuries ago with their 'discovery' by Paris society, led by Ramond. Just as Columbus' 'discovery' of America was destined to revolutionise the lives of the inhabitants, Ramond and the visitors who followed him were to transform the Pyrenees, in a process which is continuing today.

The mountains are changing physically, the animals which inhabit their slopes and the humans in the villages are changing and, most importantly, our perceptions of them are changing.

Physically, rhododendrons are replacing grass, to be replaced in turn by scrub and trees, even before global warming takes its toll. New tunnels are being gouged through the foothills and new roads are climbing the slopes.

The animal population is in a state of flux with the arrival of the *mouflon* and the *marmotte*, the disappearance of the *bouquetin*, and the continuing efforts to improve local breeds, like the Pottoks.

And the humans are not the same either. Once a population in decline, subsisting on the fruits of the land, those who have stayed have seen their way of life influenced by miners and foresters, winter skiers and summer walkers, who have brought with them not only the opportunity of new sources of income, but also a threat to the traditions which have bound the *montagnards* to their mountains.

New perceptions of the mountains are being imposed from outside. The unfinished battle over the reintroduction of the bears is only part of the story, a story of human intervention at all levels. Where once nature held sway, at best we now find a 'managed wilderness'.

At one time isolated, with more in common with their mountain neighbours on the other side of the watershed than with the inhabitants of the plains, the French Pyrenean *montagnards* are turning round to look the other way, towards France. Reluctantly or willingly, depending on the individuals, faster or slower depending on the area, the Pyrenees are changing.

Annotated bibliography

- Many of the statistics quoted in this book come from: Pierre Minvielle (1980) *Les Pyrénées des Quarante Vallées*. Paris: Denoël, an indispensable guide to life in the Pyrenees up to 1980. I have quoted him on superstitions, the Chemin de la Mâture, the Mines d'Arre, extinct species, the failed project to create a National Park in the Ariège, and Rancié.
- Another excellent overview of the Pyrenees is: A. Lévy (ed.) (2000) *Le Dictionnaire des Pyrénées* (2nd edn) . Toulouse: Privat.

The references below are listed in the order they first appear.

- One of the most extensive websites on the Pyrenees is http://www.balades-pyrenees.com/. This is my main source for details of the Treaty of the Pyrenees, and the place name Séculéjo.
- Basque houses and culture are discussed in Peio Etcheverry-Ainchart and Alexandre Hurel (2001) *Dictionnaire Thématique de Culture et Civilisation Basques*. Urrugne: Pimentos.
- The official site of the Friends of the Chemin de St Jacques is: http://www.aucoeurduchemin.org/
- For bears: Olivier de Marliave (2000) *Histoire de l' Ours dans les Pyrénées* (p. 153). Bordeaux : Sud Ouest.
- For the place names of the eastern part of the Pyrénées-Atlantiques see Marcellin Berot (2002) *La Vie des Hommes de la Montagne dans les Pyrénées Racontée par la Toponymie*. Éditions Milan.

- For guides, including Barrau, and the Vignemale race, see Antonin Nichol (2002) *Les Grands Guides des Pyrénées*. Oloron-Sainte-Marie: Monhélios.
- For an entertainingly personal view of the exploration and literature of the Pyrenees in the 19th century see the seven volumes by Henri Beraldi (2001) *Cent Ans aux Pyrénées* (originally published 1898–1904). Pau: Librairie des Pyrénées et de Gascogne
- Several travellers' accounts of 19th-century voyages through the Pyrenees are collected in André Gabastou (ed.) (2001) *Voyage aux Pyrénées*. Urrugne: Pimientos. This collection is the source of the various quotations on Cauterets.
- The Pyrenean Romantics are dissected in J. Fourcassié (1990) *Le Romantisme et les Pyrénées* (2nd edn). Toulouse: ESPER.
- The greatest Pyrenean of all time, Henry Russell does himself justice in: Henry Russell (1999) *Souvenirs d'un Montagnard* (1st edn 1878, revised 1888 and 1908). Pau: Pyré Monde. But there are also some interesting insights in R. Bailey (2005) *The Man Who Married a Mountain*. London: Bantam. She also mentions the renaming of Canigou as Pic Pétain.
- Statistics and other information on the National Park are available at http://www.parc-pyrenees.com/
- The battle of Solferino is described in Henry Dunant (1986) *A Memory of Solferino* (first published 1862). Geneva: ICRC. The book is available online at http://www.icrc.org/
- For avalanches, the Service for the Restoration of Mountain Terrain, and Barèges see Christophe Ancey (1998) *Guide Neige et Avalanche. Connaissances, Pratiques, & Sécurité* (3rd electronic edn). On WWW at http://www.toraval.fr/livre/guide.php.
- Saint-Lary-Soulan: http://www.saintlary.com/
- Although scathing of any other views, the pro-bear http://www.loup-ours-berger.org/ contains much useful information.
- The first book about the Pyrenees from the man who 'invented' them is: Ramond de Carbonnières (1813) *Travels in the Pyrenees* (trans.

F. Gold). London: Longman, Hurst, Rees, Orme, and Browne. The original *Observations Faites aux Pyrénées* was republished in 2000 by the Librairie des Pyrénées et de Gascogne, Pau.
- On Luchon see: Philippe Francastel (2004) *Le Pays de Luchon*. Biarritz: Atlantica.
- For the bear cubs at the Hospice de France see: *Pyrénées Magazine*, 113, 49. The magazine is a useful source of current information.
- Glaciers: Association Morain, www.moraine.fr.st and the *Revue Pyrénéenne* (2007), no 119.
- For a dispassionate pro-bear view of the reintroductions see: F. Benhammou *et al.* (2005) *L'Ours des Pyrénées*. Toulouse: Privat.
- On the other hand, for a passionately anti-bear stance, see: V. Berot (2006) *Pourquoi Nous Disons non à la Réintroduction de l'Ours dans les Pyrénées*. On WWW at http://www.nonalareintroduction.com.
- The Biros valley: http://biros.free.fr/biros_histoire.html.
- For an academic study of the relationship between peasants and foresters in the Ariège (and the Alps) see T.L. Whited (2000) *Forests and Peasant Politics in Modern France*. New Haven and London: Yale University Press.
- The Ariège Natural Park has a website at www.projet-pnr-pyrenees-ariegeoises.com.
- For the Canigou bonfire see: www.acg66.org/focs%20de%20Sant%20Joan.pdf
- Pyrénées-Orientales: Marc Calvet *et al. Pyrénées-Orientales Roussillon*. Bonneton.
- Resistance in WWII: Pierre Cantaloube (2002) *Évades de France Internés en Espagne*.

Printed in Great Britain by
Amazon.co.uk, Ltd.,
Marston Gate.